# HOLD ON, MY CHILD...
## JOY COMES IN THE MORNING

R EBECCA M AY B ROWNING

LifeRich Publishing is a registered trademark of The Reader's Digest Association, Inc.

LifeRich Publishing books may be ordered through booksellers or by contacting:

LifeRich Publishing
1663 Liberty Drive
Bloomington, IN 47403
www.liferichpublishing.com
844-686-9607

ISBN: 978-1-4897-4817-1 (sc)
ISBN: 978-1-4897-4818-8 (hc)
ISBN: 978-1-4897-4820-1 (e)

Library of Congress Control Number: 2023911199

Print information available on the last page.

LifeRich Publishing rev. date: 09/08/2023

*To the brokenhearted.*

# CONTENTS

Part 3

Part 4

Part 5

# ACKNOWLEDGMENTS

I would especially like to thank my wonderful, supportive, and loving family for their faith in my endeavors. A special thank you to my son-in-law for lending his time, expertise, and awesome technical skills.

# INTRODUCTION

I have often heard it said that our lives, much like the pages of a book, can be divided into three parts: a beginning, a middle, and an end. Since the average life expectancy of a woman in Canada is eighty-four years of age, my life could be divided into three twenty-eight-year periods. Twenty-eight years is also the approximate length of a generation in our culture or the age at which a woman first gives birth. In my case, I gave birth to my first child, my son Will, at twenty-seven. I was living in Goose Bay, Labrador, and was working as a nurse. I was a young wife and mother with most of my life still in front of me, full of hopes and dreams for the future.

Toward the end of the middle part of my life, at the age of fifty-four, I was a retired empty nester, married to the same man for thirty-one years, but I was preparing to leave him and put my entire life behind me—suddenly and in secret. At the time, we were living in northern Ontario, where I was far away from most of my close family and friends, who lived on the east coast of Canada. It was a very frightening and lonely time for me, to say the least. I was facing the biggest crisis of my life, during which time I had to make many drastic decisions by following my gut instinct, trying to trust God, and listening to what I thought He was telling me to do.

Twelve years later, I am well into the third and final act of my life. I feel very blessed indeed that I was able to not only survive my very difficult marriage but also that I was able to get out and start over. Thankfully, there *is* life after divorce, but that doesn't mean that things will always be easy. As long as we are alive, we will have many challenges to overcome, as well as life lessons to learn. I will be a lifelong student.

Reflecting back, I realize that where a person ends up is much more important than where they began. For some reason, I have lived a rather unusual life; not many women have the ability or opportunity to share their painful story with others. It took me many years to understand and acknowledge to myself what was happening in my own life. I was a registered nurse, but I had little understanding of addictions or mental health. When I finally discovered that my husband was leading a double life, it was almost too late. Over the years, however, I have worked with many women and children in my capacity as a public health nurse, and I have learned a lot from them. Hindsight, as they say, is twenty-twenty.

I believe that my cautionary tale may help others who are struggling in a relationship and wondering, *Should I stay or should I go?* Please know that you are *not* alone in your journey; with faith in God and the help of family, friends, and professionals, you too can begin to heal. It is *never* too late to start over, and this is *not* your fault.

# PART 1

# CHAPTER 1

# In the Beginning

In the beginning, my life was full of hope and promise. I was born in the small town of Woodstock, New Brunswick, which had a population of about five thousand people. It was a very pretty rural setting nestled along the Saint John River Valley, a home to mostly farmers, local businessmen, and agricultural producers. I lived with my parents, Joseph and Martha, as well as my maternal grandparents, a Boston terrier named Pug, and a marmalade tabby cat named Cookie. The year was 1956, and it was the beginning of a simple and nostalgic time in my life. We lived in a white vintage farmhouse perched upon the banks of the river, a few miles across the bridge and up the road from Woodstock.

The name of our village was Lower Brighton, where my father's ancestors had been founding pioneers, stretching back several generations. In fact, my paternal grandmother's ancestors were United Empire Loyalists; they'd remained loyal to the British crown and moved to western New Brunswick from New England following the end of the American Revolutionary War in 1783. Most of them were now resting peacefully in the cemetery down the road.

It was a small community by anyone's standards, consisting mainly of large, rambling farmhouses and barns, expansive fields of strawberries, potatoes, and grain, as well as a Wesleyan church just across the road from where we lived. Back in those days, there were no local stores, schools, or services of any kind in Lower Brighton, and it pretty much remains the same today.

My father worked for the railroad as a welder, while my mom was

1

a homemaker. They were both hardworking, salt-of-the-earth people, well respected by their friends and family alike. Dad's parents owned a large grain farm in Lower Brighton, and he came from a family of seven brothers. Two of his younger brothers died tragically from Spanish influenza many years before the flu vaccine was discovered. They had been healthy young boys and passed away within days of each other. Dad was born in 1909, a middle child. To say that their family struggled would be an understatement. Although they usually had both extended family and hired help working on the farm and in the kitchen, Dad shared with me that his mother wore herself out by her early fifties and died an early death from heart disease. I sometimes wonder if she may have had broken heart syndrome, which is now an actual medical diagnosis. As a parent myself, I can only imagine how devastating the loss of two beautiful sons would be, especially so close together. Their names were Gregory and Thomas, and my eldest brother was fondly named after Gregory.

My mother was born in 1911 in a large white clapboard house located in the tiny hamlet of Fosterville, New Brunswick. It was also near a large lake named North Lake and was in close proximity to the American border in northern Maine. The geography defined my mother's early life; in the summer, the children swam in the lake, and in the winter, they skated on it. They became good friends and neighbors with their American counterparts and traveled rather freely back and forth across the international border. Like my father, my mother, too, was a middle child, except that unlike Grammy Matilda, Mom's mother eventually married three times. Grammy May had two daughters by her first husband (who died an untimely death), followed by Mom, two younger sons, and her youngest daughter by her second husband, Frank.

As fate would have it, Mom's father also died prematurely from a logging accident after developing secondary pneumonia when a tree fell on him in the woods. I believe that Mom was fairly young when she lost her father, around eight or nine years of age, and life became very hard for their entire family for several years. Her little brother Kenneth also died suddenly and tragically when he was four years old from eating rhubarb leaves in the spring of the year. Apparently, it can be a deadly poison, and there was no ready antidote in such a remote country village.

Throughout this period, Grammy May kept the family going by taking

2

in boarders until she married her third husband, the wonderful man I came to know and love as Grampy Clyde. Mom told me that their family always managed to have enough food to eat growing up, as they usually kept a cow for milk and hens for eggs; Grammy also planted a large vegetable garden in the spring. Although they did not have any running water, electricity, or even an indoor toilet, she was very industrious; she cooked and baked all their food from scratch and preserved many jars of jams, jellies, fruit, and pickles each summer and fall.

Grammy was an excellent seamstress and made most of her children's clothing by hand with an old Singer sewing machine; she also made many hand-sewn quilts and knit numerous socks and mittens to keep little feet and hands warm during the long, cold, and bitter New Brunswick winters. For Christmas, Mom and her siblings would each receive a couple of handmade toys, such as a rag doll or a pair of homemade skates, with an orange and some candy tucked into their stockings for good measure!

They had extended family living with them off and on, including a young man named Uncle Jim, who was unofficially adopted by Grammy May's parents. As Mom often said, "There was always room for one more at the table." Like Dad's family, Grammy May's family had emigrated from New York State to Saint John, New Brunswick, as United Empire Loyalists following the end of the Revolutionary War in 1785. Mom's father's family were of English and Scottish origin, with her paternal grandfather immigrating to New Brunswick directly from Scotland. Trained as a Presbyterian minister, he was also very well educated, having studied at both Oxford and Cambridge universities, and he spoke several languages.

I sometimes wonder why he decided to leave everything behind in Scotland to begin a new life in the New World. It must have taken a lot of courage on his part, and I imagine he felt that he had a mission to fulfill. Both Mom and Dad came from a strong Christian heritage, although they were quiet about sharing their faith, and indeed, Dad was not saved until the age of seventy. Mom gave her life to Christ when she was just thirteen years old and was later baptized in the large lake near their home.

Mom and Dad lived about an hour's drive away from each other, which would have amounted to a much longer journey by horse and buggy back in their day. They both attended a one-room schoolhouse, where they also both chose to repeat grade eight, since neither one of them could afford to attend the regional high school, which was in Woodstock. For Mom, that would have meant boarding in town, a luxury her family simply could not afford. Her dream was to become a nurse; instead, she worked as a cleaning lady and lived at home until she was married.

Her two older sisters both got married at the tender age of sixteen, but Mom held out on marriage until the ripe old age of twenty-one. I'm not quite sure how Dad managed to make a living in those early days; I do know that he traveled to rural Saskatchewan as a teenager for several summers in a row to help bring in the grain harvest. He was a lifelong hobby farmer and grew many acres of strawberries and soldier beans, also occasionally raising beef cattle. He became a welder during the Second World War and began working full-time for the Canadian Pacific Railroad (CPR) when he returned home in 1945.

Mom and Dad met through her older half sister, Phyllis, who was married to Dad's oldest brother, Archie. They were introduced to each other at a local dance hall in Fosterville, where Mom used to attend the weekly dances with her sisters. Dad did not dance, so that must have been interesting, to say the least! I have an old photo of Mom dressed as a flapper, which was taken during the roaring twenties when she would have been just a teenager. They were married in 1932, when Mom was twenty-one and Dad was almost twenty-three years old. Mom told me that they had no money for a real wedding, so they went on their own to the local parson and were married in his home.

Their short honeymoon was spent on an island in a francophone area of northern New Brunswick, and they later settled happily into married life in Lower Brighton. They moved around frequently during their early years, from one ramshackle house to another, until they bought the home that I lived in up to the age of four. True life can be stranger than fiction—two brothers married two sisters, both couples went on to have two boys spaced three years apart, and then they each had a daughter twenty years later! The only difference was that our cousins were all older than us, and my female cousin, Sybil, struggled with heart issues all her life.

My parents were humble country folk, yet they still played a pivotal role in history, as they lived through not only the Spanish influenza and Great Depression but also the First and Second World Wars. Dad left for Scotland (and eventually England) with the Carleton York Regiment

(Canadian Army) in 1941 and did not return home until after they helped to liberate Holland when the war ended in 1945. He was thirty years old when he left home and was the oldest man in his unit. By the mercy and grace of God, he managed to live through it, but he rarely talked about his experiences in Europe, except to jokingly repeat some French and Italian phrases that he had learned overseas. He was left with a love for the opera and some shrapnel in one of his legs when a landmine exploded near him.

Dad, a lance corporal in the infantry, worked on the motorcycles and Jeeps, but he was still close to the action. He lost several good friends, but amazingly, he and his youngest brother, Carl (who was named after their father), also deployed to England with the army, both returned home safe and sound. When I once asked Dad why he decided to volunteer, he said he wanted to serve his country, and the money would provide a good income for his young family back home.

Mom kept the home fires burning while looking after two little boys for all those years. I believe her parents lived close by and helped her out as much as they could. No one had much money, and food and staples were closely rationed. When Dad finally returned home in 1945, she sent my two brothers, then twelve and nine years of age, to the train station in Woodstock to meet him. My youngest brother, David, had no memory of Dad at all, and it is safe to say that there must have been a big period of readjustment for the entire family. Although all of this happened long before my time, I am very thankful that my father survived the war, as I most certainly would not be here to write this story if he hadn't! My parents were, for sure, part of the Greatest Generation of our time. Strangely enough, Mom once told me that those were the happiest days of their lives.

# CHAPTER 2

# A Big Shock!

Since Mom was forty-five and Dad was almost forty-seven when I was born, it caused quite a commotion back in 1956! Mom used to say that well-meaning strangers assumed that my parents were my grandparents when they took me out and about to show me off. I'd come as a big surprise to them as well, since Mom believed she was going through menopause when she was first pregnant with me. Her pregnancy was only confirmed by the passage of time when the obstetrician could finally hear my heartbeat at around twenty weeks' gestation. The other outcome would have been that Mom had an ovarian tumor, so pregnancy was definitely the lesser of two evils! Even today, having a viable, healthy pregnancy at the age of forty-five is rather rare.

My brothers and I were twenty and twenty-three years apart in age, and I remember Mom telling me how shocked my oldest brother was when he arrived home from Toronto in April 1956 for a visit. Mom was wearing one of Dad's shirts, and it was obvious that something "big" was about to happen soon! Sure enough, I was born by caesarean section on the tenth of May, scheduled one month prior to Mom's due date. I was healthy but small, only five pounds and thirteen ounces, and Dad could hold me in the palm of one hand. They were thrilled to have a beautiful baby girl after raising two boys, and their large extended family on both sides were pretty excited too!

Mom said that despite having had lots of previous experience, they were very nervous parents. She took me back and forth to the pediatrician in Woodstock many times during the early weeks until the doctor finally got fed up and told her, "Just relax and try to enjoy parenting!" I am sure it didn't help that I was one of those colicky babies; Mom reported that in my early weeks, she would walk the floor with me during the daytime, and Dad would take over when he arrived home from work in the evening. They were indeed very doting parents, but I was also spoiled by both of my wonderful big brothers, who brought home many storybooks, dolls, and toys for me to play with on their periodic visits back to New Brunswick from Ontario. As a young man, Gregory lived in Ottawa and was enlisted in the air force, while David worked for various tire companies in the southern part of Ontario.

My earliest memories, believe it or not, are of lying in a baby carriage in our expansive farm kitchen, gazing up at the toys attached to the handle. I must have been very young at the time but was still old enough to remember! I also recall sitting upon a large blanket on the kitchen floor, surrounded by my toys and stuffed animals. Our nearest neighbor, Bonnie, would give me her car keys to play with when she visited. Raised like an only child, my best friends were an imaginary duck named Paddy (from a book I loved) and his girlfriend Louise. Early on, I learned to use my imagination for play, as my young country friends were few and far between. My mother did, however, throw large birthday parties for me, where I remember playing musical chairs and pin-the-tail-on-the-donkey. I have nothing but happy memories of my early childhood, which could easily match those in *Leave It to Beaver* or *Father Knows Best*.

In addition to my parents and me, Grammy May and Grampy Clyde also lived with us for several years. I was reportedly a very precocious child who loved to climb on top of the upright piano in our parlor, and I somehow managed to use Mom's old Singer sewing machine to get on top of the fridge next to it! It is remarkable that I did not sustain any broken bones, even after tumbling down a back flight of hard wooden stairs from the master bedroom to the landing by the kitchen floor! I remember the incident well; Mom had been changing the upstairs beds and must have taken her eyes off me for a few seconds. If there were baby gates back then, we did not have them installed.

Another time, I pulled a little red wagon holding a kitten all the way up the highway to our neighbor's farmhouse, which must have been a good distance for a small child to walk. I clearly remember wanting to go visit them so that I could feed their baby lamb milk from the bottle! God must have been looking down upon me favorably that day for sure, as I reached their home totally unscathed.

I seemed to have a penchant for getting into trouble. One day, I decided to go into the game drawer in the large bathroom off our kitchen. The problem was I closed the bathroom door first and then pulled the adjacent drawer open. Unfortunately, I was not strong enough to close the sticky drawer shut again, and I then became trapped inside the bathroom! Grampy came to my rescue that day when he used a big butcher knife to wedge open the door. I can't remember being spanked for that escapade, but Mom was the disciplinarian in the family, and I did receive more than my fair share of spankings. She also kept a paddle on the wall "just in case," but to my recollection, it was never used. Simply walking by it gave me goose bumps!

I had a few lesser crimes to my credit as well. My mom loved to dress me in frilly frocks with crinolines and big bows and put my blonde hair up into long ringlets. Aunt Alice (Uncle Carl's wife) once told me, years later, that my favorite thing to do after getting dressed up was to place both hands into my hair and promptly ruin my new hairdo! There are numerous photos of me scowling into the camera and pictures of me with my back to my poor, long-suffering mother. How I hated having my picture taken, as the bright flash hurt my eyes!

When I think of my mother, I remember how she was always working, whether inside or outside of our home. Back in the fifties, housework was much more demanding than it is today. She used an old wringer washing machine to wash, rinse, and wring out the sheets, towels, and clothing, and then she hung everything out to dry on the clothesline. In the winter, which was always very cold and snowy, the laundry would freeze onto the line, and Mom would then transfer all the items onto smaller lines in either the kitchen or the sunroom, where an old homemade swing also hung. No wonder she had bad arthritis in her hands.

She ironed absolutely everything and cleaned the house each week, getting down on her hands and knees to scrub the floors. Each year, the entire month of April was devoted to spring cleaning, when she would wash and scour every surface of the house, including light fixtures, walls, doors, windows, cupboards, and closets, from top to bottom, inside and out. She also baked several times a week and was renowned for her mouthwatering fruit and meringue pies, cookies, cakes, fried doughnuts, squares, delicious brown bread, and fluffy white rolls. Mom was an all-round great cook, and every dish was lovingly homemade. She excelled in making cooked jams and jellies each summer and put up a variety of pickles and mincemeat in the fall.

Mom especially loved to be in the great outdoors, whether she was cultivating roses in her own backyard or helping Dad in the strawberry fields. Working together, they planted a huge garden each spring, from which we enjoyed a multitude of fresh vegetables throughout the summer and fall. In the spring of the year, they looked forward to going out to pick fiddleheads, which grow in the wild, usually along the banks of the river or in other wetland areas. Fiddleheads can be very difficult to clean (Dad once tried to use our vacuum cleaner!) and are an acquired taste. Nevertheless, they are delicious—once boiled or steamed and loaded with butter, vinegar, salt, and pepper.

Back in those days, it was also common for the ladies of the Women's Institute to gather in one another's homes for quilting bees. Over the years, Mom made many beautiful, hand-sewn quilts and hand-knit afghans, some of which I still own today. Like her mother before her, she loved to knit wool socks and mittens all winter long, which we always wore to help keep us warm. Unlike her own mother, however, Mom was not a dressmaker, but she used her sewing skills to make short, flowery curtains and multicolored pillows to decorate our home.

Poor Mom. I really don't know how she managed to care for a very busy toddler as well as her own elderly mother, who was bedridden for several years due to a stroke and Parkinson's disease. As a nurse and a mother, I marvel at how she did it at all; I know she hired a local girl to help her out from time to time, which may have kept her sane. My own memories of Grammy are limited to me standing on a step stool by her hospital bed, rubbing her hands. Mom said that Grammy sometimes tried to communicate with me, and I would usually respond by calling out, "Mommy, Grammy wants a grapefruit," or, "Grammy wants some porridge."

I have very fond memories of Grampy giving me piggyback rides around the house and of sitting on his knee in an old homemade rocking chair while he read storybooks to me. I dearly loved to read and had memorized most of my books by heart. My grandfather often smoked a corncob pipe, and he really was quite a character. He was a sergeant in the First World War and rode his own horse; he was also the local game warden in Lower Brighton for many years and was known to break a few of the rules!

My early recollections of Dad are rather vague, probably because he was often away working on the railroad in the winter or out in the strawberry fields in the summer. Like Mom, he always seemed to be working. I do remember sitting on his lap playing games, as well as playing outdoors with him. He would chase bunny rabbits, catch them for me, and put them in a pen behind the house. When I went out to visit them the next day, they had often magically disappeared from their home overnight!

My brother Gregory seemed to visit home more often than my brother David, as he was always very attached to New Brunswick. He moved back to Woodstock from Toronto in the late fifties, got married, and began a career with the federal civil service. Both of my big brothers loved to tease me, and I clearly remember some of the drama surrounding my little dog, Pug. One day, when we were in nearby Grafton visiting Gregory and his young wife, Betty, Pug ran away and did not come back. Tragically, we had to return home that night without him, but early the next morning, we went back to the scene of the crime, my doll carriage in tow. I had trained Pug to jump into the toy carriage when I shook the handle, and using this as a ploy, we stood at the foot of the big hill behind my brother's house and shouted Pug's name over and over while rattling the carriage handle as loudly as we could. It didn't take very long for Pug to come running down the hill as fast as his short little legs would carry him and promptly jump into the carriage!

When Pug died prematurely, a year or so later (he was struck by a large truck on the highway in front of our home), it was Gregory who took me down to visit his grave by the Saint John River, which was just behind our house. There, we held our own private funeral, where Gregg put up a little cross and said a few words. I remember crying hysterically, and eventually, my mother must have heard the commotion. She promptly marched down to the riverbank to comfort me and fetch me home. Gregg most assuredly got a big piece of Mom's mind that day!

All things said, he was a *great* big brother, as was David, whom I got to know much better as I grew older. David married my sister-in-law Barbara when I was just four years old; they later moved from Ontario to Halifax, Nova Scotia, where Dave bought a tire store and started his own business. I proudly remember wearing a long, yellow, satin gown as the flower girl in their wedding in November 1960. When Gregg had married Betty the previous year, I'd apparently decided to become part of their wedding party as well when I walked up the aisle behind the bride and stood on her train! I guess you could say I was spoiled for choice.

It was also Gregg and his young wife who gave my "elderly" parents a break and offered to take me with them to Old Home Week, which was held on Island Park in Woodstock in July each year. At the carnival, I would ride the merry-go-round over and over and go for more than one pony ride, often refusing to get off the small horses. Gregg also loved to give me rides on our miniature red farm tractor, which he had nicknamed The Pony. He had a pet name for everyone; David was Cub, I was Becky Bear, and when his daughter Jessica was born, she was Jessie Bear. I also vaguely remember going to the local drive-in theater during the summer as a third wheel to my brother and his wife. It was a big treat for me because I would get to drink pop and eat lots of potato chips and candy, and I stayed up extra late. I couldn't tell you what we watched on the big screen, but it was certainly a positive experience for a little girl and a much-needed reprieve for my exhausted parents.

# CHAPTER 3

# Baby Grows Up

After both my grandparents passed away less than a year apart, my parents decided to build a new house a few miles downriver in the small village of Grafton. We officially moved homes in 1960, and I can still remember watching my mom and Betty sitting on outdoor scaffolding, painting the clapboards of our bungalow white and the window trimming green. Our brand-new, well-laid-out home was a labor of love, built by my mother's uncle Jim and my parents' good friend Charlie, who was British and well renowned for being an excellent builder. Mom later told me that she and Dad had decided to leave Lower Brighton and move to Grafton in order to provide me with a better education. That was very important to them both, as they had never had the opportunity to complete their own schooling. A modern elementary school located about a ten-minute walk down the road from our house was to be completed the year I entered grade one.

Having a shared love for the water, Mom and Dad purchased a large piece of land alongside the St. John River, right across from the town of Woodstock. We enjoyed a beautiful view of the town from our big picture window all year long. In the summer, we sometimes watched small fishing boats go up and down the river and occasionally even people waterskiing; during the cold, frosty winters, the river was covered with a thick coat of ice and snow. It was always a big event for us when the ice flowed in the river in late March or early April of each year, when we'd watch with childlike fascination huge icebergs drifting slowly past our house. There was often the risk of flooding when occasionally the ice would become

12

jammed under either the train bridge or the century-old bridge upriver in Hartland, which boasted being the "longest covered bridge in the world."

When I was a little girl, the bridge between Grafton and Woodstock was a lifeline, located a few miles down the long, winding road below our house. I remember riding my snazzy gold bike over the old rickety bridge to take the causeway down to Island Park. The large island was located near the mouth of the Meduxnekeag River and was shaped like a teardrop. It sported a large park, including a camping and picnic area, ball diamond, grandstand, racetrack, and parade grounds, as well as an outdoor swimming pool and arena, where I took swimming lessons in the summer and learned how to skate in the winter.

Over time, New Brunswick Power raised the floodwaters at the Mactaquac Dam below Woodstock near the city of Fredericton, and the landscape along the river gradually changed. Today, that area along the river is an overgrown jungle, reclaimed by nature itself. After Island Park was flooded in 1968, a new bridge was completed around 1970 just above our home; many of the houses downriver from us were subsequently bought out by the power commission and moved off the land, as the water levels were just too high. Fortunately, our small home was spared. It was all in the name of progress, but it was a sad sight to see just the same.

It is very true that we don't tend to miss the key people and essential elements of our life until they are no more. Compared to today, the time I lived with my parents in that sweet little home seems simple and uncomplicated. Mom and Dad owned a large lot with extensive front and back lawns, including room for a huge vegetable garden and raspberry patch in the backyard. Each year, they grew so much produce that they gave a lot of it away and sold the remainder to the local hospital and nursing home.

Dad continued to cultivate several fields of strawberries in the nearby countryside on land he rented from the local farmers. It was his hobby, and he was good at it! Mom was always by his side in the berry shack, directing the traffic while keeping a close eye on the crates of ripening strawberries. I will forever associate the smell of summer with strawberries. The extra berry money certainly helped to supplement their income, as Dad now worked as a foreman for the CPR, while Mom kept busy looking after me and working in our home.

Mom also loved picking apples each fall in North Hampton, which was a small settlement located a few miles downriver from us. The family of one of my school chums, Susan, owned the expansive orchards, which are still active to this day. Mom additionally worked for a short period of time in a strawberry box factory that my uncle Gabe owned, and when I was a teenager, she worked evenings at the hospital, delivering snacks and drinks to the patients. Mom and Dad were both friendly, kind, and generous people and had many friends. Mom once told me that when she and Dad were first married during the Great Depression, it was common for strangers to come knocking at their door. They were the hobos, men who rode the rails, often originating from the northwestern United States, looking for work. Mom said she could never turn a person in need away and would always offer them a free meal and a warm bed in the barn for the night.

I clearly remember my mother walking me back and forth to school on my first day of grade one. It was about a fifteen-minute walk along the river, with neighbors' homes spread sparsely throughout on the opposite side of the road. Grafton was still more countrified than gentrified back then, and for a small child, it was rather scary! On the second day of school, she encouraged me to walk by myself, which I did. Coming home for lunch was another matter entirely; I started out from school just fine but somewhere along the way became convinced that I had spotted a big bear lumbering along the riverbank. Since I was still quite a distance from our house, I walked up to one of the homes to ask for help. Their teenage son John ended up walking me the rest of the way home, and my poor mother had to recommence her duties after that. The one and only time I pretended to be sick, she personally walked me back to school, quickly squashing my childish deception!

Back in those days and in that neck of the world, no one locked either their house or car, and children were free to walk, bike, or play within a few miles' radius of their homes. Nothing bad ever seemed to happen, although we now know that not to be true. Bad things *did* happen to children, but they were often covered up. Grafton was just a glorified village without any stoplights back then, but there was a small business just up the road where the local kids would go to buy penny candy, chips, chocolate bars, and soft drinks. The owner was a real creep, and I later heard that he had allegedly molested more than one child there over the years. I am very thankful that I was not one of those innocent young children. God had His hand on my life even then.

I completed all my primary years at Grafton Elementary School, which were filled with mostly happy and carefree moments. Overall, I was a very good student and loved to read and write. I had several friends I would often play with, either after school or on Saturdays. I also had a second cousin, Patricia, who lived just behind us and was two years older than me. She and I used to play together until she grew up and discovered new friends. I also remember going to birthday parties and even the odd pajama party, which was lots of fun for me, since I had no siblings at home. I could sometimes coax my mother into playing card games, such as Old Maid, or board games like Mousetrap or Monopoly with me after school. When I was very small, I loved to play with my dolls, and my friends and I would take turns playing house, school, or nurse—the career options were rather limited for women back then! Cut-out paper dolls and Barbie dolls were my favorites, though, and I played with them until I was almost thirteen years old.

Mom enrolled me in piano lessons when I was six, and I continued taking weekly lessons until I was fifteen and decided to focus on other activities. My friend Susan also took piano lessons from the same teacher, Mrs. Jones, and was in Brownies as well. I dearly wanted to become a Brownie, too, but for some strange reason that I will never understand, Mom said no, and that was that; when Mom made up her mind, there was no changing it!

Two major world events stand out from my childhood: the assassination of President John F. Kennedy in November 1963, when I was seven years old, and the moon landing in July 1969, when I was thirteen. I remember watching the unfolding news on our old black-and-white television in the living room with my mom but not really understanding the significance of either day. Walter Cronkite was the undisputed king of the news in the 1960s and 1970s, earning his reputation as "the most trusted man in America."

Back then, our evening entertainment consisted of watching Canadian TV shows like *Don Messer's Jubilee*, *The Pig and Whistle*, and *The Tommy Hunter Show*, with Dad watching *Hockey Night in Canada* every Saturday night. I reserved Saturday mornings for my cartoons, while Sunday evening we all sat transfixed by *The Wonderful World of Disney* and *The Ed Sullivan Show*. Mom had her favorites as well. She had a huge crush on Dean Martin and never missed an episode of *The Lawrence Welk Show*. *All in the Family* first aired in 1971, and almost instantly, satirical entertainment rose to a whole new level. That was around the same time that Grafton finally got cable, and to celebrate, Dad went out and bought a brand-new color console TV. What a treat it was for us, after years of watching very limited television programming in basic black and white! Aside from our television viewing, most Sunday afternoons were reserved for a family drive in the car, usually somewhere along the picturesque backroads of New Brunswick.

During my early childhood, our small town consisted of a rather bustling downtown area, full of the usual essentials and amenities that most people take for granted today. There was a large discount department store; several clothing and shoe stores; a couple of drugstores; three or four grocery stores; several specialty shops, banks, and churches; a post office / government building; and finally, two very old and historic buildings that housed both a library and a courthouse. What we couldn't buy in town, we ordered from either the Sears or Eaton's catalogues, and we would then pick up the parcel a few days later at their service depot.

The *Sears Wish Book* came out a few months before Christmas each year, and I would spend hours and hours picking out the toys that I wanted Santa Claus to bring me that year. When I was old enough to print, I would painstakingly write my note to Santa and place it in our woodburning fireplace for the elves to magically dispatch to the North Pole! Although I didn't always get exactly what I wanted, I was never disappointed on Christmas morning, as there was always a large array of toys and dolls crowding for space around our redbrick fireplace hearth.

Even though we hardly ever ate out, I remember one charming diner, the Whoa Daddy, located inside of what resembled an old train car; beside it was an old-fashioned ice-cream and soda fountain shop. The office of one of the first newspapers in Woodstock, the *Sentinel Press*, was also down by the river, and my sister-in-law Betty worked there as a secretary for several years. Most impressively, Woodstock boasted the Capitol Theatre, an original old-time movie theatre (first built in 1885 as the Graham Opera House), where I sometimes went on Saturday afternoons with my cousins or my friends to watch classic children's movies, such as *Mary Poppins*, *The Sound of Music*, *Chitty Chitty Bang Bang*, and *That Darn Cat!* How I loved Hayley Mills and longed to be like her in every way!

# CHAPTER 4

# The Wonder Years

The good people of the Saint John River Valley lived in what is still called the Bible Belt, and a big part of my life was attending Sunday school and church at one of the several large churches in Woodstock. For years, Dad would drop me off for Sunday school in front of the church and then come back for me when church was over. Neither one of my parents went to church at that time, and Mom later told me that she did not feel comfortable or even accepted there by certain people. Woodstock was once a rather class-conscious town, and if a person did not have the right last name, income, or social status, they were looked down upon. What a sad commentary for both the church and the town; I sincerely hope that things are different there now. When I left for university at the age of eighteen, I never looked back.

One Sunday in June, after I had just turned thirteen, I was sitting in church with Gregory and Betty. That morning, the minister had invited a traveling evangelist to preach the sermon, which turned out to be a fire-and-brimstone message for sinners! Despite being so young and not a child to get into any serious trouble, I felt very convicted by his message and was compelled to go forward when the preacher gave the altar call. Like Billy Graham, he recited one of the most familiar verses in the Bible, John 3:16, "For God so loved the world that he gave his one and only son, that whoever believes in him shall not perish but have eternal life." That promise was something I did not want to miss out on!

Two older boys in the congregation went forward first, and as I hesitated, I heard a loud and commanding voice inside my head telling me,

*"Go."* Thinking back, I am sure that was the voice of the Lord speaking to me, and I obeyed that call and walked up to the front of the church. I gave my life to Christ that day and have never regretted my decision for even one minute since. After we drove back home and I told my parents what had happened, Mom was speechless. Despite being a born-again Christian herself with a deep faith in God, she had missed out on the whole affair because her pride had kept her from going to church. When I was baptized a few weeks later, Mom was sitting in one of the front pews of the church, and she rarely missed a service after that! How true it is that a child can often lead us back to our own faith.

Holidays were a special source of joy for me, especially Thanksgiving and Christmas, as we would always have family members come over to visit. I fondly remember sitting around our big dining room table with my parents, my brothers, and their families, eating my fill of turkey with all the trimmings while Mom waited on us hand and foot. Of course, it was all home-cooked food—simple but always delicious. By the time I was ten, I was an aunt to my brother Gregory's daughter (who was seven and a half years younger than me), as well as to my brother David's two sons (who were six and ten years younger than me). We pretty much grew up together, although I did not see a lot of the boys, since they lived in Halifax, and my niece was much too young to be a playmate. David and his family would visit us every summer for a week or two, usually when Old Home Week was on. I saw a lot of Gregory, Betty, and their little girl, Jessica, up until Gregg took a job with the provincial government in Fredericton, and they moved there. Fredericton was an hour's drive away from us, and we would often go there to visit them or to shop, as the selection in the small town of Woodstock was rather limited.

We also saw quite a bit of my uncles, aunts, and cousins during the summer, since people tended to visit one another more often during the warmer months. Those were the days ... Mom and Dad would usually host a big corn boil in their backyard toward the middle of August, where there would be twenty-five to thirty very hungry people eager to eat Mom's good food! We sometimes had family who lived in British Columbia staying with us, or Dad's brother Carl and his wife, Alice, visiting us from Toronto. My first cousin Dale and his family lived right next door to us for several years, which gave me a warm feeling of family unity. One thing I learned from both of my parents was that family *always* came first, even if there were some strained relationships here and there over the years. In my experience, it is rather rare to receive a sincere apology from most people. Time seems to have a way of healing, though, and often, a person must try to forgive and forget. Mom and Dad were often the peacemakers in their respective families.

The long, hot days of summer seemed to go on forever back then as Grafton took on a Mayberry-like essence. The latter part of June and all of July were taken up with Dad's strawberry endeavors, in which the whole family played a role. Dad ran the show, of course, and Mom was his second-in-command; I played a bit part by picking berries each day. My niece Jessica spent most of her summers with us, and although she hated picking strawberries, she tagged along. Sometimes even Gregg or David would help Dad out when he was planting, fertilizing, irrigating, or covering his beloved plants.

Those mornings started very early, and by 6:00 a.m., we lowly workers would all be rounded up into the back of my father's pickup truck, which had a homemade box over the top of it. Off we would go to the berry field, which was located several miles outside of Grafton on Betty's parents' farmland in Newbridge. The pay was low, and the conditions were poor, but we always had a lot of fun anyway, and my first summer job gave me pocket money to spend on comic books, magazines, and candy. Mom and Dad never really gave me an allowance, but they always seemed to provide me with enough money for whatever I needed.

Unlike other families, we were never able to take summer vacations when I was young, as Dad and Mom were always so focused on tending their strawberries and huge vegetable garden. Mom made a home-cooked meal every single night, and the three of us always ate supper together at the family dinner table. I guess we never really knew how the other half lived, except on TV, but we were happy just the same. The highlight of our summer was always the last week of July during Old Home Week, which was kicked off by a big street parade full of floats and marching bands from all over the Maritimes and northern Maine. This yearly event featured a large carnival (my personal favorite); a variety of horticultural, baking, and livestock exhibits; a country and western concert; stock car and harness racing; tractor pulling; and the Miss New Brunswick Beauty Pageant. The festivities had been relocated from Island Park to Connell Park (on the mainland) back in the late sixties, when our "fantasy island" was no more. Always popular with the locals and tourists alike, this summer celebration endures even today.

When I turned twelve years of age, I had to take the school bus each day to Richmond Corner to attend Southern Carleton Junior High School. It was in the countryside, close to the New Brunswick/Maine border, and the journey to and from school took at least an hour each way. I can't say that the time I spent in grades seven, eight, and nine were the happiest years of my life, as I suffered from social anxiety and a general lack of self-esteem, trying to navigate my way through my early teens. I felt like such an ugly duckling, and having little or no athletic ability, I found it difficult to fit in. To top things off, I was in a much larger school setting and rubbing shoulders with a lot of kids I did not know. Most unfortunately, I became shortsighted and had to be fitted for glasses when I turned fourteen. I greatly feared that this terrible affliction was the end of life as I knew it, and the remainder of my time in school was a blurry experience, to say the least!

The summer I turned thirteen, my parents put me on the train to Halifax to go visit Dave, Barb, and their family. I spent a week or so with them while they showed me around Halifax and the surrounding area. I had a great vacation, and when it was time for me to return home, Gregg and Betty drove the seven hours to Halifax to pick me up. Tragically, during the drive back through a treacherous stretch of wet highway on the backroads of New Brunswick, we endured a terrible car accident. Gregg was driving his brand-new car, a Chrysler Le Baron (which he was extremely proud of), when suddenly a car came careening down the big hill in front of us and swerved into our lane. Gregg had no option but to pull the car over into the ditch to avoid a head-on collision. Our car rolled over several times, leaving the three of us hanging upside down by our seat belts! I was sitting in the back seat with only a lap belt around me, but by the mercy and grace of God, I was relatively uninjured, as were my brother and his wife.

To say that we were very shaken up would be putting it mildly, but not one of us had so much as a scratch or a bruise on our bodies. We ended up spending the next few hours in a nearby home speaking with the police.

Sadly, Gregg's beautiful new maroon car was a write-off, but we were all safe and sound. Not all injuries can be seen with the naked eye, however, and I suffered from what we now know to be PTSD (posttraumatic stress disorder) for weeks following the accident, each time I would get into a car. Eventually, things returned to normal for all of us, but one thing I know for sure is that God and His angels were protecting us that awful day.

# CHAPTER 5

# Happy Days!

Sometimes a change is as good as a rest. In 1971, I had to make another big transition in order to attend high school, which was just across the river in Woodstock. I somehow still managed to spend an hour on the school bus twice a day, but things improved a lot with my social life. I gradually made new friends and became more secure in my own body. Like in the storybook, the ugly duckling slowly turned into a graceful swan, and as my self-esteem grew, I developed new interests and hobbies. In grade ten, I became a cheerleader for the junior boys' and girls' basketball teams. Not only were the practices lots of fun, but the games on the weekends were exciting, as was the odd road trip with the team! Throughout high school, I hung out with a great group of friends who were all good kids and (mostly) followed the rules. I continued to do very well in school and usually got along great with my teachers. Mom and Dad were very experienced parents by this time, and they seemed to know just how short a leash to put me on; they expected a lot from me, and in return, I tried not to disappoint them.

My best friend, Olivia, lived in Woodstock, and we would often walk to her home for lunch and spend most of the hour watching *The Young and the Restless*. We practiced cheers together and eventually worked together on the weekends. I remember how touched I was when she lugged a homemade birthday cake, decorated with sixteen candles, into my grade-ten homeroom to surprise me on my birthday. She was, and still is, my best friend to this day.

The summer I turned fifteen, I developed a very bad case of hay fever and, alas, had to retire from work in the berry field! By that time, I was glad to give it up, and the next year, my parents wasted no time in encouraging me to fill out an application for a job with the Canada Employment Agency. Lo and behold, the phone rang a day or two later, and I was offered a summer position at our one and only local department store, Stedmans Department Store. My first real job turned out to be a whole lot of fun, as I worked side by side with Olivia and some of my other friends in the stockroom, on the floor, or at the cash register near the front. I continued to work every Friday night and almost every Saturday throughout high school and was able to earn enough money for many of my own teenage needs, including clothing, magazines, and makeup.

I also had a wonderful wardrobe full of miniskirts, maxi dresses, peasant blouses, bell-bottoms, and hot pants throughout my teen years, thanks in large part to a dear friend of my mother who was a talented seamstress and made a lot of my clothing. Every so often, Olivia and I would drive across the border into Houlton, Maine, to buy blue jeans, painter pants, or overalls, and each Labour Day weekend, our family would take an extended trip to Bangor, Maine (usually with Gregg, Betty, and Jessica), for back-to-school shopping. "Penney's" was a favorite stop of mine!

During the summers following grade eleven and grade twelve, I was fortunate enough to secure a position working as a tour guide in a local museum. It was my job to walk tourists through the first courthouse established in Carleton County, built in 1833. This also gave me the chance to practice my French language skills with tourists from our bordering province of Quebec. My friends and I had a lot of fun working there, but on the days when I was alone, it was not unusual to hear mysterious sounds coming from the room behind me, which housed a lot of the military artifacts from that era. There were tales of a ghost inhabiting the old historical building, and although I don't believe in ghosts, the eerie sounds were very real, which was most disconcerting to a young lady with a vivid imagination. As a result, by the end of each summer, I was more than happy to have a change of venue!

During my growing-up years, I suffered from the usual range of maladies that afflicted young children during the sixties, such as chicken pox, scarlet fever, rubeola (red measles), and rubella (German measles). When I was just five years old, I had surgery at Carleton Memorial Hospital in Woodstock to remove my tonsils, an experience I will never forget. As it happened, the hospital was located directly across the river from our bungalow in Grafton. I stood for what seemed like hours in front of the big hospital window, gazing at my house while sobbing inconsolably for my mother. (This would be the very hospital I later worked in for two summers as a student nurse while attending university.)

None of these ailments compared to the terrible health crisis that befell me one fall morning during my grade-eleven year. The moment I woke up, I knew something was terribly wrong. When I opened my eyes, there was a bright light in the middle vision or macula of my right eye that would not go away. Mom and Dad, much to their credit, reacted immediately, taking me that very day to see the ophthalmologist who practiced in Houlton, Maine. Even after a series of examinations, he seemed baffled as to the origin of the problem but reassured us that I could be diagnosed and treated in Boston, Massachusetts. Needless to say, this was extremely alarming news to a young girl of sixteen with her whole life still in front of her!

Over the next few weeks, I saw no less than five other eye specialists in Fredericton, all of whom were just as perplexed as the first one had been. They finally came up with a diagnosis of toxoplasmosis, a parasitic infection that can be found in cat feces, undercooked meat, infected water, and unwashed produce. The disease initially begins with flu-like symptoms and can later travel to infect other parts of the body, including the eyes, lungs, or brain. Since my mother always overcooked our meat, and we had clean well water and produced most of our own vegetables, it was surmised that I had probably caught the disease through close contact with cats. Because Mom only allowed me to keep parakeets and small turtles for pets after we moved to Grafton, it was a big mystery as to where I might have encountered the pathogen.

Unfortunately, the bleeding in the back of my retina continued to spread, and more bright spots began to appear in my vision. The disease was virtually untreatable in 1972, so I was sent home from the doctor's office uncertain of what the final prognosis would really be. Those first few months were a waiting game for me, but eventually, by Christmas, the bright lights disappeared entirely, leaving only a few tiny scars when I closed my left eye. I was so thankful to God that He was able to sustain me throughout that trying time and that I was able to come out of the whole terrifying ordeal relatively unscathed.

The funny thing is, one night during this same time period, I had the strangest dream where it felt like I was watching myself in a movie. I sat up in bed, and Jesus was standing before me in a long white robe with flowing, light brown hair. With a gentle and loving expression on His face, He reached out and touched me. For many years, I tried to remember what He said to me, but I have since learned that as a Christian, God puts a hedge of protection around us, which nothing designed by the devil (our enemy) can penetrate. I believe that when Jesus touched me, true healing began. Dealing with my eye disease was probably the first big test of my faith, and as we often say in jest, "What doesn't kill us makes us stronger."

The remainder of my time in high school was mainly happy and carefree. I spent most school nights listening to rock music on the local radio station while hitting the books. Anything by the Beatles or Elton John was a favorite of mine, and I knew all the words to their songs by heart. For posterity, I even recorded their music on a cassette recorder that my parents had given me one Christmas.

I pursued an academic stream in school, studying English, math, French, history, geography, economics, chemistry, and biology. Olivia and I also decided to take a typing course together, which really served me well over the years. In grade ten, we took driver's education at the local vocational school, and I eventually learned to perfect my newfound skills by driving around Woodstock in my dad's pickup truck.

In 1972, the English carpenter (and family friend) who built my parents' home had his grandniece and grandnephew from England come over to stay with him and his wife for the summer. I spent a lot of time showing them around town while trying to explain how things were done in Canada. I always did have a fascination with everything British ever since I became enamored with the Beatles!

Throughout my high school years, I had a huge crush on one boy who unfortunately already had a girlfriend, so any relationship between the two of us was not meant to be. As a result, I didn't date much, although toward the end of grade twelve, a few boys did ask me out. I was never really that interested in anyone, but I did double-date with my friend Susan once. Because of this mindset, I didn't attend my prom, which is something I regret to this day. Other events leading up to graduation day were exciting, though, as was the big day itself, which took place in late June 1974. With my family present in the Connell Park Arena to cheer me on, I graduated near the top of my class and secured a scholarship to the University of New Brunswick.

I sometimes reflect on how it was that I never got into any trouble during high school when all around me there were kids in my class who did just that—they smoked, abused alcohol, and did drugs. A couple of "good girls" from good homes even got pregnant and had babies in grade ten. I grew up during the tumultuous sixties and seventies when hippies were common, young men had long hair, and kids partied at the lake; none of this, however, seemed to touch my friends or me. I was obviously sheltered by my parents, and being a natural rule keeper, I always aspired to tell the truth and do my best. I think I inherited this trait from my father, who was somewhat of a perfectionist. My brother Gregg was cut from the same cloth, while Dave used to say, "Easy come, easy go!" Of course, it certainly didn't hurt that I had a praying mother who kept a close eye on me and spent quiet time each day reading her Bible.

Following graduation, my parents decided to treat both themselves and me to my first big vacation: a trip to visit Dad's younger brother Gabe, his wife, Evelyn, and their family in Nanaimo, British Columbia. Toward the end of August, we flew to Vancouver, where we met up with their family of five. From there, we set out on a camping trip, driving in their big suburban (hauling a tent trailer behind it) through Alberta and British Columbia. Our final destination was Vancouver Island, where we toured beautiful Victoria and then spent the rest of our trip in the small city of Nanaimo. It was wonderful to spend quality time with my parents and our extended family while experiencing the magnificent vista of the Rocky Mountains for the first time. We even ran into some black bears in Jasper National Park, which livened things up a bit! This shared family vacation was very precious to me and was indeed one of the last defining moments of my childhood.

CHAPTER 6

# The End of Innocence

It's a very true saying that graduation from high school in no way prepares you for life in the real world. As sophisticated as I thought I was, I was not at all prepared for the reality of making all my own decisions and being entirely responsible for myself! By the end of the summer of 1974, I had to make two of the biggest decisions of my life—which school to attend and which program to take. I had applied to several different universities in the Maritimes and fortunately was accepted into each one of them. I ultimately decided to attend the University of New Brunswick (UNB) in Fredericton for several reasons, not the least of which was that my brother Gregg lived there and had most generously offered to give me free room and board during my time at school. Since our family income was quite modest, I qualified for a large bursary each year, but I also had to take out a student loan for the entire four years. Living with my brother and his family would certainly help pay the bills.

After considering a career either as a journalist or working as an interpreter, I decided upon nursing (at the last possible moment), believing that it would always provide good job opportunities for me. Upon reflection, I think this idea must have been God inspired, as previously I had never, ever had a burning desire to look after anyone! I never even babysat that much as a teenager. More than once in my life, however, my career choice has proven to be a real godsend. As it happened, I had a good friend from high school, Kathy, who was also enrolled in the faculty of nursing. In early September, I hitched a ride with her and her parents to the Fredericton campus and blindly followed the other freshmen around the big auditorium, trying to figure out which courses I should take. The curriculum was a mixture of arts and science courses with nursing at its core. With the hurdle of registration behind me, I then settled into my tiny bedroom in Gregg and Betty's small bungalow, which was located a few miles off campus.

During the week, they would drop me off at the bottom of the big hill leading up to the UNB campus on their way to work in downtown Fredericton. After a full morning of classes, I would usually eat my solitary lunch at the Student Union Building (SUB). At the end of the day, after the remainder of my classes, I would walk home alone. Fortunately, I could cut across the small forest bordering the brand-new Aitken Centre arena located at the very top of the hill. It was not a very long journey, but it *was* rather scary, walking through the thick blanket of trees to reach the other side where my brother's home was situated. During my four years at UNB, a few cases of rape occurred on campus, including some lesser crimes, but thankfully, I never ran into any trouble during my travels.

I would like to say that my freshman year was a fun-filled year of firsts, but truthfully, it was a very lonely time for me, as I felt I was missing out on all the fun on campus. On weekends, I would either take the bus home to Woodstock or catch a ride home with an engineer who worked at the Aitken Centre during the week but lived in the nearby town of Hartland. I would spend most of Saturday studying, and on Sunday afternoon I would once again make the one-hour trek back to my brother's house. To make matters worse, there was a lot of tension in their home, as my brother and his wife were having marital problems, and a big black cloud seemed to constantly hover in the air. I really appreciated all that they were trying to do for me, but it turned out to be a rather miserable year. Living off campus, I also made few new friends and dated very little. I found the academic transition from high school to university difficult as well and barely passed chemistry. My first-year marks were ho-hum at best, but I did okay and proceeded on into the second year.

Each year, May and June were devoted to working in different hospital settings, which provided me the opportunity to move into a new home. Toward the end of my first year, I worked on the medical/surgical floors at the old Fredericton hospital, the Victoria Public Hospital, which was located downtown by the river. I moved into a quaint but rambling

Victorian house owned by the university with a few other student nurses and biked back and forth to work each day. That summer, I moved back home and worked on the medical floor of our small hospital in Woodstock. It helped pay the bills and gave me some valuable experience in the medical field.

When Mom and Dad realized how isolated and lonely I had felt living with my brother and his family, they made sure I would have a better experience during the remainder of my school life. With their blessing, I applied to move into student residence and was accepted into Lady Dunn Hall in the fall of 1975. Most of my friends also lived there, and I loved being a coed! Although I was officially a sophomore, my hazing was complete when my dormmates threw me into the shower, fully clothed, and covered me in shampoo from head to toe! During second year, I shared a room with a quiet freshman from the Miramichi, and in my third year, I roomed with another friend from Woodstock who was studying education. Living with Jenny proved to be much more exciting because she was fun-loving and a little bit wild! In my fourth and final year, I wanted my own space, so I splurged on a private room with a shared bathroom (with Dorothy, another nursing friend).

I had so much fun, even though I was weighed down by heavy coursework as well as work commitments at different times of the year, both in the hospital and in the community. It was a stark contrast to the first year of my university life. Despite spending most Friday and Saturday evenings at different pubs on campus, I worked very hard, and my marks improved significantly. There is a lot to be said for having a good work/life balance! My social life was also much improved, as I mixed with other students and started to date. There were lots of social events and formals to attend throughout the year, with either the Faculty of Nursing or functions at Lady Dunn Hall.

I spent May and June of my second year in Saint John, New Brunswick, completing my psychiatric practicum. That summer, I decided to return to Fredericton, so I took a job working on the orthopedics floor back at the old hospital. I once again lived with my brother, but by then, I was using my dad's second vehicle to go back and forth to Woodstock on the weekends, which gave me more freedom.

Third year was our make-or-break year, and some of our professors seemed to take great delight in trying to ruin our blossoming careers. More than one girl ended up dropping out of nursing that year. Our studies concentrated on maternity, pediatrics, and community nursing, with increasing time spent in both the hospital and the community settings. By the fall of 1976, a brand-new hospital opened in Fredericton; our maternity and pediatric experience was completed there, but I fell totally in love with community nursing, right from the start. It would, however, be many more years before I worked in that area of nursing.

I managed to emerge from my third year relatively unscathed and returned to work at the Carleton Memorial Hospital in Woodstock in July and August 1977. I was fortunate enough to get a job working on the maternity floor, which included labor and delivery, postpartum, and the nursery. Although I gained practical experience in each area, my favorite spot to work was in the nursery. I loved bathing, holding, and feeding the tiny infants, as well as sitting with them in our big rocking chair to lull them back to sleep. During that time, it was the nurses rather than new parents who mainly looked after the babies, as the rooming-in policy of today wasn't yet in place. What a wonderful summer I had, made even more perfect when I met my first true love!

On my days off that summer, I would hang out with a few old friends from high school, including my best friend, Olivia, who had a summer job working for the telephone company. She had also decided to study nursing but was taking her degree at Mount Saint Vincent University in Halifax, Nova Scotia. The two of us saw a lot of another good friend, Christie (also studying nursing in Saint John, N.B.), who drove a little orange VW Bug all over town. Christie was a force to be reckoned with, as she loved boys, shopping, and having a good time—all in that order! Indeed, it was difficult to keep up with her. Many warm summer evenings were spent biking around the town of Woodstock for exercise and for something to do. It really was a one-horse town back in those days, without any fancy restaurants, bars, or discos. The young people would congregate in the parking lot of the largest grocery store in town, which is where I had my first glimpse of Bobby.

He was sitting behind the wheel of his sleek black sports car (a Firebird, as I recall), looking very handsome and cool. Right away, I noticed his thick, wavy blond hair, beautiful white smile, azure-blue eyes, and cheeky dimples. He was *indeed* very good-looking but had a quiet manner about him. I felt an immediate attraction to him, and I believed the feeling was mutual. Coincidentally, Christie had dated Bobby's older brother, who died tragically a year or so before in a motor vehicle accident. Bobby was a couple of years younger than me and was the third child out of four brothers; he still lived at home with his parents and younger brother on the family farm. Located just outside of Woodstock, they operated a large and very prosperous dairy farm.

I can't remember exactly how it happened, but we started dating, and our romance quickly blossomed into what I thought was lasting love by the end of the summer. Bobby was a great guy and was a lot of fun to be around. I remember sitting beside him in his car with the windows rolled down and the music turned up, listening to tunes on his eight-track player, including America, the Eagles, Fleetwood Mac, Foreigner, and all the other big names from the seventies. How exhilarating it was to be young, carefree, and in love! We also had lots of fun with our mutual friends and attended more than one kitchen party that summer when unsuspecting parents were not at home. Of course, that never included my house because Mom and Dad were usually there!

Bobby's parents also had a cottage at Skiff Lake, and we loved spending time there, where I tried to learn how to waterski. Unfortunately, I never did quite get the hang of it! One night, as we were all driving back from the lake, we had the misfortune of getting a flat tire on the gravel road, which made us very late arriving home. Although my parents really liked Bobby, my mother was waiting up for me as I walked in the door. She thought that we had been "up to no good," but that was certainly not the case. After much explaining, she finally believed my story and let me go to bed. By that time, I had already turned twenty-one, but that held little or no weight with Mom!

On the weekends, we enjoyed going over to the nearby town of Houlton, Maine, for our evening entertainment. Just across the border, there was a rather raunchy bar with a dance floor that hosted (very bad) hard rock and country and western bands; we somehow managed to have fun anyway! The state trooper there always checked our IDs because we probably looked younger than we actually were. By this time, although I never smoked or took drugs, I did drink alcohol when I went out on the weekends. I usually did not drive, but I did share rides with other people who were under the influence; most fortunately, we never had an incident of any kind. We lived in a different era back then, although the problem of impaired driving seems to be just as serious, if not more so, today. Once again, by the mercy and grace of God, we were protected from any harm.

I certainly regret some of the careless and stupid things I did as a young person, and irresponsible drinking is among them. I have been blessed my whole life in that I have never experienced any problems with addiction; rather, I tend to have a more disciplined personality and can be very hard on myself. My love-hate relationship with food has proven that over the years; I am always watching my waistline, counting calories, and trying to get enough exercise into each day. It is always a challenge.

As summer inevitably drew to its sad ending and September rolled around, I was excited to be entering my fourth and final year of university. Bobby and I continued to see each other on the weekends when he would come down to UNB to visit me or when I would occasionally go home to see my parents. My coursework was more manageable than it had been the year before, although I still had to complete a research paper and write an article for publication. Our hospital experience was focused on time spent in the cardiac care unit (CCU) and intensive care unit (ICU) that year.

I enjoyed the privacy of finally having my own room in residence, which was on the second floor of Lady Dunn Hall and overlooked the entire campus. There was still time for socializing at dorm parties held on the weekends or during the more formal dinners and balls held throughout the year. I occasionally attended a Baptist church in downtown Fredericton with my brother, who would pick me up on Sunday morning and return me back home after I had enjoyed lunch with him and his family. Even though I was not actively practicing my faith during my university years, I never once stopped believing in God or knowing that He had a master plan for my life. Despite this, it was easy to get off track while living in residence and trying to fit in with everyone else.

When Valentine's Day in 1978 came and went with no valentine card, flowers, or even a phone call from Bobby, I suspected something was terribly wrong. When I finally talked to him one evening on the dorm phone, he began making excuses as to why he couldn't come down on the weekends to visit me. When I was able to go home one weekend in

March, prior to exams, all my hopes and dreams for our future together ended abruptly. Bobby took me out on a date and then promptly broke up with me when he brought me back home, explaining that he thought I was "too serious." He was obviously young and immature and not yet ready to settle down. Never one to hang on, I tearfully kissed him goodbye in my driveway, my heart broken beyond repair. He had been my first true love but would not be my last. It is said that everything happens for a reason, and I rather doubt I would have made a very good farmer's wife!

After I returned to school, I tried to focus on preparing for final exams, which continued throughout the month of April. In early July, after finals, we had to write the dreaded RN exams, which were rumored to be very difficult and exhausting. Although I certainly had a full plate to take my mind off my love life, little did I know what—or rather, *who*—was waiting for me around the corner!

# CHAPTER 7

# A Blind Date

Sometime during the second week of exams, my good friend, fellow dormmate, and (second-year) nursing student Lydia set me up with the roommate of the guy she was dating. Lydia had once lived in Woodstock, and although she and I had never met then, I had been friends with her older sister in high school, and their father had also been one of my teachers. Coincidentally, Brian, Lydia's current boyfriend, hailed from the small town of Hartland, which was just up the river from Woodstock. Jake was one of Brian's three roommates (all attending UNB), but he originated from St. John's, Newfoundland. Brian was studying business administration while Jake was studying forest engineering. Although I was still nursing a broken heart over Bobby, I trusted Lydia's judgment and, after carefully pondering the matter, agreed to go out on a blind double date with the three of them. The timing was not great, but it was a welcome distraction after the pressure of the previous few weeks.

I took great care in choosing my attire, which was rather limited by then, but I really wanted to make a good impression. I ended up borrowing a pair of Frye boots from a friend, which looked great with my favorite pair of burgundy corduroy culottes! I shampooed and blow-dried my medium-length blonde hair (parted in the middle), applied a bit of makeup, and was ready to go!

I still remember my first sighting of Jake; the guys were waiting for us in the front entrance of the Dunn lobby. He was tall, dark, and handsome, sporting a small Afro and moustache and wearing skinny black corduroy bell-bottoms with a checkered shirt under a long, reddish-brown leather coat. He also wore a black fedora hat angled to one side, which gave him an old-time gangster movie appearance. My first impression of him was mixed at best because, in addition to his odd apparel, he seemed to be extremely thin and was recovering from a bad cough and cold.

His manner was very subdued, and he rarely looked at me or tried to engage me in conversation during the entire course of the evening. He did seem to be a gentleman, however, as he helped me settle into the front bucket seat of his huge black Camaro, with Brian and Lydia sitting in the backseat. I later learned that his friends called him the "Codfather," which we thought was hilarious at the time but may have been a bad omen of things to come. One thing was for sure: he seemed to have more money than the rest of us poor university students put together. He also had nice wheels, which was once again rather unusual.

The setting for our first date was a small restaurant called the Baker's Oven, located in the trendy Neapolitan Club, which was a large part of the nightlife in downtown Fredericton at that time. The Neo was a hip disco dance bar back in the day, a place where university students would occasionally go if they wanted a change of pace from the pub life back on campus. I can't remember exactly what we ordered, but I think the food was pretty good there. The guys paid the bill at the end of the evening, which gave them full marks in our books! By the end of our fourth year, most students were poorer than church mice and carried a huge student loan debt to boot. After our first date, I was not quite sure what to make of Jake, and I wondered if I would ever hear from him again.

During the following week, I was preoccupied with studying for my final two exams, so I tried not to think about Jake. He eventually called me in the middle of the week and asked me out on a date for the upcoming Saturday night. I was happy to hear from him again, since I believed that he *might* have been boyfriend material, and our second date went much better than our first. We went to the cinema and saw *The Goodbye Girl*, which from then on was always known as "our movie." It was a teary love story but quirky and funny at the same time. Over the course of the next few weeks, Jake proceeded to wine and dine me. We went out to a few local restaurants, pubs, and discos and sat in the very first row to watch *Grease*. It was well worth the pain in our necks to see John Travolta and Olivia Newton-John dance and sing together. What a golden couple they were!

35

After we both wrapped up our final exams at the end of April, I moved out of residence for the last time. Jake continued to live alone in the basement apartment of a large bungalow located just off campus. His roommates were mostly undergrads and had already returned to their respective hometowns. I moved back home to Woodstock with my parents and started preparing for the RN exams, slated for the first week of July. In early May, Jake and some of his classmates flew out to British Columbia for a field trip that they had arranged prior to graduation. On the morning of my twenty-second birthday, the tenth of May, I woke up to the sound of a delivery man knocking on our front door. I still recall how surprised and pleased Mom and I both were to discover that Jake had sent me a dozen red roses. They were probably the most beautiful flowers anyone had given me since I'd been the flower girl in my brother's wedding! He certainly made a good impression on all of us that day, including my father.

When Jake returned to Fredericton from B.C., around the middle of May, we resumed seeing each other. He still had his car and would drive up to Woodstock to see me at least once during the week and once on the weekends. Graduation was toward the end of May, and we were both excited to finally receive our hard-earned degrees and to get on with the next stage of our young lives. On the big day itself, I joined the graduating class of 1978 in the massive Aitken Centre arena. It felt extra special for me, as my parents, both of my brothers, and their wives were in the audience to watch me graduate. I fondly remember walking up the steep hill with my fellow graduates in the warm sunshine of late spring and later walking proudly across the stage to accept my degree in nursing. Anne Murray, a famous Canadian recording artist, had also graduated from UNB several years before and gave the keynote address that day. She was, in fact, a good friend of one of my nursing professors, who held a doctorate degree in nursing—a person we all admired but secretly feared!

In addition to his forest engineering degree, Jake also received two university rings: one honoring his service with the student union (SU) and one for his involvement in student affairs. For fun, he had worked on the forest engineering newsletter and also played for their ice hockey team. As an elected representative of the student union council, one of his favorite jobs had been interviewing and hiring rock bands to play at university events, including bands such as Rush, April Wine, Trooper, and The Guess

Who. Compared to Jake, I felt like an underachiever, as I had focused on completing my degree while having a good social life. It soon became clear to me that Jake was indeed a good catch!

As well as being very bright, he was hardworking and had many friends. He seemed to have a lot going for him, and I was slowly falling in love with him. It was not a case of love at first sight, as it had been with Bobby, but I hoped and prayed that perhaps this kind of love would be more substantial and everlasting. Unfortunately, Jake already had a date for the big UNB ball on graduation night. She was rumored to be very beautiful and had once been a model in her home province of Newfoundland. Jake insisted they were just friends, so I ended up asking one of my friends from high school to escort me to the final event of my university life. Sadly, I don't remember it being a very memorable night for either me or my poor neglected date.

In early June, Jake drove home to Newfoundland, taking the ferry from North Sydney, Nova Scotia, to Argentia, which is on the southernmost tip of the Avalon peninsula and about an hour-and-a-half drive from St. John's. After a short visit with his parents, he traveled to his summer job in Beaverton, a tiny town in the middle of the big island. He had a temporary position working in a logging camp, mapping sections of the dense forest. I don't think it was an easy assignment in terms of the amenities, as the showers were scarce, and the blackflies were relentless, but he did get out to visit civilization once a week. In the meantime, I was still at home studying for my RN exams; our frequent, long love letters to each other kept us going until we could meet again.

I took a break from studying sometime toward the end of June when Jake invited me to fly over to St. John's to meet his parents and little sister, Debbie, who was almost seven years younger than him. His father's elderly mother also lived with the family at that time. Although I was a little hesitant to go at first, Jake generously offered to pay my way; so, putting any doubts aside, I hopped onto a jet and flew the short distance to his family's home. It was an opportunity to meet not only his immediate family (who were very hospitable to me) but also his favorite aunt and uncle, who lived just outside the city limits on a huge, century-old farm. Jake's family also lived very close to another aunt and uncle as well as to their son, daughter-in-law, and two children. They seemed to be a tight-knit, middle-class family, with both of Jake's parents working full time. His mom, Joan, was an elementary school teacher, while his dad, Tom, was a carpenter and part-time fisherman.

They lived in the small home that his father had built with his own hands back in the fifties. It was in a charming little coastal town called Herring Bay, located about twenty minutes outside of St. John's. Herring Bay had originally been settled by the Spanish way back in the 1600s and was one of the oldest settlements in Canada. It was extremely picturesque and directly across the bay from Fairyland Island, which had once been famous for its rich stores of gold. Two ferries crossed back and forth to the mainland several times a day to transport the locals who still lived there.

During the few days that I was there visiting, I met most of Jake's family while we toured around the quaint, old city of St. John's and its surrounding area. It all seemed very foreign to me, since I came from a family of farmers, not fishermen, and the scenery looked more like the craggy cliffs of Ireland than the soft, rolling hills and valleys that I was accustomed to. Our drives along the coastline were breathtakingly beautiful, and the stark yet majestic landscape is still hard to put into words. I was treated to traditional "Newfie" fare, including fish and chips, fish and brewis, cod tongues, Bannock, and Jiggs Dinner; all were very tasty but not ideal for the waistline! Before I returned home, Jake's cousin Gary made sure I was properly "screeched in," which involved having me drink a shot of the strong, locally made Screech rum, reciting a short poem, and then kissing a cod fish! (I think I may have skipped the last part.) That informal ceremony made me an honorary Newfoundlander, although I still could not understand much of what they said, especially Jake's dad, who had a very strong accent. It was really rather embarrassing for me, since it was hard to answer his questions with any semblance of intelligence! All in all, though, my trip went well, and I had a great time.

After I arrived safely back home in New Brunswick, I settled down once again and focused on my upcoming exams. In early July, I stayed with Gregg's family in Fredericton and proceeded to write two different nursing exams each day, over a one-week period. I was relieved when it was all over, but since the exams were mainly multiple choice, it was hard to tell exactly how well I had done. I tried not to worry too much about it and instead started sending off résumés to several different hospitals in the

Maritimes, hoping that I would eventually land a good job. Things moved much more slowly back then, as we all relied on "snail mail" for almost everything, but it wasn't too long before I heard back from one of my top picks, the King George Hospital in Halifax, Nova Scotia.

The head of human resources phoned me one bright, sunny morning and offered me a position working as a graduate nurse on their burn unit. It was the burn center for Atlantic Canada at the time and would provide a good opportunity for me to get my feet wet. Thankfully, I would only be working with adults and not children, because I didn't think I could handle treating children with bad burns. I mulled it over for a couple of days, and after discussing it with my parents, I decided to accept their offer. Mom was happy to have me broaden my horizons, but I will never forget how sad my father was to see me leave my home province. He had been secretly hoping I would stay in Woodstock or move to Fredericton and work closer to home.

To complicate matters further, Mom (now sixty-seven years young) suffered a heart attack sometime during the latter part of July, but after spending a week or so in our local CCU, she came home. Thankfully, the damage to her heart was minimal, but since she had been overweight for many years, she knew the time had finally come for her to lose the extra pounds and get her health back under control. Once Mom set her mind to something, there was no stopping her, and she did indeed lose a lot of weight over the next few months. More significantly, her blood pressure and blood glucose levels returned to normal, and she said she felt so much better. A big bonus for her was that she could shop for clothing with ease, and her wardrobe soon expanded accordingly! I now had a brand-new mother, and I was *so* proud of her huge accomplishment! Following her big health scare, Mom became much more self-confident and self-aware and, most importantly, never put the weight back on again.

All in all, I felt very badly about leaving my parents behind, but I knew there would be more opportunities for me if I was working in a larger hospital setting. I also loved Halifax and was very excited to be moving to the same city where my best friend, Olivia, and my brother David and his family already lived. Thankfully, Dad eventually came around to accepting the idea of me working so far away from my hometown and was genuinely excited for me. Jake was another matter entirely; he had already been accepted into a joint law/MBA program at UNB for the upcoming fall and was not at *all* happy that we would be living so far apart.

By now, we both firmly believed we were officially boyfriend and girlfriend, and we were wondering just where our relationship was headed. Jake ultimately decided to apply to the master of business administration (MBA) program at Saint Mary's University (SMU) in Halifax so that he could be nearer to me. Fortunately, by the end of the summer, he was accepted into their program and turned down the placement at UNB. At the time, I wasn't sure he had made the right choice, but I decided to leave the decision up to him. In the meantime, I began to fill my own oversized, big blue steamer trunk with all my worldly possessions. The difference now was that this move would be my very last time leaving home.

# CHAPTER 8

# Life in the Big City

If memory serves me correctly, I made my move from the small town of Woodstock to the big city of Halifax around the end of July. Gregg had generously offered to drive me down in his car, which pulled a small U-Haul trailer behind it. The trailer held all that was dear to me, including clothes, shoes, some small household items Mom and I had purchased together, my beloved stereo and record collection, and other treasured mementos from my childhood. My bedroom dresser, cedar hope chest, and big blue trunk were also jammed into the small space. To top it off, Gregg had offered to deliver some strawberries to Halifax for my father, so as we drove down the long and winding road, the sweet smell of berry juice filled the car. A year or so after our shared journey together, Gregg gave the toast to the bride at my wedding, cautioning the groom, "Watch out, as Becky never travels lightly!" That was all too true.

My temporary destination was my brother David's home, with all my odds and ends stored in his back shed. They were kind enough to take me in for a couple of weeks until I found a permanent place to live. My sister-in-law Barb took me under her wing, and together we looked through the two Halifax daily newspapers for an affordable place to rent. After we made a (very) short list of possible rentals, we spent a few days checking out the apartments in downtown Halifax, near enough to the hospital to allow me to walk back and forth to work each day. The King George Hospital (KGH) was located close to all the other hospitals in the pricey south end of Halifax and was also near to both Dalhousie and Saint Mary's universities. In midsummer, the streets were draped with beautiful elm trees, and the petunias, begonias, and impatiens were in full bloom; it did not take long for me to fall in love with this quaint but still modern city on the harbor! Unfortunately, there were not many housing options to choose from, and the prices were very high for a young nurse who did not yet have her official RN designation or, worse still, any savings!

In the end, I chose a bachelor apartment located on busy Robie Street, on the seventeenth floor of a one-year-old high-rise building overlooking the Halifax Commons. It was clean and modern, and the view from the long bank of windows in the great room was spectacular! Once again, I quickly fell in love with my new abode, although it was situated a few miles away from the hospital, which would mean taking the city bus to and from work. Fortunately, the bus stopped right in front of my building, and since I have never been a morning person, this turned out to be a godsend for me. On fair-weather days, I could even walk home at the end of my twelve-hour shift.

It was a good compromise, and even though the rent was a whopping $280 a month, the heat and lights were included, making it *just* affordable for me. My only extras would be cable, phone, food, transportation, and entertainment. I hoped my clothes would last for a while, but I knew I would have to buy several new nursing uniforms and at least another pair of good shoes. With a student loan to repay, money would be tight. By my calculations, my hourly wage would be a little over six dollars an hour, but it would go up a bit when I passed my RNs. The results of those exams could not come soon enough!

David, along with his two teenage sons, Jamie and Brent, and another friend, helped move me into apartment 1703 in early August 1978. Immediately, I noticed that I was shy of a few essentials. With my parents' help, I ended up furnishing my tiny dwelling with a single brass bed; a small, round orange-and-white dining set; and a chocolate-brown sofa bed with a matching chair. In addition, I borrowed a round, glass coffee table from Dave and Barb as well as a small black-and-white TV. I decorated the entire apartment with bright orange accents to complement the table and chairs, which helped pull the whole room together. The unit also had a separate galley kitchen with a full stove and fridge, which was more than sufficient for my limited cooking skills! (The microwave oven was not a common feature of most kitchens back in those days.) Finally, I spent my last bit of money buying basic dishes, pots and pans, cutlery, and items for the bathroom. I soon realized that the luxury of living alone would not come cheap!

My first two weeks of work at the KGH were spent in a classroom, learning more about burns in general and how to assess and treat patients with first-, second-, and third-degree burns. There was a lot to learn, and most of it was new to me. The floor itself was divided into an isolation burn unit with separate rooms, and there was a larger plastic surgery section, which housed patients who required the repair of injuries and skin graft surgery for severe burns and gunshot wounds. Some injuries were accidental, while some were intentionally inflicted. All in all, it was a real eye-opener for me, since these patients often suffered from mental health issues, such as severe depression and a lack of self-esteem. Most unfortunately, they could also be extremely sarcastic and manipulative, and because the majority were comprised of men, the all-female nursing staff often had to put up with offensive and sexist remarks.

The burn patients were almost always in extreme pain and were on high doses of morphine, which the nurses would administer intravenously. They always came in as an emergency admission directly onto our floor and required immediate medical attention and intervention. They were vulnerable to excessive loss of blood plasma as well as infection and could not regulate their body temperature well due to the loss of skin and/or body fat. They endured normal saline baths in a huge stainless steel tub, several times a week, where we would use scissors to debride the dead tissue from their bodies. They would then be coated with copious amounts of white medicated cream and wrapped up in several layers of sterile gauze bandages. The dressings were completed both morning and evening in reverse isolation to protect the patients from infection and to promote healing. The nurses, nursing assistants, and plastic surgeons were always dressed in full gown, gloves, mask, and booties in the burn unit. It was a hot, demanding, and tiring place to work, and some of the personal stories were just heartbreaking. It was difficult to get those patients out of my mind at night, since not everybody pulled through.

Nevertheless, 9 West was known as a good floor to work on, as we had a great head nurse with a high level of staffing. It was a supportive environment overall, which cannot be said about many workplaces. It was where I first learned *how* to become a nurse, putting my schooling into real practice. I got along well with most of the girls I worked with, and quite a few of the single girls socialized together as well. Later that August, I finally received the results of my RN exams through the mail, and thankfully, I did well. I had easily passed each area and was now officially a real nurse!

Toward the end of August, Jake moved from the Rock (a.k.a. Newfoundland) into a small apartment building in Bedford. Bedford was a suburb of Halifax and was nestled along beautiful Bedford Basin. It was close to where my brother lived in Rockingham, a subdivision that was situated higher up on a steep hill, overlooking almost all of Bedford Basin. Luckily, since Jake had a car, he could easily commute back and forth to Saint Mary's University each day.

In truth, Jake ended up spending a lot of time at my apartment on my days off, so his place was sorely neglected. I worked twelve-hour shifts, including both day and night shifts, but had a long weekend off every other week. Besides socializing with my friends, we gradually developed a new group of friends, mostly fellow MBA or law students, whom Jake had met through school. Most of them were a bit older than us and were already married or in serious relationships. One of his former UNB roommates, Peter, eventually married Carol, one of the nursing assistants I worked with. (Jake and I had introduced them.) We had a lot of fun that year and enjoyed going out on the town to explore new pubs, restaurants, and discos. One of our favorite discos was known as The Palace and featured live bands, some of them quite famous. I remember we once heard Joe Cocker perform at the Misty Moon, which was an unbelievable experience. It was the height of the disco era, and we loved to dance! There were also many small artisan shops, boutiques, and bistros along the waterfront to explore together on our days off. I quickly grew to love fresh seafood, especially lobster, as Halifax is a seafood lover's paradise!

That Christmas, while Jake went home to visit his parents, I worked through the holidays. When he arrived back at my apartment on the third of January, he presented me with a beautiful diamond solitaire engagement ring! With a puppy-dog face, he confessed that he had planned to propose on Valentine's Day, but he just couldn't wait any longer. I was delighted but not completely taken by surprise, as although we had only been dating for less than nine months, we had already lightheartedly discussed the idea of marriage. Our relationship did seem to be moving quickly, however, since Jake was still in school, with at least a year and a half to go before graduation. We were also very young; Jake was about to turn twenty-two, and I would be twenty-three in May, but we both felt mature for our age at the time.

Despite our concerns, we knew we were in love, so we decided to be reckless and throw caution to the wind. A few days later, we got dressed up and went downtown to a fancy English restaurant located on Barrington Street called the Manor House. Despite the damp and chilly winter weather outdoors, I fondly recall the warm, romantic ambiance of soft candlelight, dried flowers on the tables, and romantic music playing quietly in the background as we discussed our plans for the future. It felt very grown-up and serious indeed to have a fiancé!

I am sure that our parents must have had some misgivings about our engagement, but if they did, we never heard about them at the time. With thinly veiled excitement, we phoned each of them to share our good news. Everyone seemed to be very happy for us, and we looked forward to celebrating our wedding sometime during the upcoming summer. Already, the crunch was on, as I had only a few short months to plan and organize the wedding of my dreams! In late winter, we had our engagement photos taken, and in addition to having an announcement put in the newspapers, we had our picture placed on the front of our invitations. All that winter and the following spring, on my days off work, I carefully perused bridal magazines for ideas about my wedding dress, the bridesmaids' dresses, the flowers, and possible locations for our wedding, reception, and honeymoon. We also had to select the menu, hire a photographer, and decide what to do about the entertainment.

Thankfully, Jake took charge of picking out the attire for himself and his attendants as well as planning and organizing our honeymoon. It had always been my dream to travel to the UK, and Jake was happy to oblige. Together, we visited a travel agent to get brochures and ideas for our itinerary, and with a growing sense of excitement, we booked our airline tickets to London for late August.

We soon learned that before we could do anything else, we would have to set a firm date for our big day. We settled on Saturday, August 25, since it was toward the end of summer, but the weather would still be warm enough to host a beautiful wedding and hospitable enough in September to travel around England and Scotland. Most importantly, Jake would not miss any time at school. We decided to wed in Fredericton; it held a special place in our hearts, as we had both attended university there. When I told my parents that we would not be getting married in Woodstock, they were very disappointed, but they soon accepted our decision. It helped to soften the blow a bit when we chose to get married in the same church I had attended with Gregg, a very old and quaint Baptist church in downtown Fredericton. Jake was fine with letting me decide which church to choose; he had been brought up in the United Church and told me he was a Christian, although we never had any deep conversations about what that meant to him. We also never discussed the topic of having children, and I just hoped we would eventually have them.

In the days before wedding planners, organizing a wedding in another city proved to be a whole lot of work, but eventually, things started to come together. We each picked out our attendants carefully; I chose my niece Jessica and Jake's sister Debbie, who were both fifteen years old at the time, as well as my friend Olivia from high school. My friend Lydia from university was to be my maid of honor. For groomsmen, Jake chose two of his roommates from university (Brian and Peter), as well as my nephew Jamie, who was seventeen years old. Jack, his best friend from home, would be his best man. We wanted to celebrate with our nearest and dearest family and friends and settled on a guest list of about one hundred twenty-five people. That was plenty big enough for us, as our funds were limited, and all of Jake's family had to travel from either Newfoundland or Ontario. Thankfully, our parents offered to help us out with the cost of the wedding, and they ended up splitting a large part of the bill. The reception was to be held at the oldest and most stately hotel in Fredericton, the Lord Beaverbrook Hotel, which was located along the St. John River and had a rich history in the old Loyalist city.

During one of my numerous trips back to Woodstock that year, I decided to drop into Levine's, a popular department store in downtown Fredericton. I was still searching for my wedding dress; Mom, Barb, and I had previously scoured Halifax with no luck. That day, looking by myself, I fell in love with the first one I tried on. It had a classic high neckline, an empire waist, and pleated, full-length sleeves and was covered from top to bottom with white lace and pearls. With the salesgirl's help, I also picked out a Juliet cap and long veil, fit for a princess bride. I had recently cut my blonde hair and had it styled in long, loose curls; the snow-white, pearl-encrusted cap was a perfect match to the long, romantic gown I had chosen. Jake had already ordered black-and-white tuxedoes for himself, his best man, and his groomsmen, while my maid of honor and bridesmaids were wearing breezy, off-the-shoulder, long and flowing dresses. Each dress was a different pastel color: pink, peach, yellow, and blue. Together, Mom and I picked out the design for the peach, three-tiered wedding cake (complete with the traditional figurines of a bride and groom on top), and we hired a local lady in Fredericton to bake it. As well, Jake's mom was bringing a homemade fruitcake from Newfoundland for the groom to pass out to our guests. At last, the scene was set for romance!

My final trip to Woodstock was a week or so before the wedding to complete the final preparations for our upcoming nuptials. Although the practice of throwing a bachelorette party had not yet come into vogue, no less than three separate bridal showers had been planned for me. One was a community shower held in Grafton; one was hosted by my cousin Dale's wife, Elaine (who had at one time lived next door to us in Grafton); and the third was held by my good friend Olivia in her home. The first two showers were household themed, while the last one was lingerie themed and was meant for a few close girlfriends. I felt very special and honored indeed to have such a supportive and loving group of family and friends!

The best man, Jack, and the maid of honor, Lydia, arrived with Jake a couple of days prior to our wedding. Lydia stayed with me at my parents' home, while Jack and Jake stayed in a hotel in Fredericton with their family members, who had traveled to New Brunswick for the festivities. Several of Jake's uncles, aunts, and cousins had driven from both Newfoundland and Ontario, including his mom's mother, who was in her early eighties. She had been a midwife in her day, delivering most of the babies in her tiny coastal town, located a couple of hours outside of St. John's.

The rehearsal was held on Friday, August 24, and that evening, family members and close friends alike congregated in my brother Gregg's small home in Fredericton. It was literally packed to the gills with both people and wedding presents. I remember we opened a few of the smaller gag gifts, such as a Newfoundland tea kettle that was just a large tin can with a cord taped to the side of it! We shared a lot of laughs that night as both sides of the family met for the first time and began to get acquainted. Later that evening, Jake and I said our last goodbyes to each other; the next time we would meet would be at the altar. I remember feeling a mounting sense of excitement and trepidation, both at the same time. There would be no turning back now.

# CHAPTER 9

# Our Wedding Day

Saturday, August 25, broke as a warm, foggy, and drizzly day. I woke up bright and early, around 7:00 a.m., as I didn't want to miss out on even one moment of this special day! I was disappointed about the rain, however, because that meant we would not be able to take any outdoor photos, but I consoled myself with the old saying that a marriage was blessed by the rain. In the Bible, rain signifies favor and a special blessing—that was my hope and prayer, anyway. Following a leisurely breakfast, Mom, Dad, Lydia, and I packed up everything we would need to take to Fredericton for the wedding and the honeymoon. Jake and I would have a six-hour drive from Fredericton to Halifax, where we planned to catch the flight to London on the evening of August 26. There was a lot to coordinate and get right. It was a good thing that I was a planner, wanting things to go as well as they possibly could, if not perfectly! The rain put a wrinkle into those plans for sure.

We had reserved several rooms at the hotel in order to relax and prepare for our late-afternoon wedding, scheduled for 4:30 p.m. I shared a room with Lydia, where we each took our time getting ready. I soaked in the luxurious bathtub and then did my own nails, hair, and makeup. Luckily, my hair went into place on its own as I applied blush, powder, mascara, and lipstick. I never used a lot of makeup because I preferred a fresh, natural look. It was 1979, after all, the age of CoverGirl and Christie Brinkley! Lydia helped me get into my wedding gown, while the two younger bridesmaids ran back and forth from room to room with anticipation. I wore "something old," Jake's favorite aunt's antique pearl hair pin; "something new," my garter; "something borrowed," also the hair pin; and "something blue," also the garter! The florist had already delivered our huge, colorful bouquets, full of exotic flowers and daisies, and soon we were all camera ready for the photographer. I had several sweet, sentimental shots taken with my parents—Dad resplendent in a formal gray tuxedo and Mom looking radiant in a filmy, long blue gown. They probably resembled my grandparents more than my parents, but I couldn't have been prouder of either one of them that day.

David always owned expensive vehicles, and he had very generously volunteered to drive Lydia, Dad, and me to the church. I surely felt like Cinderella, stepping out of his big white Lincoln Continental that day as he helped me onto the sidewalk. Inside the church, I knew my groom was waiting for me behind the wide, wooden doors of the sanctuary. As we stood outside the entrance getting ready to go in, my heart started to pound, and for a moment, I thought I was going to faint. I was so thankful that I had my dad's arm to hold onto. I now believe I had a premonition about what was to come while I wondered for a few seconds if I was making the wrong choice; was Jake really the right man for me? It was much too late for cold feet, however, and the feeling soon passed as I stood by my father's side, listening to our wedding singer croon the lyrics to the song "Romeo and Juliet." Moments later, the familiar strains of "Here Comes the Bride" started to play. The sweet little flower girl and adorable ring bearer began the procession, followed by my lovely young bridesmaids and the maid of honor.

Taking our cue, we slowly walked down the aisle, gazing at the rapt faces of our family and friends looking back at Dad and me. Meanwhile, Jake and Jack were standing at the front of the church waiting for us. The expression on Jake's face was serious, and I wondered if he was also having second thoughts about our marriage. Once Dad and I reached our designated spot on the floor and Dad and Mom gave their blessing for Jake to marry me, I tried to relax and enjoy the moment. The flowers adorning the front of the altar were tall, multicolored gladiolas; the beautiful arrangements alongside the warm glow of candlelight made for a magical setting in the age-old church. I listened intently to the minister's words as he cautioned us that marriage was a lifelong institution created by God and not intended to be entered into lightly. The soloist, a man from my hometown, performed two more love songs, "If" by Bread and "The First Time Ever I Saw Your Face" by Roberta Flack. The lyrics of both songs were soulful and timeless, and I was hoping and praying that our marriage would be as well.

After reciting our wedding vows, we exchanged rings, and the minister declared us "man and wife." Jake lifted my elegant white veil over my head and kissed me; for the first time ever, we were "Mr. and Mrs." As we exited the church to the organist playing the wedding march, a sense of euphoria came over me, and I could sense that Jake felt the same way. Now that the solemn and formal part of our day was complete, we could celebrate and party with our friends and family!

While the wedding party posed for photos at the church, our guests gathered in the St. John's ballroom of the hotel. I had arranged for a pianist to play music on the grand piano during the cocktail hour, catered with small canapés and drinks. After the photographer was finished with us at the church, we drove back to the hotel, greeted our guests in a traditional reception line, and then took our seats at the head table with our attendants. I remember the menu well; the entrée was Cornish game hen with all the trimmings, and I am sure it was delicious, but I think I was too excited to eat much of it. Following dinner, there were the usual speeches, but the only ones that stand out to me, forty years later, were the two that my brothers made.

Gregg was in charge of giving the traditional toast to the bride, but it seemed more like a *roast* than a toast! He fondly looked back upon his memories of his little sister, sharing with Jake that I had been stubborn from day one and liked getting my own way. Of course, it was all in good fun, although it did have a ring of truth to it. Afterward, Dave stood up and toasted both Jake and me, wishing us a long and happy marriage. Strangely enough, I don't recall how Jake responded to these two toasts; he was not a natural-born public speaker. There were also several telegrams sent to us from family and friends in Newfoundland who could not be with us in person. The only one I remember was from a cousin of Jake's, and it read "Long may your big jib draw." This old-fashioned saying is Newfie talk for "May your sails always catch wind," or, in other words, "Good luck!"

The rest of the evening was filled with the typical dances. Our rock band played "You Needed Me" by Anne Murray for our first dance together as husband and wife. This song choice would eventually come back to haunt me, but at the time, I had no idea how much it would resonate in the years to come. At the end of the long evening, after we passed around the wedding and groom's cakes, I tossed my bouquet, and Jake threw my garter. My friend Carol from work caught the flowers, and in response, her future husband-to-be, Peter, put the garter on Carol's leg! Afterward, I went back upstairs to change into my long and diaphanous going-away outfit, and we collected our luggage. Jake and I said a last goodbye to our guests, jumped into his car, and took off for our honeymoon suite at another hotel; all the while, colored confetti flew out of the vents into our hair and eyes and onto our clothes. It seemed like someone had gotten there ahead of us!

The next morning dawned warm, bright, and sunny, unlike our wedding day, and since we had all day to get to Halifax and board our flight, we decided to visit Gregg and Betty after breakfast. They seemed surprised to see us but offered us coffee and doughnuts before sending us merrily on our way. I remember feeling so happy, young, and carefree as we drove those few hours down the highway to embark on our much-anticipated honeymoon. The thought of an overseas flight was more than a little daunting to me because I had only flown three times before, all of which had been domestic flights. This time would be different, as we were taking an international flight over the Atlantic Ocean. I was hoping and praying all would go well.

I felt exhausted when we finally landed at Heathrow Airport after six and a half hours. I had slept very little on the plane, probably because I was so excited to finally see jolly old England! I had dreamed of this trip for most of my life, and now Jake was making all my dreams come true. We ended up spending five days in London, seeing many of the sights that great city had to offer. I remember touring Buckingham Palace, the Parliament Buildings and Big Ben, the Tower of London, the Tower Bridge, Westminster Abbey, Piccadilly Circus, and Trafalgar Square, as well as visiting different pubs, restaurants, and shops.

One of my favorite finds was a beautiful deep-blue satin peasant top, purchased at a huge outdoor market in Notting Hill, long before the movie with Julia Roberts and Hugh Grant made the area famous. One evening, we attended a dinner theater called the Beefeater, where we ate with nothing but steak knives, similar to the time of Henry the Eighth; for more cultured entertainment, we went to a London showing of *Jesus Christ Superstar*, a highlight for me. I had seen the movie at the drive-in theater in Woodstock years before, and it had left a big impression on me. The live version did not fail to disappoint either!

The soles of our sandals were starting to wear down as we walked for miles and miles along old cobblestone streets, such as the infamous Abbey Road. We strolled along the Thames River and hiked through parks such as Hyde Park, where at Speaker's Corner, any Tom, Dick, or Harry could step up onto a small podium and pontificate over any topic they wished. When we got too tired at the end of the day, we would hop onto a red double-decker bus to return to our hotel, where we could relax and soak our feet. Jake had a big interest in photography back then and owned an expensive camera, which made him the official photographer for our trip.

We had our first big fight as husband and wife near the end of a perfect day of sightseeing. I honestly don't remember what it was about, but I think he got tired of carrying around the tote bag with his camera and all our other stuff in it. He didn't say much but walked off in a big huff, leaving me to sit alone on a park bench in front of a big building, with no idea of where I was. I tried not to panic and just sat there, hoping he would eventually come back. I was not great at reading maps at the best of times, and he had the map!

This would become a pattern in our marriage; instead of talking things out, Jake would usually stuff down his negative feelings until days or even weeks afterward, when his behavior would suddenly erupt like a volcano, spilling over onto me. Often, he would go behind my back or even lie directly to my face about things. I tend to be more of an open book, my thoughts and feelings often plastered across my face for all to see. (I have never been a very good actress.) Since I had never dealt with passive-aggressive behavior before, it took me a while to figure out what was going on. Simply put, I trusted him and thought he loved me. Although I had studied psychology and psychiatry in university, it was, alas, not my strong suit in my early adult years. Our first fight ended when Jake finally sauntered back to where I was sitting, with an insolent look on his face. He was still mad at me but was not willing to talk about it. In the end, I suggested we take turns carrying the tote bag, and the remainder of our trip went smoothly.

After our time in London was over, we rented a car and drove up to Scotland through the Lake District, located in the northwest corner of England. Jake offered to do the driving, since I was hesitant to drive on the left-hand side of the road. He did a good job of it, and the only close encounter we had was with a lazy dairy cow in an overgrown, grassy lane filled with buttercups! We soon discovered that the Lake District was filled with numerous crystal-blue lakes and rugged mountains as we slept in rustic cottages along the way. The English countryside did not disappoint us; neither did the Highlands of Scotland, which were breathtakingly beautiful.

It was a bit of a trek up to Edinburgh but well worth the journey; as we approached the ancient and historical capital of Scotland, Edinburgh Castle loomed high above us on its foggy hill with the city perched below it. I had never seen anything more spellbinding in my entire life as we slowly wound our way up toward the castle. Edinburgh is known as the city of festivals, and there was one going on that September. A bagpiper greeted us while we drew nearer to the old, stalwart castle, and the hair on the nape of my neck stood up as I listened to his lament ... it must have been my Scottish roots coming out! We toured around Edinburgh for a few days, where I especially enjoyed browsing through the many wool shops the city had to offer.

Later, driving up through Scotland, we went to the city of Inverness and stopped by Loch Ness to visit Nessie. Unfortunately, there were no sightings of her that day. We took our time returning to London, stopping along the way to pick the purple heather blooming on the hills of the Highlands. We even spent two magical nights in an authentic Scottish castle that had been turned into a small hotel. I still recall two memories involving our unusual lodging: on the day that we checked into our room, we were terrorized by a bat flying around our bathroom; the next day, through the high-arched windows, we spied several deer grazing in the nearby fields. Our first wildlife encounter was very frightening, while the second one was truly majestic!

One evening, while we were eating in the small restaurant downstairs, we overheard several other guests talking about a tragedy that had occurred a few days before in Ireland. The Irish Republican Army (IRA) had bombed the fishing boat of Lord Louis Mountbatten, the cousin of Queen Elizabeth and uncle of her husband, Prince Philip, the Duke of Edinburgh. Three people, including Lord Mountbatten, died that day; this terrorist attack was considered a massive crime against the royal family and treason against the nation as a whole. Being a huge fan of the royals, I felt badly about it, and as we were leaving the castle, to make matters worse, I came down with a heavy head cold.

I tried to make the best of it as we went on to spend a day or two in Glasgow, but that cold, rainy, and gloomy city did little to cheer me up. As our vacation wound down to its inevitable close, I felt more than ready to return to Nova Scotia, which is also Latin for "New Scotland." Overall, we enjoyed a wonderful holiday and honeymoon, but it was time to go back home and embark on real married life.

# CHAPTER 10

# We've Only Just Begun

After our plane touched down in Halifax and we collected our luggage, we were met by David and Barbara at the arrivals section of the airport. It was so good to see their familiar, smiling faces and to get a welcome-home hug. We regaled them with tales of our recent adventures during the drive back to Bedford, where our brand-new home was waiting for us. Just prior to our wedding, we had signed a one-year lease on a two-bedroom apartment, since neither one of us had a suitable place for two people to live together. Our previous homes were both too small, and we had fallen in love with a modern, two-story apartment building, nestled in the woods just off the Bedford Highway. It was cheaper than living in the city and was only a twenty- to thirty-minute commute to both my workplace and to university for Jake.

Most of our old furniture was already in the apartment, but we did splurge on a new solid-pine cannonball bedroom set with the money we had been given for our wedding. I set about decorating our new love nest with a combination of furniture from both of our previous homes, as well as filling the kitchen cabinets with our new dishes and other small items from my bridal showers. We still owned only one car, so the plan was for Jake to drive me back and forth to work. His hours were somewhat flexible, whereas mine were not.

There was one small problem, however; I technically had no job to go back to. I had resigned from my position in the burn unit at the KGH just before our wedding, as I had become quite miserable working there over the past year. Although I felt I was good at my job, and I worked hard while

I was there, I had started to dread going into work. Working in isolation was just not my cup of tea, and I found the patients to be demanding, with most of their situations being quite dire. Almost all of them were scarred for life, both physically and psychologically, and were facing multiple surgeries to repair the damage from their burns or injuries. I could not see myself working there long-term.

So, the first item on my to-do list, after we were settled into our new home, was to find another job. I sent out résumés to several local hospitals and quickly landed a job at Mariner Bay Hospital (MBH) on 5S, a very busy surgical unit. Nursing jobs were plentiful back in the 1970s, and I most certainly needed one as soon as possible! I would be supporting both of us for the next year until Jake graduated with his MBA. He had worked for a pulp and paper mill in a nearby town from May through August, but our wedding and honeymoon expenses had eaten up most of our savings. With my new job offer, it seemed that God was once again looking after us and meeting our needs.

In the middle of September, Jake began his second year at SMU, while I started my new nursing position that October. I was once again working both day and night shifts for twelve hours at a time. In reality, few of my days actually consisted of twelve hours, as 5S was an incredibly busy and demanding place to work. It was definitely a case of "out of the frying pan, into the fire!" Some of the doctors could also be difficult to deal with, and there was one surgeon who would sometimes go into fits of rage and throw hard metal charts at the nurses in the nursing station! I witnessed only one such incident, and, thankfully, no one was injured during his tirade. In today's culture, he would have been charged with assault and possibly gone to jail. Shortly before I arrived on the scene, it had also been the practice for nurses to stand up and give surgeons their chairs when they entered the room. With the passage of time, this antiquated custom fell by the wayside, but many of the doctors still thought they were our superiors. Of course, there were respectful doctors as well, and some of the nurses could also have bad attitudes. Suffice it to say, I worked the hardest I ever have, before or since!

Our floor was large, comprised of about forty beds, and was divided up into two sections with a small step-down unit across from the nursing station. Our most seriously ill patients would stay there, and it became like a mini-ICU. The RNs practiced total patient care; on days, each nurse would have eight patients to care for, and there was also one nurse dedicated to administering most of the medications for the whole floor. The individual nurses were still responsible for providing the PRN (as needed) medications for their own patients, such as injections for pain control or nausea.

We had three services: thoracic, abdominal, and vascular, and our patients came in with a variety of surgical needs, most of which required both preoperative and postoperative care. The medications, IVs, dressings, tracheotomy care, chest tubes, catheterizations, colostomy care, and other surgical procedures were numerous, and in those days, nurses also did complete bed baths on the patients who required them. We offered nightly back rubs and changed the bed linens every other day or as needed. We also hung blood products, administered TPN (total parenteral nutrition), and drew bloodwork on our patients after hours. It was backbreaking work and only for the young, in both mind and body. On nights, there were only two RNs and one nursing assistant assigned to look after the whole floor and to complete all the required paperwork before morning. Needless to say, there was a very high turnover of staff.

While I was busy running around trying to keep up with my new job, Jake was working away at his MBA program. By the fall of 1979, he was in his second year and due to graduate in May 1980. Unfortunately, unbeknownst to me, he was struggling with an accounting course, and sometime during the winter, he announced that he would like to extend his program to include another semester. His plan was to take some extra courses in order to get another qualification of some kind. He never once mentioned that he was having any problems or failing the course. I was happy to oblige, so I agreed to his plan, and we decided to keep our apartment for a second year. In the meantime, I typed up and edited most of his term papers on my days off, which was a big help to someone who typed with only two fingers!

My good friend Lydia graduated from the nursing program at UNB in the spring of 1980 and was now also living in Halifax. Her roommate, Carrie, worked on the same floor as me at Mariner Bay Hospital, and often, Jake and I would swing by their apartment on Quinpool Road to pick them both up for work early in the morning. Lydia worked at the children's hospital, which was close to MBH. We continued to socialize with our friends who were attending SMU with Jake as well as with Jake's friend Peter and my friend Carol (who was fun-loving and could be rather wild at times). All in all, it was an enjoyable and entertaining couple of years, during which time we got to know and love Halifax.

On Thanksgiving weekend of 1980, my parents came down for a visit. We ended up inviting our whole family over for dinner, including my brothers, Gregg and Dave, with their families, as well as Lydia and Carrie (Olivia was now living in Orillia, Ontario). Mom was happy to cook the turkey, as that culinary skill had not yet made its way into my meager repertoire as a young wife! I really enjoyed having Dave and Barb living so near to us, and it was wonderful to drop over to visit them or go out to dinner together.

Jake and I agreed on most things, although we did have the occasional argument or fight. Once, when Lydia and I were driving across the MacDonald Bridge after a shopping trip to Mic Mac Mall, crossing from Dartmouth back to Halifax, I came too close to the side of the toll booth and peeled the chrome off the side of Jake's treasured car. Of course, I felt badly about it, but I secretly hoped that he would somehow not notice. Unfortunately, he did, and he was not at all happy with me. Another time, Jake slept through his alarm and neglected to pick me up after my long night shift. I sat in the lobby of the hospital for at least an hour and a half, waiting for him to materialize. Getting more and more upset by the minute, I kept dialing our home number on the pay phone until eventually he picked up. Suffice it to say, we had a big argument, which ended up with me demanding that he stop the car when we were halfway home. I opened the passenger door and stubbornly walked most of the rest of the way home, but he did finally come back for me, and we later made up. Our lack of maturity certainly showed up at times.

I remember the summer of 1980 being a particularly difficult one for both of us because Jake was unable to get his old summer job back and was unsuccessful at finding work anywhere else. Forestry/engineering jobs were few and far between in Nova Scotia back then. He ended up receiving employment insurance that summer but was none too happy about it, while I continued to support us both through my nursing job.

By Christmas 1980, Jake had finally earned his degree and was preparing to graduate. The official ceremony would happen in May 1981, but until then, it was imperative that he find employment. He had taken out a big student loan to finance his MBA, although his parents had very generously paid for his undergraduate degree. I was slowly trying to pay off my own student debt, which was well over $6,000—a small fortune to us back then. Jake cast his net wide in his job search and was quickly offered a top position within the province of Newfoundland and Labrador. Armed with his newly minted MBA, it was a fantastic job opportunity for a rookie graduate.

Jake was one of the few people I knew who not only enjoyed going for job interviews but excelled at doing them! He was intent on taking this job, although I was rather less than enthusiastic about it. For one thing, I loved Halifax, and I did not want to leave either the city or our family and friends behind. I also had no knowledge of Labrador, and it seemed like a very foreign and strange land to me. We would be very isolated there, living in the town of Happy Valley-Goose Bay, which was only accessible by air. There was a gravel road between Goose Bay and Labrador City (which borders the province of Quebec), but that would be of no help to us. We would have to fly into Goose Bay from St. John's, Newfoundland, while all our belongings and furniture would have to be shipped first by ferry and then by cargo plane. Our move would take place in January, the worst of all months, when the temperature could dip to a frigid minus fifty degrees Celsius.

When we told our family and friends about this "amazing" opportunity, I imagine they must have thought we were making a huge mistake. Secretly, I thought the same thing. However, being a supportive wife and aware that Jake might never get another chance like this again, I reluctantly agreed to go and immediately put in my notice at work. We also gave notice on our apartment, hired movers to look after all our worldly possessions, and packed our bags. We spent that Christmas with Mom and Dad in Woodstock, where we all said our tearful goodbyes. They were happy for us and never complained once about our decision to move so far away. We then said farewell to all our family and friends in Halifax, and sometime near the middle of January, my brother and sister-in-law sadly waved us off. This time it would be for good; we were starting our young lives over in a land far, far away. It was a big adventure but also a giant leap of faith.

# PART 2

# CHAPTER 11

# The Call of the Wild

After surviving a perilous winter ferry crossing across the Cabot Strait from North Sydney, Nova Scotia, to Port Aux Basques, Newfoundland, we drove our car across the icy Trans-Canada Highway to St. John's. Jake had decided to sell his old car to someone he knew in the area, so we left it behind. We enjoyed a brief visit with his family in Herring Bay and then embarked on our journey to Goose Bay. It was an hour-and-a-half flight, and I clearly remember the short brown-and-white rabbit skin jacket I wore that day. Fur was in fashion back then, unlike today, and I was hoping it would keep me warm in the chilly temperatures of Labrador.

Stepping off the jet onto the frozen tarmac, I allowed my first impression of Goose Bay to wash over me; it felt like I had left civilization behind and just landed on the surface of the moon. Although it was a bright, sunny day, the scenery was very different from beautiful Nova Scotia. The evergreen trees were extremely tall and spindly due to the short growing season, and there were towering banks of snow everywhere. CFB Goose Bay is also an air force base, hosting military from all over the world, including Canada, the United States, Great Britain, Germany, Italy, and the Netherlands. They use Labrador as a training ground for their fighter pilots because the landscape, with its numerous lakes, trees, mountains, and tundra, resembles parts of Europe. In fact, a large portion of northern Labrador remains completely uninhabited.

Goose Bay is also a convenient refueling stop between Europe and North America for aircraft of all kinds, so it was not unusual to have celebrities such as Christopher Reeve or John Travolta refuel their private airplanes at the

Goose Bay Airport. Prince Philip loved to hunt in northern Labrador, and he was also a "frequent flyer." The base was, in fact, a beehive of social activity in the 1960s and 1970s, hosting big acts for the air force, including Bob Hope and Phyllis Diller. Even the town itself seemed very foreign to me as we headed off to the best (and only) local motel, the Northern Lights Inn. Our plan was to stay there until we found a place to live. It was very comforting, however, that Jake's cousin Brenda and her husband, Blake, also lived in Goose Bay at the time, and they warmly welcomed us to our new home.

It turned out that the Northern Lights Inn was not a five- or even four-star motel, but it did have a restaurant where we could get our meals and was reasonably clean. We quickly found a local real estate agent and started looking for a home right away. There was not a lot to choose from, but we finally found a small wartime home in a subdivision that backed onto CFB Goose Bay. It was compact but had four bedrooms, including a basement and a small second floor, and was perfect for two people. The best thing about it was the price; we paid approximately $21,000 for it, which we thought was a great bargain in 1981!

It is true that Goose Bay has one of the longest runways in the world. Our one disadvantage was that we had a landing strip parallel to and directly behind our house, where fighter jets could land at any hour of the day or night. All that separated *us* from *them* was a high chain-link fence. I used to worry that one of the aircrafts would crash into our home while we were sleeping, as the Europeans especially were known for taking chances and pushing the limits. In fact, there were usually a couple of bad crashes each year involving fatalities. Thankfully, our small home was spared, although our houseguests found it very disconcerting to be suddenly awakened at two or three in the morning by the high-pitched sounds of a fighter jet landing just yards away from their bedroom. Over time, Jake and I got used to the noise and eventually learned to sleep through it.

Our next step was to purchase a car, since the town of Happy Valley-Goose Bay, located beside Lake Melville, was spread out and was not ideal for walking. Once again, we would be forced to make do with one vehicle, having very limited funds. We purchased a preowned white VW Rabbit, which had surely seen better days. It was both tiny and very cold to drive in, especially since there was a large hole on the driver's-side floor that allowed snow and frigid air to freely creep into our boots. I later discovered we could put our foot right through the hole, which was rather disconcerting when driving! To put it mildly, this car was a big comedown from our beautiful but ancient black Camaro.

While Jake began his new job, I slowly decorated our new home. I hired a young man to repaint the inside of the house, including the kitchen cupboards, which were transformed into a bright orange to match our kitchen table and chairs. We also had solid maple shelving built into our den to hold our many books, while the other bedroom on the main floor became our dining room. Most of our furniture fit nicely into the small home, although it had sustained some damage from the rough ride over. There was one large furniture store where appliances could also be purchased, so we splurged on a new stove, fridge, deep freeze, washer, and dryer. We were now all set to keep house!

My next priority was to find a job for myself, and wanting a change from working in the hospital setting, I applied for the position of child management specialist that a friend of Brenda's had told me about. Kate worked at the local hospital, and she and her husband, Bruce, a social worker and lay pastor of a church in nearby North West River, eventually became close friends with us. This job would be a stretch for me, although I was qualified for it, since I had my nursing degree. If I became the successful candidate, I would be doing developmental assessments of children from birth up to the age of five years and afterward completing care plans for the parents to follow with the child in their home. I would be making home visits, which was right up my alley, as I had loved working in the community setting when I was in school. Once again, God was in my corner, because I soon received a phone call from the main office in St. John's, informing me I had been chosen for the position!

I couldn't have been more delighted and arranged to fly over to the island in May 1981 for three weeks of training at their head office. During that time, I stayed with Jake's parents in Herring Bay and got to know his family a bit better. I enjoyed brushing up on my knowledge of infant and child development as well as learning the ins and outs of the various assessment tools I would be using. I also had to learn about the different methods of fostering child development, how to write up a plan of care for each individual child, and how to model the plan for the parents of children who were developmentally delayed. The parents were the ones who would do the heavy lifting with their child each day, and I would then go back the next week to reassess their progress and adjust the plan. I loved the concept and was excited to get started!

Toward the end of May, Jake and I flew back to Halifax for a few days for his MBA convocation from SMU. All our parents, Dave and Barb, as well as his sister and favorite aunt and uncle from St. John's, Aunt Bess and Uncle Harry, were also on hand to celebrate with us. Upon our return to Goose Bay, I began my new job and worked out of the same building as Jake, which was ideal for our commuting needs. We would drive together to work each weekday morning and travel home together at the end of each day. I had my very own office, where I would score and interpret the results of the children's tests and then prepare lesson plans for them to follow with their parents. I loved working independently, although it could be a bit isolating at times. I especially enjoyed getting to know the families and helping the young children meet their goals. It was mostly rewarding work, but there were some sad situations that had to be handled gently. Just upstairs from my office, Jake was also settling into his own job and loved being the boss. He usually did administrative work but could also go out into the field, if he so desired.

Once a month, I would travel to the small coastal community of Brookdale, which was only accessible by bush plane, helicopter, or the seasonal ferry, which operated only during the summer months. There was no road into or out of the area. Obviously, the ferry would not work for me, so I usually shared a helicopter with other folks—sometimes even with my own husband—when we would fly in and out on the same day. I had never flown in a helicopter prior to this and found the experience to be both exhilarating and terrifying; the young pilots often liked to show off by flying fast and low over the Mealy Mountains before landing. The scenery higher up proved to be spectacular, though, as we could sometimes see huge herds of caribou or hundreds of harp seals on ice flows, migrating between the summer and winter months.

Unfortunately, if fog suddenly descended upon Brookdale, the helicopter could not land or take off, and we once got stranded there for three days before the weather improved. In addition to the local Roman Catholic school and church and RCMP office, there was a nursing station where one nurse/midwife permanently lived and worked. On that trip, I ended up sleeping in her spare bedroom, but as I remember it, she had lived in near isolation there for many years and was not the most hospitable of hosts. I made do, however, and cooked my own meals in the small kitchen. I shopped at the only store in town, the Hudson's Bay Company store, which had a very limited selection of certain items, such as milk, fresh meat, fruit, and vegetables, especially toward the end of the winter. Food was also extremely expensive, and I was so thankful that I lived in the much larger and less isolated community of Goose Bay, where groceries were regularly flown in all year long.

My home visits in Brookdale were interesting, since the people who lived there were mainly Inuit or Eskimo, and although most of them spoke English, their customs were quaint, and they were generally very poor. There was a lot of unemployment, but they supplemented their meager income by traditional means, such as trapping, hunting, and fishing. A favorite treat for the children was to eat frozen, raw caribou (a.k.a. reindeer) meat. There was also no real need for vehicles there, so the main source of transportation was by foot in the summer months and by snowshoes, snowmobile, or snow sled in the winter.

One of the homes I visited had only rough wooden walls (with daylight peeking in between the cracks), a dirt floor, and a potbelly stove to heat the home all winter long. It was just one big room. During the winter months, I found it to be very chilly, and I can only imagine how cold the children must have been. At least they were always dressed in warm outdoor clothing, often homemade and trimmed with beautiful beading, sealskin, and fur. Due to the geographic isolation of the village, the locals often intermarried and had large families, which caused a lot of genetic mutations with resulting developmental delays for their children.

The Inuit typically made their own home brew, which caused numerous issues with addiction and other subsequent health and social problems. In fact, it was rumored that one of the small coastal communities dotting the southern coast of Labrador had suffered a recent tragedy where, due to lack of care, a baby had fallen headfirst into a large bucket of home brew and drowned. It was horrible to contemplate and must have been much worse in real life. Having said that, the Indigenous people dearly loved their children, seemed to be content with their lives, and were welcoming to the outsiders who came in to provide services for them. They usually appreciated any attention they could get.

I also made weekly home visits to a children's group home that was located near a small village about a half hour outside of Goose Bay. A small Innu (First Nation) Federal Reserve was situated a couple of miles away from this residential facility and was infamous for its many socioeconomic, health, and addiction issues. Alcohol, illegal drugs, and solvent abuse plagued the reserve, leading to many physical and mental health issues, suicide, domestic violence, and the neglect and abuse of children. Many of the young residents in the group home ended up being put into care and lived there long-term. Some of the children I visited had FAS (fetal alcohol syndrome) or FASD (fetal alcohol spectrum disorder), which are debilitating and permanent conditions, caused when a woman consumes alcohol during pregnancy. The result is often profound developmental and behavioral problems that the child and then adult exhibits throughout their lifetime. Since most of the children did not speak or understand English, a local interpreter accompanied me during those visits. The lack of easy communication made things more difficult for all of us, but it was better than nothing.

One day, when I was at the group home, I noticed that all the workers and children were gathered in rapt attention around the TV in the common room. It happened to be July 29, 1981—the much-anticipated wedding day of Prince Charles and Lady Diana Spencer. Despite the language barrier, even this remote corner of the world was enthralled by the grand fairy tale playing out before us all that day! How tragic that their marriage did not fare nearly as well as their magnificent royal wedding.

Just outside of North West River, I also made weekly visits with my interpreter to an Innu family, who chose to live the traditional way by hunting caribou, moose, and small game off the land. They lived in a teepee or tent, both winter and summer, and heated their home with a small stove, where the exhaust escaped through an opening in the top. They cooked all their meals over an open fire, including bannock, a delicious fried mixture of flour, salt, and baking powder. Once again, they welcomed me with open arms, happy to get the much-needed help for the children they so loved. My new job came with its downsides, though; sometimes the endings to people's stories did not turn out nearly so well. That was the kind of dismal outcome that would keep me awake for hours and hours during the long winter nights.

# CHAPTER 12

# A Joyful Hello but
# a Sad Goodbye

Life in Goose Bay was busy for us workwise, but socially, things happened much more slowly. It took some time for me to get a real feeling for the land because it was so unlike anything I had ever experienced before. I would say that Jake took to life "on the Goose" like a fish to water, while I was slowly dipping my toe in. In addition to the landscape being so unusual, the weather patterns and seasons also seemed alien to me. The winters, though often displaying amazing aurora borealis, or northern lights, were long and extremely cold, with snowbanks that could reach several feet in height. By contrast, the summers were short and sweet, often arriving quickly after a brief spring, and could be intensely hot. As a result, the summer growing season was condensed, and a lot of the typical perennials and annuals did not grow well there.

One thing that did thrive on the hills and in the valleys was berries. In particular, the partridgeberry, a tart, bright red berry, was picked in the early fall and was very delicious in baked goods. The apricot-colored bakeapple berry was popular with the locals and had its own peculiar flavor, of which I was not a big fan. Brenda, however, adored bakeapples and picked as many as she could each August. They made good jams and jellies, which Newfoundlanders had long been known to beg, borrow, or steal for. (My mom had bakeapple jam stolen from her hotel room in St. John's when she and Dad and David and Barbara were once visiting Jake's parents.)

Due to Labrador's northern latitude, the daytime hours during the winter were short (approximately seven hours), and in the summer, they were long (about seventeen hours). This could be challenging in several ways; the lack of daylight in the winter led to long, dark afternoons and evenings, while the extra daylight in the summer made it difficult to get enough sleep. I remember going to bed around midnight with the setting sun and waking up to bright sunlight around 4:00 or 5:00 a.m. Some nights, it never seemed to get fully dark at all. Thankfully, we eventually got used to this, just like the noisy landing strip behind our home!

What I never got used to, though, was the annual infestation of every fly known to humankind. It started during the spring and continued throughout most of the summer until the first frost arrived. Window and door screens were a must, as was the use of copious amounts of insect repellant whenever we ventured outside. This great horde of insects made outdoor living during the spring and summer difficult, to say the least, but Labradorians were tough and braved the elements.

Indeed, the outdoors ruled in Labrador. Recreational and extracurricular activities centered around fishing, camping, and hiking in the summer, while in the winter, people loved to hunt, icefish, ski, skate, snowshoe, and go snowmobiling. Just outside of town, there was a downhill ski resort called Snow Goose Mountain, and although I never hit the ski slopes myself, I did occasionally borrow skis or snowshoes to go cross-country. As part of our work agreement, both Jake and I had been provided with hardy and warm outdoor clothing and snow boots, but I still always managed to come home with chilled feet anyway! Did I mention that I have always been more of a summer person than a winter person? The highlight of our summer was the big air show hosted by the base; it featured airplanes and jets from all over the world, both on land and in the sky.

Since I have never been a big follower, I decided not to follow Jake's lead when he became a member of one of the local service clubs in town. I was, however, more than happy to help Brenda lead her weight-loss group on Friday evenings. Afterward, we usually went over to Brenda and Blake's home to watch *Dallas*, as they had two small children, while we were footloose and fancy-free. One bonus of attending the weekly meetings was that I lost twenty-five pounds during the first few months I lived in Goose Bay! We also often saw our mutual friends Bruce and

Kate on the weekends, usually for dinner at either our home or theirs in North West River.

One of our favorite meals was Arctic char grilled on the barbecue and stuffed with crabmeat. Jake sometimes flew by helicopter to Nain, the most northernly community on the coast, where he went fishing with the locals and brought back garbage bags filled with the delicacy, which we then put in our freezer. Once, after I had been gone overnight on a business trip, I arrived home to a putrid smell, hanging like a heavy fog in our small kitchen. Jake had taken the opportunity while I was away to try his hand at baking seal flippers, a local favorite. Another time, when I ventured into the basement to do the laundry after being away for a few days, I opened the door of the cold room only to find an enormous, hulking caribou hanging from the ceiling! Jake had gone hunting inland with some friends from work and had killed and brought home the poor animal to butcher for winter meat and later store in our freezer. Sadly, our options for eating out were limited to Chinese food at the Shanghai Restaurant or pizza at our local pizzeria.

Occasionally, we would go to our one and only movie theater, where, since it was located on base, we were asked to stand to attention and sing a combination of "God Save the Queen" and "Oh Canada." The nightlife in Goose Bay was also limited to the air force base, where each country had its own officers' mess—a place to eat, drink, socialize, and dance. We sometimes went to the British or Canadian mess on a Friday night for a change of pace. I remember one time when Jake and I were invited to go to a formal dinner at the RAF mess; after I got home from work, I suddenly came down with a bad case of the stomach flu. Jake decided to go on his own, which at the time I thought was a strange thing for a married man to do. It was also rather hurtful, as I lay in bed, sick as a dog. When he came home later that night, it was clear he had enjoyed himself, and I was less than impressed!

As the winter of 1982 set in, Jake and I both started to get cabin fever. We were now "in the money," as we were a double-income family with a low mortgage. Our biggest monthly expenses were our electric lights, oil heating, and home phone bill. Despite the huge hydroelectric project at Churchill Falls, Joey Smallwood, the first premier of Newfoundland and Labrador, had signed a disastrous deal with the province of Quebec in

1969. He literally gave away millions of dollars' worth of electric power well into the next century. Meanwhile, we locals paid for our electricity through the nose. Jake and I also talked to our parents on the phone once a week, if not more often, and the cost was through the roof back in those days.

In addition, most of our food was flown in, so groceries were generally expensive. Fortunately, we had two stores to choose from—the Hudson's Bay Company and the large cooperative food store. Mom would regularly mail me parcels full of my favorite coffee and baking powder, since she knew how much I loved coffee and homemade biscuits. She purchased these items in Houlton, Maine, as they were not available in Canada at the time. Little treats like that kept me going, especially through the long, dark winter months.

Since our mortgage was very affordable, I was paying down my student loan as quickly as I could, though Jake did not agree with my thinking; he thought I should space out the payments for as long as possible. I have never liked owing money, so I was intent on getting rid of my one big debt as soon as possible. Jake's parents had long since paid off the student loan for his MBA, so from where I was standing, he had no right to criticize either me or my methodology. In fact, even though he was the businessman in the family, I was always the one to write the checks and pay the bills for our household needs. He seemed to have little interest in budgeting or humdrum things like managing our money.

Since things were going so well financially, we decided to book a Caribbean cruise for April of that year. It was something I had always dreamed about, and once again, Jake helped make my dreams come true. We sailed away on a large ship, departing from the port of Miami, with stops in Nassau, the Bahamas; San Juan, Puerto Rico; and St. Thomas, the British Virgin Islands. It was a one-week, all-inclusive voyage, and I treasured each day of it. Once again, the landscapes were foreign to me, but they were at the other end of the spectrum from Labrador; we had left five feet of snow behind in Goose Bay to walk hand in hand on the beautiful, sandy beaches of Nassau. The sizzling sun quickly transformed our pale skin into a rosy sunburn. It felt like we had landed in paradise, and I never wanted to go home again!

Later that week, as we began to cruise through the breathtaking entrance to San Juan, the temperature changed dramatically, and the air became extremely hot, sultry, and oppressive. While standing at the railing, I suddenly developed severe abdominal pain and quickly ran back down into our tiny bathroom. I knew that my period was due, but for some strange reason, it had not materialized that month despite the intermittent cramping. Thankfully, toward the end of the week I felt better and tried to enjoy the remainder of our trip.

When the cruise was over, we disembarked in Miami once more and rented a car, planning to drive up to Gainesville, Florida, to visit our married friends from SMU, who were now both attending the University of Florida. As it happened, Aunt Alice had a new boyfriend (Uncle Carl had passed away a few years earlier), and they lived in a rural area in nearby Jacksonville. We planned to make a second stop to see them as well. Amid all the excitement, Jake left our passports and airline tickets on the back seat of the taxicab we had used to get to the car rental agency. Halfway up Interstate I-75, we realized they were missing, and panic set in!

We knew the crime rate in Miami during the mideighties was very high (our hotel had armed guards inside its locked gates), as the drug culture was reflected weekly by the TV show *Miami Vice*. In fact, it seemed like the odds of getting our documents back were not very good. Unbelievably, though, the cabby was an honest man and turned them in to the airline's booth at the airport, where we could later pick them up. After having a huge argument over the mishap, we heaved a collective sigh of relief and checked into our motel in Gainesville. We felt like we had dodged a bullet, but I truly believe God orchestrated everything to work out in our favor.

The rest of our trip went well, and we had a great time visiting Mickey Mouse and Cinderella in Orlando with our friends. It turned out that my adventuresome aunt lived in a house on stilts by the banks of the Swanee River, where armadillos and alligators were free to roam. We spotted one of the former but, thankfully, not the latter! Aunt Alice even introduced us to her neighbor, who had just been released from jail and drove around town with a rifle attached to the back window of his pickup truck. That was a little unnerving to see but was not unusual for the place or the times.

Back at home, when my period failed to materialize for the second month, I wasted no time in making an appointment with our one and only obstetrician in Goose Bay, Dr. Smith, who hailed from New Zealand. Lo and behold, I discovered I was pregnant, which explained the terrible cramping I had experienced in San Juan the month before. It was surprising to me but not totally unexpected, as I had gone off birth control a few months before and was monitoring my cycles by taking my body temperature. My method was clearly less than 100 percent effective, but I was not at all disappointed! According to Dr. Smith, my pregnancy was around eight weeks' gestation. Later that night, when I told Jake my exciting news, I could see that he was not as thrilled about it as I was, but he seemed to be okay with the idea of impending fatherhood. We immediately phoned both sets of parents to share our big news with them, and they were all very ecstatic for us.

As fate would have it, tragedy struck in early June when my baby was around twelve weeks' gestation. I awoke early one morning and noticed right away that I was spotting. I also had some cramping, which I knew was not a good sign. We had British midwives in Goose Bay who worked out of our hospital, so I immediately phoned the maternity floor and spoke to one of them. She advised me to rest at home and monitor my situation closely. Most unfortunately, things only got worse as the morning progressed, and I eventually phoned for Jake to come home and take me to the hospital. I was admitted right away and had emergency surgery later that day. Sadly, I had lost our baby. I was well and truly devastated, as although I had just gotten used to the notion of being pregnant, I had already bonded with our precious baby.

It is very true that nobody understands what it is like to lose a baby, unless it happens to them. I soon discovered that most people felt uncomfortable talking about it around me and preferred to pretend it had never happened. There was also no counselling for miscarriage back in 1982, so I was left alone trying to process my loss and move past it on my own. Even Jake did not seem to understand the intense pain and grief I felt over losing our unborn baby. Indeed, it was hard *not* to blame myself for what had happened, and I began to wonder if our cruise had been the cause. Unaware that I was pregnant, I had had a few drinks, and the weather had also been stifling hot. Trying to reassure me, Dr. Smith told me that miscarriages often happen due to problems with implantation of the fertilized egg into the lining of the uterus, and I was not at any increased risk for another miscarriage. At the time, my one consolation was that I knew my unborn baby was safe and sound in heaven, and one day, we would meet face-to-face.

Feeling a little bit better, I thought that a brief trip to visit my parents in New Brunswick would be good medicine, and coincidentally, it was their fiftieth wedding anniversary at the end of June that year. I flew home alone and helped my brothers and sisters-in-law throw a reception for my parents, who were all very happy to see me. Although the visit did me some good, I continued to feel sad and depressed as spring turned into summer, and I found it extremely painful to work around young children. After much reflection, I ended up resigning from my position at work and took some time off to rest and recover from my devastating loss.

# CHAPTER 13

# The Rainbow After the Flood

Time is a great healer, and by the fall, I was ready to return to work but thought that a change of scenery would do me good. I ended up taking a position at Mealy Mountains Hospital, working in the outpatients/emergency department. It meant doing shift work once again, but this time my shifts were eight hours instead of twelve and included days, evenings, and nights. I enjoyed the work right from the start and generally liked the nurses and doctors I worked with. Most of the doctors and many of the nurses were foreign-born, and they were well trained, and on nights, I could help the midwives with their deliveries.

In outpatients, every day and every patient were different, and the work was fast paced but not overwhelming. During the days, we held wart clinics and fracture clinics, where I learned how to remove warts using liquid nitrogen and how to support bones using gauze and plaster strips. I also removed casts and sutures, changed dressings, occasionally drew up chemotherapy, and assisted the doctors with dental extractions on children. It was very much a mixed bag.

In the emergency department, we saw everything and everyone under the sun, including people of all ages presenting with injuries related to motor vehicle accidents, broken bones, and bad lacerations, as well as medical emergencies, such as asthmatic attacks, heart attacks, and strokes. One evening, an entire family came in with injuries from a bad motor vehicle accident (including a woman who was pregnant), with only myself and one attending physician present. Another night, I received a call over the emergency radio system from the air force base, alerting me to a possible aircraft disaster, but, thankfully, that emergency never materialized. Our nights were usually quiet, and I would often keep the switchboard operator company. We would spend the time talking and knitting or completing other craft projects.

One of my saddest memories involved the cardiac arrest and subsequent death on the ski slopes of a friend's husband; since I was the nurse working evenings, and I knew him personally, it was my job to visit the morgue to identify the body. Another time, a baby girl was brought in by ambulance early in the morning; an eight-month-old plump Inuit baby, she had passed away from SIDS (sudden infant death syndrome) sometime during the night. In the words of Forrest Gump, "My mama always said, 'Life was like a box of chocolates. You never know what you're gonna get.'" The sheer variety and uncertainty of the job kept me on my toes as I continued to learn and grow in my role as a nurse.

In the meantime, while my depression gradually lifted, the desire for another child grew; this time, we intentionally tried to get pregnant. God once again blessed us with new life when I discovered I was pregnant toward the end of November that same year! Our baby was due in early August 1983. From the very first moment that my pregnancy was confirmed by the doctor, I started praying for a healthy baby. Thankfully, I had an easy pregnancy this time around and continued to work without any problems. I never had so much as even one day of nausea or heartburn, which was fortunate, since I was still doing shift work. Although Dr. Smith performed one ultrasound, I chose not to know the sex of the baby. I truly wanted it to be a surprise for both Jake and me. This limited our choices for both baby clothes and decorations for the nursery, so I decided to go with neutral colors, such as mint green and pale yellow.

All that winter, I eagerly began to prepare for our new arrival, ordering baby furniture from Sears and painting the small bedroom across from ours a pretty, mellow yellow. I went with a Winnie the Pooh theme for the white crib with a colorful animal mobile over the top. My work friends threw me a large baby shower at one of their homes, where I also received a change table, much-needed baby clothes, and other items. Meanwhile, on quiet nights at work, I knit an entire infant layette, consisting of a mint-green blanket with matching sweater, bonnet, and baby booties. But our biggest investment by far was a brand-new silver VW Jetta with a top-of-the-line car seat—two purchases I considered absolute necessities to safely bring home a new baby. A few months before my due date, Jake and I took Lamaze classes together, even though I had taught them in my last year of university. I thought it would be a great way to get him more involved in the birth, although he had a hard time taking the breathing seriously!

That spring, I took a few days off work and once again flew home to New Brunswick to see my parents. During the flight over, I suddenly felt my baby do a huge somersault in my abdomen, which scared me for a few minutes but didn't seem to make any difference afterward. He or she was very active, so I simply put the experience down to a change of position. Back home, Mom, Dad, and I went shopping in Fredericton for baby clothes and supplies, since there was not much to choose from in Goose Bay. We were all very excited and impatient for this baby to arrive! On my journey home, I finished reading the La Leche League book, *The Womanly Art of Breastfeeding*, as I was intent on providing my precious newborn with no other nourishment than all-natural breastmilk. Jake heartily supported the idea because he would not have to share in the responsibility of getting up every two hours throughout the night to feed a crying baby!

The summer in Goose Bay that year was an intense one, consisting of long, hot, sweltering days, with no air-conditioning anywhere of any kind. Over the course of my pregnancy, I slowly put on thirty pounds, which was a healthy weight for a pregnant woman, but I *felt* enormous and was very uncomfortable. I spent a large amount of time on my days off in front of the fan, trying to catch my breath and cool down. My big day could not come soon enough! During the second week of July, I suddenly got a big burst of energy and felt a strong desire to clean out all the kitchen cupboards I had been staring at from my chair in front of the fan. Upon further reflection, I now realize that standing on top of a kitchen chair to wash high cupboards and move around dishes was not a great idea for a woman who was so close to giving birth! This nesting instinct is common toward the end of pregnancy, and I was no exception.

I had decided to take an early maternity leave, as I was feeling very fatigued, so I spent the day at home resting on Monday, July 18. While I was climbing the stairs after supper that evening, the first labor pain suddenly came upon me. It is impossible to describe the intensity of the pain or put what labor feels like into words, but it is hard work for sure! Immediately, I doubled over, unable to walk down the stairs without assistance, and I called out frantically for Jake. Luckily, he was home, and after timing my contractions, which were already about five minutes apart, we wasted no time in calling the labor and delivery floor of the hospital to tell them I was coming in. After I was admitted by one of the midwives, Dr. Smith examined me and discovered the baby was a transverse lie—in a horizontal position across my uterus. This baby would be a breech delivery for sure, and an emergency Cesarean section (C-section) was called for.

Things happened very quickly after that, and the next thing I remember is counting down from ten as the anesthetist put me to sleep. Today, a spinal or epidural anesthetic would commonly be offered, but in 1983, a general anesthetic was the practice, so it was imperative not to use too much because it could be harmful to the baby. It was also important to get the baby out quickly for the same reason. Unfortunately, the doctor did not use quite enough of the drug, causing me to wake up from my deep sleep while Dr. Smith was still suturing me up. I could not open my eyes, talk, or move, and I seemed to be racing through a dark tunnel. My hearing was normal, though, because I could hear the doctors and nurses laughing and joking around with music playing in the background, although I could not understand what they were saying. I could also feel every excruciating stitch as my doctor closed my incision, which seemed to go on for hours but was most likely just a matter of a few minutes. I was aware that something very important was happening to me, yet I could not comprehend exactly what it was, and I wondered if I could be dying.

Eventually, I woke up completely and was greeted by the wonderful news that I had delivered a beautiful, healthy baby boy, weighing seven pounds, twelve ounces, at 8:30 p.m. that evening. My two doctors felt badly when I told them that I had been semiconscious while they were closing my incision. Since I knew them both through work, they personally wheeled me back to my private room on the postpartum floor. All my pain was quickly forgotten, however, as I was soon gazing into the dark blue eyes of my little strawberry-blond-haired son. Jake had been with me throughout the evening, but the rules were different back then, and he was only allowed to watch the surgery through a small window.

I believe my hospital stay was unremarkable except for when the hospital lost its hot water for several days, and I was forced to boil the tea kettle over and over in order to partially fill up the bathtub. I must have been in the hospital for at least a week, since I was recovering from surgery, and new mothers were kept in much longer back then. I certainly received lots of tender, loving care, as I knew virtually all the midwives and the doctors. Indeed, I was treated like royalty, and better yet, the breastfeeding went off without a hitch. We decided to name our new bundle of joy William, or Will for short, and he was one baby who never had a bottle!

I would say that I took to motherhood like a duck takes to water. I treasured each moment I had with Will, and he seemed to be the perfect baby. I loved showing him off in his brand-new blue corduroy carriage while we took daily walks through our neighborhood. As he grew, he developed beautiful brown eyes and curls like his father, but unlike Jake, his hair was blond like mine, creating an unusual combination. He was a happy, jolly baby and shocked his pediatrician when he intentionally smiled at her around three weeks of age. I faithfully recorded each milestone in his baby calendar and spent hours filling in his baby book. In addition, Jake and I both took many photos of Will to commemorate each step of his journey. We also had both sets of grandparents as well as other family and friends visit us that first year to meet the newest member of the family. Most unfortunately, though, Brenda and Blake and our close friends Bruce and Kate moved away around the time Will was born, and I soon became lonely for adult company.

To help deal with my growing feelings of isolation, I flew back east with Will several times during his first year. I fondly remember carrying him in his snuggly as we roamed around the streets and boardwalk of downtown Halifax with my friends. He was one heavy baby! Jake, Will, and I spent both his first Christmas and first birthday with my family in Woodstock. In July 1984, on our flight over from Newfoundland, Will and I accidentally ran into Olivia in the departure lounge of the Halifax airport. Her family home had just burned down in Woodstock, so she was going back to help and support her mom. I don't usually believe in coincidences, and I am sure God brought us together that day. We sat side by side on the airplane and visited a lot with each other over the course of the summer, which I am sure was a real blessing to both of us.

Toward the end of my maternity leave, I made the difficult decision to stay at home with Will, as we had no family nearby who could look after him, and I could not fathom putting him into day care. It was a no-brainer for me, but Jake was not happy about losing the extra income. Around the same time, a management position opened in St. John's, which Jake decided to apply for. It was not his dream job by any means, but it would get us out of Labrador and back to quasi-civilization in Newfoundland. A big positive for us as well was that Jake's family lived in Newfoundland and would be a good support for our growing family. We would also be closer by air to my family in New Brunswick. There was always the inclement and fickle weather to deal with, but I felt it could not be any worse than dealing with the cold, snowy weather and geographic isolation of Labrador.

When Jake learned he was the successful applicant for the job, no one was happier than I was, although I think his parents may have come in a close second! They were thrilled to have us finally living so close to them, especially now that we had little William. In October 1984, we called the movers and packed up all our belongings once more. Our small home sold quickly, and we made a good profit on it, which was a bonus for us. We knew that it would be challenging to find affordable housing in St. John's, and we were anxious to begin our search.

CHAPTER 14

# A Mainlander Moves
# to the Rock

We spent our first month in Newfoundland living with Jake's parents while we diligently combed the area for a new home. It was very tight quarters for six people, as we slept in their spare bedroom downstairs, with Will sleeping in his playpen on the floor. One night, a few days after we arrived, we were abruptly and loudly awakened by a blood-curdling scream coming from Jake's younger sister's upstairs bedroom. We soon learned that a huge rat had run across her face while she was sound asleep in her bed! Oh, the perils of living in a seaport city!

Following that harrowing encounter, it was very unsettling for me to stay alone in the house during the daytime, especially with a young toddler who liked to play on the floor. In fact, if Will and I remained quiet, I could sometimes hear the crafty rodent stealthily moving around the house. Thankfully, the horrible creature eventually turned up inside the insulation of the stove, where it had become trapped and could not escape. Jake's father was often in a rush, and we surmised the animal must have entered the house from the small stream behind their fence when he had accidentally left the back door open. After that, we tried to ensure that the door was always shut tight, but it was a constant worry. What a disconcerting welcome to Newfoundland—I hoped and prayed things would only get better.

It was a rather limited housing market in 1984, and since we knew we could not afford to live right in the city, we searched high and low in the surrounding area. We narrowed down our options to three potential homes and finally settled on a large home in the small community of Topsail. It was still listed well above our price range but was best suited to the needs of our growing family. The house was about a thirty-minute drive south from Jake's office in St. John's when taking the arterial highway and about the same distance from his parents' home in Herring Bay when driving on the backroads and along the coastline.

Topsail is located on the eastern shore of Conception Bay and was part of a string of small communities comprising the town of Conception Bay South in 1984. I fell in love with this pastoral, unspoiled land right from the start; we had only one corner store, a post office, and a couple of churches and elementary schools, but we could easily see the Atlantic Ocean from our backyard. During the spring and summer months, we would often see huge icebergs floating down from western Greenland and the Canadian Arctic. Topsail Beach was also nearby and was ideal for taking long walks, year-round. Just down the road in the Manuels River area was a world-famous excavation site for prehistoric trilobite fossils.

We put in an offer on the house and purchased it for $85,000. It doesn't sound like much money by today's standards, but back then it was a small fortune. At the last minute, Jake's uncle Harry and aunt Bess offered to give us an interest-free mortgage, which we thankfully accepted. Their generosity turned out to be a huge help to us financially, since I was still at home with Will. Once again, I began the arduous task of unpacking our belongings and decorating our new house.

This multilevel, four-bedroom home was much larger than our little starter home in Goose Bay; it had an eat-in kitchen, powder room, living room, and dining room as well as a sunken family room and den on the main levels, with a finished basement downstairs. The upstairs held three good-sized bedrooms and a full bathroom. For Christmas that year, Jake surprised me by buying us a lovely set of silver-blue living room furniture. His parents kindly bought us a set of solid oak dining room table and chairs with a matching buffet and hutch, which tied the two rooms together. Over the next few months, Jake and his mom did some painting and wallpapering, while I painted all the wooden windows a bright white. I eventually splurged and had custom draperies made for the living room and dining room, which I felt was well worth the money.

The one thing missing from our beautiful home was an attached garage, but we felt that was an addition that could come later. The other problem was that I stayed at home with a toddler and had no vehicle, so Will and I had to walk everywhere. The good news was that there was really no place to go, except to the post office or corner store, which I tried to do on most fair-weather days. In the spring, summer, and fall, I would put Will into his navy blue corduroy stroller, and we would head out for some much-needed fresh air. In the winter, it was more difficult, but if there was enough snow on the ground, I would pull Will on Jake's ancient red wooden sled. It must have been at least a mile or so each way and was a good workout for me.

Back in those days and in that neck of the woods, there were no baby or parenting groups like there are today. Our only other outings were to the local public health unit for Will's immunizations or to see our family doctor in St. John's, either when he was ill or for routine checkups. Since I had no transportation for these excursions either, Jake's father, Tom, who was now retired, would come over and take us to wherever we needed to go. Jake's mother, Joan, still taught school in St. John's, but they both turned out to be real life savers for me and wonderful grandparents to Will. On Sundays, our small family would faithfully drive over to their house for a home-cooked dinner, often visiting with other members of the family as well. It helped lessen the loneliness I felt at times for my own family and friends who lived on the mainland.

We did eventually make new friends with our neighbors as well as with some of Jake's coworkers. Our best friends, Kelly and Trevor, lived in nearby Mount Pearl, and we saw them almost every weekend. Trevor worked with Jake, while Kelly was an ICU nurse at Our Lady of Peace Hospital in the city. Like me, Kelly originated from New Brunswick, and she and Trevor had also both attended UNB, although they were a little younger than us and had no children. For that reason, and because we had a young child, they would often come over to our house to socialize. We also became good friends with Lucy and Ted, who lived in St. John's; Ted was in management and had originally hired Jake to work in Goose Bay. Lucy was a gym teacher at a junior high school in St. John's and was a fun-loving person with a high amount of energy. They were a few years our senior and had two grown boys.

We did our fair share of sightseeing during the first few years we lived in Newfoundland. On weekends, we explored the usual tourist attractions, such as Cape Spear, the most easterly point in North America, and the iconic Signal Hill, which overlooks the city of St. John's and the historic Narrows, where it is alleged that John Cabot landed in 1497. In addition, it was from the top of Signal Hill that the first transatlantic telegraph message was received from Europe by Marconi on December 12, 1901. Actually, St. John's is the oldest city in North America and sits upon a quaint harbor lined with pubs, restaurants, shops, and bars. Many a mainlander has been "screeched in" on the infamous George Street in downtown St. John's, with a mammoth headache to show for it the next day!

Geologically, Newfoundland is called the Rock for good reason; most of the landscape on the Avalon Peninsula is composed of 550-million-year-old volcanic rocks, with numerous crystal-clear lakes and streams, multitudes of evergreen trees, and a few native deciduous trees. Due to the harsh climate, the growing season is condensed, so most Newfoundlanders only grow root vegetables and quick-maturing plants, such as lettuce, radishes, and onions. There are no fruit trees of any kind on the large island; however, blueberries, wild strawberries, bakeapples, and cranberries abound on the hills and in the fields. We spent many carefree hours picking blueberries in a large, grassy meadow located high above Jake's parents' home.

Tom still fished as a hobby; he put down lobster traps and jigged cod when the season was open. Most Newfoundlanders are a jack-of-all-trades, and Tom was no exception. Always a hard worker, he owned a piece of land across from their home, where he had a small vegetable patch filled with carrots, onions, potatoes, turnips, and beets. There was also a large area filled with fish flakes, which were large racks used to dry and salt the cod fish he caught in the Atlantic Ocean. Will spent many a happy hour with Papa and Nana, helping them with the vegetable garden and preparing the cod. As Will got older, Tom and Jake would sometimes take him out in a small dinghy to go fishing in the bay. Dressed from head to toe in yellow rain gear and rubber boots, it was not unusual for them to return home soaking wet with stories of whales approaching and sometimes surrounding their small boat; thankfully though, there were never any close calls that I was aware of. They probably wouldn't have told me anyway!

The weather was another matter entirely; a person could quite easily experience all four seasons in one day in Newfoundland. In fact, the weather was always doing something; often it was rain, drizzle, and fog, but when the sun decided to shine down on a warm summer's day, there was never a more beautiful place on God's green earth. The scenery was then and still remains absolutely spectacular along the long and winding coastline, often leaving a person lost for words.

One of our favorite spots to visit was Logy Bay-Middle Cove-Outer Cove, where Jake's uncle Harry and aunt Bess lived. It was adjacent to the town of Torbay and about a ten-minute drive from the city. They had no children and had recently sold their old, sprawling family farm to the city of St. John's, which had big plans for the property. They had reportedly made a small fortune on the deal and subsequently retired to enjoy life in their new home. In addition to spending quality time on the weekends with both of them, we loved the scenery of the surrounding area. Their large home overlooked huge cliffs, which dropped off to a rocky beach. In the spring, hundreds of people flocked to this beach to watch the capelin, a species of small smelt, come in. The endless sea of silver fish lining the beach and floating in the water was a sight to behold. They were also delicious to eat, which was a bonus for us! Men, women, and children brought fishing nets and large white buckets and scooped them up by the handfuls.

Despite enjoying all that Newfoundland had to offer, I looked forward to returning home to New Brunswick each summer for a holiday with my own family. Unfortunately, we were unable to go in 1985 for several reasons. First and foremost, money was tight, as living in Newfoundland was not cheap. I had managed to pay off my student loan debt while we still lived in Labrador, but despite Jake's generous salary, it was difficult to keep up with our mortgage payments of $700 a month, as well as our pricey utility bills. We heated our large home with electricity, the cost of which had literally gone through the roof in recent years. Our home phone bills continued to be high, and the price of groceries was atrocious, since most fresh food had to be flown onto the island. To offset all of this, I tried to be mindful about buying clothes and not paying too much for travel or entertainment. Despite being frugal, we still struggled not to go into debt each month, and unfortunately, we relied on credit cards more than we should have.

We were also unable to visit my parents that year, as they were finally forced to sell their home to the New Brunswick Power Commission. NB Power planned to raise the dam at Mactaquac just above Fredericton, so most of the older part of Grafton would be flooded out and uninhabitable. As a result, Dad impulsively bought a newly built home in Grafton Heights, which sat up high on a big hill above their old home just a couple of miles away. Apparently, he never thought to tell Mom about it until after the contract was already signed, but thankfully, she loved the large bungalow, and they moved in toward the end of the summer. That made it impossible to visit them that year. I was shocked and truly devastated by the fact that I would never again set foot inside my old childhood home; my deep feelings of loss were even worse than when my mom sold my piano a few weeks after I left home for university. Once again, I had to say goodbye to something I cherished, so I tried not to dwell on the inevitable and instead moved on as best I could. *C'est la vie,* as the French would say.

An opportunity for advancement unexpectedly presented itself to me that summer. My friend Kelly told me that Our Lady of Peace Hospital was hiring nurses for their ICU, and she encouraged me to apply for a position there. Since Will was only turning two years old that July, I was hesitant to return to work so soon, but with our financial pressures mounting, I felt I really had no choice. Jake was all for it, of course. As luck would have it, I got the job, and I planned to begin two weeks of orientation in early July. I don't remember how I juggled getting back and forth to work with only one family car, but for childcare, I ended up hiring a young relative of Jake's, whose family ran a small business in Topsail.

Unfortunately, she turned out to be a very unsuitable babysitter, as she failed to clean Will up properly after he became ill one day with gastroenteritis. To make matters worse, I could smell cigarette smoke in our powder room downstairs. Neither Jake nor I smoked, and I had made it crystal clear to her right from the start that I did not want her to smoke in our home while she was tending Will. I had to let her go immediately, and I decided right then and there that I was not yet ready to leave my precious son with a stranger. By that time, I had also worked a few night shifts in the ICU and discovered it really was *not* my cup of tea. All the patients were very ill, and most of them were heavily sedated and on ventilators. I liked interacting with my patients and did not enjoy monitoring a bunch of machines. At the end of the day, I was sorry to give up my paycheck but very happy to stay home with Will for a while longer. His welfare was the number one priority in my life.

A personal health issue raised its ugly head during that same period of time, when I developed chronic inflammation of the cervix. My family doctor phoned me one day with the results of an irregular PAP test, and despite treatment with antibiotics, the condition failed to improve. I was finally referred to a gynecologist and had cryosurgery of the cervix with a cone biopsy, which eventually fixed the problem. After the unpleasant day surgery, I distinctly remember asking a resident doctor what he thought the cause may have been. After pausing for a few seconds, he gave me a funny look and said, "We think it may be chlamydia, although your test was negative." I was not familiar with the uncommon medical term at the time, and when I discussed it later over the phone with my nursing friend Lydia, she said she thought it was an STD (sexually transmitted disease). I was well and truly horrified but quickly dismissed the thought from my mind, as I was certain that was not in any way possible; Jake and I had always been faithful to each other. Once again trying to be positive, I was thankful to be feeling better and hopeful we could eventually have more children.

# CHAPTER 15

# The Good, the Bad, and the Ugly

The dawning of 1986 heralded several life-changing events for me. My mother phoned me one day in early January to give me some startling news—my brother Gregg had just been diagnosed with thyroid cancer and was flying to Toronto later that week to have surgery at a top hospital there. He had recently experienced the symptoms of a hoarse, raspy voice with difficulty swallowing and had subsequently seen a specialist in Fredericton who had performed a biopsy and detected cancer. Apparently, the surgeon removing the tumor was world-class, which was why Gregory was having the procedure performed in Toronto. I immediately put on my nurse's cap and booked a flight to Toronto, so I could support Gregg, Betty, and Mom. In turn, Jake was very supportive of me and offered to stay home during the week to look after Will.

Thankfully, the surgery was a success, and after rooming for a week with my family in a residence adjacent to the hospital, I flew back to St. John's. My brother Dave arrived just before I left, so there would be lots of family support for the next few days until they would all fly back to their respective homes. Once he was back in New Brunswick, Gregg would have to endure a series of radiation treatments to ensure the cancer was completely gone. I was so happy and relieved that he was going to be okay, and I thanked God for answering my prayers and looking after my brother.

The second profound event in my life that year was wonderful news. Shortly after I returned home from Toronto, I confirmed my suspicions with a home pregnancy test and discovered I was expecting! I was so looking forward to becoming a mother once again, and Jake also seemed to be happy about it. We had been trying for a few months, and this time I was hoping to have a little girl. Like my pregnancy with Will, I had virtually no symptoms, apart from mild morning sickness during my first trimester. I felt great, and because the baby was so quiet, I sometimes wondered if I was pregnant at all! I also put on less weight than the first time, although I was healthy and ate well. I imagine running around after a small child helped me burn off the calories!

Our baby was due in early August, so I started getting things ready in the bedroom across from ours, which I set up as a nursery. Once again, we chose not to know the sex of the baby, but we optimistically painted the room a pale pink and adorned the large window with pink, frilly curtains a few weeks before my due date. We shared the big news with our families and with Will, who would be turning three in July. I even bought a storybook about becoming a big brother and tried to help him bond with the baby by letting him touch my tummy and talk to her.

While we excitedly awaited our new arrival, I received more bad news from my mother. Once again, it involved Gregg, but this time it was different. Gregg's wife had suddenly left him, and since they had been married for almost twenty-seven years, it came as a huge shock to our family. In fact, I initially thought Mom was pulling my leg. I was totally blindsided, even though I knew from the short time I had lived with them that it was not a happy home. Gregg eventually told Mom that Betty had been waiting for their daughter Jessica to graduate from university before she finally left him. This separation had been brewing for many years.

I felt so badly for him, especially since he had only just completed his cancer treatments. In retrospect, I have often wondered over the years if the unhappiness in his marriage contributed to his cancer, since there was never any explanation as to why he became ill. We now know that our emotions and mental health have a profound effect upon our immune system and our body's ability to fight off infection and to heal itself. Thankfully, Gregg had loving parents, family, and friends who helped support him both financially and emotionally until he got back on his feet. With their collective help, he eventually healed and moved on with his life.

Back in Newfoundland, things were progressing nicely with my pregnancy. Something felt different, however, on the morning of July 2, when I woke up feeling tired and miserable, like I had the flu. I spent most of the day sitting in the rocking chair in our family room, and by the time Jake arrived home from work, I knew something was about to happen. I started having mild pains in my lower back, which moved around to the front of my abdomen and got progressively stronger during the course of the evening. As time wore on, I was sure I was in labor, and knowing just how quickly a second baby could come, I called Jake's mother and asked her to come over to watch Will while we went to the hospital. When both of Jake's parents finally arrived, Joan seemed skeptical that I was in true labor and predicted I would soon be back at home. After all, this baby was not due for another month, but as the contractions became stronger and closer together, I was sure it was the real thing.

It was good that we left the house when we did because the labor and delivery nurse barely had time to strap the monitor onto me before I felt the need to push! It was a busy night at Our Lady of Peace Hospital, as all the delivery rooms were full of mothers in labor. Indeed, it felt like ages before they finally wheeled me into one of the rooms and told me I could start pushing. Much like my first delivery, the doctor was surprised to learn the baby was breech, this time in a frank position, or buttocks first. Unfortunately (or perhaps fortunately), it was too late to perform another caesarean section, as nature took over, and I successfully delivered a healthy five-pound, thirteen-ounce baby girl on the third of July at 1:08 a.m. This type of delivery is called a VBAC, or vaginal birth after caesarean, and is rather rare.

Strangely enough, my baby was born on the same day of the week as me, a Thursday, and was the exact same weight I had been when I was born. Although she arrived four weeks early, she was fully developed, and I was able to heave a huge sigh of relief! We finally had our beautiful baby girl. She was slender with long arms and legs, had a full head of brunette hair, and she looked like a little angel to me. We named her Mackenzie (after my Scottish roots), and this time, I brought her home after spending only five days in hospital. We introduced her to her big brother, proud grandparents, and Aunt Debbie and tried to settle back into a good routine.

I found it much easier to recover from a vaginal delivery than a C-section and soon got back into the swing of things at home. The breastfeeding once again went well, although Mackenzie had to be monitored every few days for breastfeeding jaundice. Her skin was yellow in color, but over the next few weeks, this gradually improved as she put on weight and began to fill out. She was a sweet, content baby and slept in a beautiful maple-wood cradle at the end of our bed. Our neighbors had planned a baby shower for me, but since the baby came first, the shower was held with Mackenzie in attendance, lying in her Moses basket on the floor. Because our house boasted a large area connecting our family room, living room, and dining room, I held the shower myself, cleaning my own home and preparing most of the food!

Soon afterward, Mom and Dad arrived for a much-anticipated visit to meet the new baby and see Will again. By this time, in early August, I was starting to feel tired and run-down. Nevertheless, I went all out, trying to make them feel welcome while looking after a three-year-old and a newborn. While they were visiting, Dad's younger brother Gabe passed away suddenly in British Columbia, upsetting him very much. My uncle had been ill with heart disease, so although it was not a huge surprise, it was still a sad event for all of us.

One morning during their visit, as I was feeding Mackenzie in the rocking chair in the nursery, I suddenly noticed a dark purple blotch in the vision of my right eye, much like the one I had initially experienced when I was in high school. I knew right away that the infection had returned, and trying not to panic, I booked an appointment with my optometrist in St. John's. After she examined me, she seemed perplexed regarding the nature of my problem, and over a series of visits during the next few weeks, she still had no answers for me. The spots seemed to be spreading, and at one point, I thought they had moved over into my left eye as well.

By then, I had been referred to an ophthalmologist who worked at our largest and newest hospital in the region. It seemed that even he was completely baffled about what to do with me and finally settled on a course of medication to treat toxoplasmosis. As a result, I had to rent a breast pump to "pump and dump" my breastmilk and then offer Mackenzie formula through a bottle, since the medication would come through my milk and could adversely affect the baby. When the treatment was completed, I got her back onto the breast, but unfortunately, thanks to the interruption in nursing and my mounting panic, my milk supply was low and not enough to satisfy a growing baby. I started supplementing her with formula from a bottle once again, and by October, she was totally formula fed. There were no lactation consultants back in 1986, and I was on my own. I was devastated by this turn of events, and by then was in such a state of anxiety and worry over the possibility of going blind, I was almost beside myself.

One day in the fall, at yet another doctor's visit (where I had dye injected into my veins), I had a complete meltdown in his office. I remember shouting at the top of my lungs, "All the while you are trying to come up with a diagnosis, I am slowly going blind!" During my lifetime, I have learned the hard way that sometimes in order to get results, you must go to the extreme. Or as my mother used to say, "The squeaky wheel gets the grease!" Following my over-the-top outburst, this geriatric doctor wasted no time in referring me to a much younger doctor across the hall that very same day.

Dr. Jonas, originally from South Africa, was familiar with my condition and, after examining my eyes, gave me a differential diagnosis of histoplasmosis, not toxoplasmosis, which had been my initial diagnosis way back in 1972. Histoplasmosis is almost always acquired during childhood, following exposure to fungal spores in the air from either birds or bats. Primarily a respiratory illness, it can also travel to other areas of the body through the bloodstream, including the eyes. This can lead to the formation of secondary blood vessels as well as bleeding in the back of the eye (the retina), which eventually results in scarring and loss of vision.

Dr. Jonas went on to explain that I had had a recurrence of the condition, possibly due to a lowered immunity following pregnancy. I now had two options: I could wait it out, and hopefully the bleeding would subside, or I could try laser surgery, which would be tricky in my case, as one of the lesions was very close to my macula, the center of my vision. If this part of my vision was affected, I would lose much of the central vision in my right eye. Before I left his office, he filled my arms full of textbooks because he knew that I was a nurse and left the decision up to me.

"Knowledge is power," as they say. I finally had a correct diagnosis for my eyes after many years of living in darkness. I would be eternally grateful to Dr. Jonas for his expertise and insight. One of my biggest worries, apart from going blind, was that I might have transferred the disease to my baby daughter through my breastmilk, but this wonderful doctor reassured me that scenario was not possible. Overwhelmingly relieved, I started reading the medical textbooks while fervently praying to God about what I should do. After several days, I made the tough decision to just leave things alone, since I hoped and prayed that the bleeding behind my eyes would completely stop, and I would eventually get my normal eyesight back.

God heard my prayers, as slowly but surely the spots and wavy lines began to fade, and thankfully, my vision returned to normal over the course of several months. From then on, I was certain all would be well, and to this very day, every time a new doctor looks into my eyes, he or she is astounded by how close I came to losing the central vision of my right eye. Today, I have almost twenty-twenty vision, which I am very grateful for every day of my life. For years, I racked my brain, wondering where I might have encountered the initial infection. I now believe I contracted it from playing beside the large henhouse that our elderly English neighbors owned in Grafton. Dad had an old pile of boards out there where I used to play for hours, making mud pies. Dr. Jonas had finally solved a big mystery, but it was a long, treacherous journey that led me back to daily prayer and a renewed faith in God after many years of putting Him on the back burner. Nothing speaks to us more than a personal health crisis.

The remainder of 1986 was less traumatic, apart from one disturbing incident. One morning, as I was upstairs brushing my teeth, I suddenly heard Mackenzie crying loudly. Only a few minutes before, I had left her sound asleep in her baby basket on the love seat in our living room. I raced downstairs and saw Will standing over her; he was looking intently at Mackenzie but was not touching her. After I picked her up and comforted her, I asked Will what had happened. He became quiet for a minute, then answered honestly, "I put my hands around the baby's neck and squeezed." Totally stunned, I failed to respond for a few moments. Not wanting to make things worse by overreacting, I finally said, very forcefully, "William, that hurt Mackenzie, and you must never do anything like that ever again."

Thankfully, he never did, but there were a few other incidents along the way, including using play scissors to cut off her bangs! Sibling rivalry is very strong, especially at that age, and the strength of children's feelings should never be underestimated. From that moment on, I never left Mackenzie unattended again. Will entered preschool that fall for three mornings a week, which greatly improved his socialization skills with other children.

Recruited by my friend Kelly, I began selling a popular skin care / cosmetics line from my home but soon discovered I was not a natural-born salesperson. I lacked the contacts and assertiveness needed in sales and gracefully retired a few months after I started. I still reap the benefits, though, as I have used their products ever since with lasting results. It also helps me keep in touch with my dear friend Lucy, who is a senior sales director for the company in Newfoundland and Labrador. When she retired from teaching many years ago and began selling their products as a hobby, even she had no idea just how successful she would quickly become! The funny thing is that Kelly also recruited Lucy but only worked for a brief time with the company herself. It's my guess that nurses are not great salespeople for good reason!

# CHAPTER 16

# A Wedding and a Funeral

In June 1988, there was cause for a big celebration in Jake's family. His younger sister Debbie was preparing to marry a man she had met while working at a summer job in St. John's. Brad had a managerial position with the company, and Debbie had just graduated from Memorial University of Newfoundland (MUN) with a degree in nursing. After the wedding, Debbie and Brad planned to move to Halifax, Nova Scotia, where he originated from. Since Debbie's immediate family was so small, our little family played a big role in the whole affair. Once again, because our home boasted the largest rooms, I hosted her bridal shower a few weeks before the wedding as well as the rehearsal dinner on the evening before the big day. Will, now almost five years old, was to be the ring bearer, I was a bridesmaid, and Jake was asked to be the master of ceremonies. Brad's niece was to be the flower girl, but because she was so shy, it was doubtful she would agree to go through with it. A few days prior to the wedding, relatives from both families arrived from Nova Scotia and Ontario.

When the wedding day finally arrived with bright sunshine and warm temperatures, the ladies all gathered at Debbie's parents' home to get dressed. Just as we had expected, the little flower girl refused to perform her role in the ceremony, so at the last moment, we put the rather large dress onto Mackenzie, who was not quite two years old at the time. You can imagine how nervous I felt with all three of us in the wedding, but because she was so young, Mackenzie had no qualms about walking down the aisle, hand in hand with her big brother. They stole the show that day in the small country church down the road, as Will patiently told Mackenzie where to stand when they reached the altar.

It was during the photo session afterward, again at our home in Topsail, when I first noticed Jake walking around with a beer in his hand. He was anxious about speaking in front of his family and friends, and I guessed that this was a coping mechanism for him. Still, it was unusual to see him drinking so early in the day. One beer led to another as the afternoon wore on. When the photographer was finally finished, we left for the reception, which was held at an old English heritage restaurant just up the road from our home, and the rest of the evening went off without a hitch. Jake, despite being ill with the stomach flu, did a good job as MC and entertained the crowd with a few jokes. All in all, we were left with many special memories of that day, but no matter how hard I tried, I could not shake the image of Jake walking around the house with a beer in his hand. In hindsight, it was a big red flag.

As June turned into July, we got ready for our summer vacation in New Brunswick to visit my parents in their new home. We borrowed Joan's Ford Bronco because we needed the extra space for the kids that our small Jetta would not afford. We drove from Topsail to Argentia, where we took the sixteen-hour ferryboat ride over to North Sydney, Nova Scotia. Since the ferry was at full capacity, we were unable to book any berths, so we lay down in the lounge chairs all night, trying to get some sleep. I remember Will curling up in one of the porthole windows, trying to sleep during the daytime, as the rocking of the large boat could be bad at times, even during the summer, and could induce either sleep or travel sickness. Sleep was definitely the lesser of two evils! Mackenzie, being little, could sleep in her umbrella stroller. Once we disembarked in North Sydney, we faced a long drive to Woodstock, at least six or seven hours back then. We were all very happy and relieved when we finally pulled into the driveway of my parents' new bungalow.

It was so sweet to see Mom and Dad again and to get reacquainted with their new abode. It was a more spacious home than their old one and overlooked the St. John River Valley, since it was suspended very high up on a steep hill. I spent a lot of time with my dad during that first week, as he was in rare form. He had recently been ill with vascular dementia, related to a series of TIAs (transient ischemic attacks), also known as mini strokes. His memory would come and go with periods of confusion, which Mom was finding increasingly difficult to manage. Amazingly, during this short window of opportunity, God granted us both precious time together to talk about our shared memories as well as what my life was like at that time.

One day while we were sitting outside on their patio, Dad asked me, "Rebecca, do you have school tomorrow?" He had obviously traveled back in time to when I was a child living at home. It was so sad to see Dad like that, but there was really nothing to be done about it. We could either go along with him or try to bring him back to the present day. We carried on with our visit and celebrated Mackenzie's second birthday with Mom and Dad as well as with my brother Gregg, who had traveled up from Fredericton to spend the day with us.

On the morning of July 13, Jake and I had planned to take the kids to visit my mom's youngest sister, Aunt Ruth, who lived in Forest City, New Brunswick. This tiny hamlet was about an hour's drive away from Woodstock, close to where Mom had grown up in Fosterville near the Canada/US border. I still have fond memories of visiting my aunt and uncle as a young child at nearby Spednic Lake, where they owned and operated a sporting camp, catering mainly to wealthy Americans who loved to hunt and bass fish there. My uncle Abe had passed away many years before, and Aunt Ruth now lived alone in the family home with their aging dog, Freckles.

I remember giving Dad a big hug and kiss as I told him I loved him before we left for the day. Mom had made him a poached egg and toast for his breakfast, since he was feeling a bit better that morning. We were excited to set out on our small journey because we looked forward to taking the children swimming in the cold, clear water near the dam by my aunt's house. It turned into a beautiful, hot, sunny day, and we had so much fun playing and splashing in the refreshing water. When we arrived home, it was late in the day, so we spent a short time with Dad before he went to bed.

After getting both kids bathed and tucked into the cozy double bed in the spare bedroom, I decided to read in bed for a while before going to sleep. The house was quiet except for the soft murmurs coming from the TV in the den, where Jake was watching a program. Just as I was about to drift off to sleep, I heard a big commotion in the hall outside my bedroom. Dad had gotten up to use the bathroom but sounded confused and disoriented. I heard Mom follow him into the bathroom and try to calm him down, but she obviously needed some help. Alarmed, I quickly got up and rushed into the small hallway, where I met my mom trying to hold Dad steady in order to get him back into bed.

As soon as I reached them, I realized Dad was in real trouble, as he collapsed into our arms, a dead weight. Screaming for Jake to come quickly, we managed to hold Dad upright until he arrived, and the three of us finally managed to get him back onto their bed. Once there, we soon realized he had passed away, and in fact, he seemed to have a small smile on his face. Mom and I stood over the bed in complete silence, gazing down at the husband and father we so loved, in total shock and disbelief.

Dad's death hit me very hard, possibly because I was not expecting it, but at the relatively young age of thirty-two, I was not yet ready to lose my beloved father. The next few days passed in a haze, as Gregg along with Dave and his family arrived at my parents' home, sharing in our sorrow. I remember breaking down completely during the visitation at the funeral home when I saw the familiar faces of family and friends from both my past and my present. Their caring and loving support meant so much to me later when I reflected on Dad's untimely passing, but it was cold comfort to me at the time.

It was very reassuring, though, to know that a few short years before his death, Dad had finally started attending the small Baptist church in Grafton and gave his life to the Lord at the age of seventy. He was just shy of seventy-nine when he died of what was probably a heart attack or a stroke. I knew he was finally at peace in heaven and that God had orchestrated the timing of his death so Mom was not alone with Dad when he passed. I also had those few precious days with him, which most surely would not have happened had we not made the trip home that summer. I was so grateful for that. As I write this memoir, it is exactly thirty-two years ago today that Dad passed away; I have now lived on this earth for the same amount of time without my father as I did with him. It always seems that life comes around full circle.

Dad's last gift to me before he died was his much-loved bronze-colored Ford Maverick car. He had not been able to drive it much for the past year and had generously offered to give it to me during one of my last conversations with him. He knew that I could make very good use out of the car. Since we now had two vehicles to bring back to Newfoundland, and I was most certainly not up to driving all the way there with two small children in the back seat of the car, we were faced with a new dilemma. Thankfully, Jake's father, Tom, came to our rescue. He flew to Fredericton and helped Jake drive the two cars the long distance home, while I arranged to fly back with both kids. To make matters worse, it was heart-wrenching to leave my poor mother behind, since she was now confronted with the stark reality of picking up the pieces of her life and carrying on without her partner of fifty-six years.

On a positive note, we finally celebrated Will's fifth birthday after we all returned home to Topsail. In honor of Dad, I ordered a long, multicolored cake in the shape of a train from our local grocery store, and Sean, the little boy who lived next door, came over to complete the small party of three. In September, Will entered kindergarten in the school located at the top of the big hill behind us, while Jake started a new position at work. He was excited about this new chapter in his work life, since he would be responsible for several different outdoor children's clubs in the province.

The premier club was a brand-new family-focused outdoor adventure program for children. Jake eventually recruited Cliff, a forester from Alberta, to help organize and start the program. He and his lovely German wife, Amelia, had two little girls close to Will and Mac in age, and because they lived only one town over, we quickly became good friends with them. When the first clubs opened in Newfoundland in 1989, Amelia and I became joint leaders of our own little group of children. Additionally, for the first time ever, I had the freedom to come and go as I pleased, using Dad's old car. Finally, things seemed to be looking up for us.

## CHAPTER 17

# My Waking Nightmare

As I relive the events of 1989, things seem so crystal clear in my memory that they could have happened just yesterday. Suffice it to say, this was the year our lives changed irreparably for the worse. With our financial pressures mounting, Jake started spending more and more time at the office, sometimes missing dinner entirely and arriving home late at night. Although I knew we were on a budget, I couldn't quite figure out where all the money was going. Since I was so busy with the children and we lived outside of the city, Jake usually paid the bills and picked up the mail at our post office each day. He also did all the banking since our bank was in St. John's. I trusted him to look after things.

One dark night in early spring, Jake arrived home in a foul mood. He seemed very angry with me for reasons I could not quite fathom, and out of the blue, he ordered me to take myself and both children back to New Brunswick to live with my mother. He went on to say he had booked flights for all three of us, which I knew could not possibly be true. He then lay down on the couch in our family room and fell fast asleep. I was not only stunned but also in a state of disbelief and confusion. As a result, I did nothing, since I could not seem to get him to wake up and talk to me about what was bothering him. Our standoff went on for several days, with Jake coming home late at night, refusing to talk to me, and then falling asleep on the couch. After a week or so of this strange behavior, Jake seemed to come around, and we never spoke of the matter again.

Another time that spring, when I went to get something out of my car, Jake locked the front door behind me, and I was stuck outside in the cold

101

for at least an hour before he finally opened the door and let me back in. Once again, he offered no explanation for his erratic behavior and certainly no apology. In addition to all of his unexplained aggression toward me, there were two more bizarre incidents, both occurring at night; thankfully, our children were fast asleep in bed.

One evening, Jake came home, late as usual, and headed straight for the living room. He seemed to be disoriented and announced that he was going to burn our house down in order to collect on the insurance money. He went so far as to get a barbecue lighter and some newspapers and then sat down in the middle of the floor to start a fire! I couldn't believe my own eyes and ears, but eventually he calmed down, and I quickly snatched the items away from him. His eyes were glazed over, and he seemed totally spaced out. I asked him if he had been drinking, and he admitted he had. With a note of desperation in my voice, I told him he needed to stop right away, as the alcohol was severely affecting his decision-making and behavior. I knew there was a history of alcoholism on both sides of his family, putting him at an increased risk of falling into the same patterns. Looking miserable, he told me he could not stop drinking because he had already tried to do so, and he had, in fact, been drinking for over three weeks straight! Horrified, I was at a loss for words.

The experts in addiction say it usually takes about three weeks for a habit to form, so that explained a lot to me, such as why he came home so late at night and went straight to sleep. The strange thing was that he rarely seemed impaired or even smelled of alcohol. I asked him once more where he had been spending his long evenings, and he insisted he had been staying late in his office, drinking by himself. I was adamant that he quit drinking right away, but I still felt something else was going on with him; I just couldn't figure out what it was.

The second incident was even worse than the first. A few days later, he once again arrived home late at night and seemed to be in a state of frenzy. This time, he went into the kitchen and took a large butcher knife out of the knife block, shouting at me that he was going to go to Topsail Beach to kill himself! He was so out of control that I could not calm him down. Frightened that he might come after me with the knife, I let him go, racing to lock the door behind him. Once again, I was totally out of my depth and unsure of what to do. I couldn't follow him in my car because I could not leave the children alone, so I considered calling the police.

Before I could do even that, he arrived back home, banging on the front door and shouting to be let in. After reluctantly unlocking the door, I made him put down the knife before he entered, and afterward, he went straight to the couch in our family room, lay down, and immediately fell asleep. Like his mother, Jake was one of those rare people who could fall asleep at the drop of a hat—anytime, anywhere. I eventually went upstairs, crawled into bed, and tried to go to sleep myself. Sleep was elusive, however, as I worried all night long about our safety, should he suddenly wake up and go off the rails once more.

Having young children in the house, I considered all my options, none of which were good. In complete desperation, I had called his parents to come over once, earlier that same year, after he had put his hands around my neck and threatened to choke me—again, for no apparent reason. He did it twice but then backed off after I called his bluff and told him, "Just go ahead and do it." When Tom and Joan arrived at our house about an hour later, they assumed we had just had a big fight, and they soon went home again, very angry that I had called them in the first place. I knew, then and there, that I was on my own with Jake.

I could hardly believe this was happening to *us*. My biggest problem was that I could never get him to sit down and have a straightforward talk with me about anything. Following this string of frightening and disturbing events, I became worried over not only his heavy drinking and driving but also the dubious state of his mental health. Unfortunately, mental illness had never been my strong suit in university, and I did not have any experience in dealing with addictions. As far as I knew, there was not a history of either one in my own family.

I wondered if Jake had started drinking to self-medicate, which in turn may have led to further depression or even psychosis, since addiction can become a vicious cycle. On the other hand, he seemed almost manic at times, like when he wanted to burn down the house and threatened to commit suicide. Putting two and two together, I feared he could possibly have manic depression, now commonly known as bipolar disorder. There was a history of depression in the extended family as well, and his own father had once had a bad bout of it after his elderly mother passed away.

Unfortunately, everything came to a head one night when I was once again sitting up late at the kitchen table, waiting for Jake to come home from work. He finally staggered through the door around 1:00 a.m., this time reeking of alcohol and slurring his speech. He was obviously impaired and had just been dropped off by Cliff, who had rescued him after he totaled a work vehicle on the arterial highway near our home. The worst had finally happened, but amazingly, like a cat with nine lives, he crawled out of that car wreck without a scratch on him, and thankfully, no one else was injured or involved in the accident.

As soon as he entered the kitchen, he started working on my emotions, begging me and threatening me at the same time to not tell anyone he had been drinking and driving. I knew a lot was at stake, including both his job and income as well as his freedom and reputation. Cliff, his work colleague and friend, was apparently unaware of just how impaired Jake really was, since Jake had become an expert at hiding the truth. As I would eventually discover, he was also an expert at storytelling. Indeed, he was learning to become very good at lying and deception in general.

I was in a terrible quandary, but before I had a chance to think things through, a knock came at the door. Right away, Jake knew that it was the police. The two officers had found the overturned vehicle with Jake's briefcase inside and wanted to breathalyze him right then and there. He flat out refused, stating that he had only started drinking once he arrived home, so they had no choice but to take him at his word and leave him alone. I don't know what he told his superiors at work the next day, but as far as I know, he was never reprimanded, and no charges were ever laid. He also seemed to be off the hook for the damage to the vehicle he had been driving, as insurance covered the cost. In the end, he was never held accountable for any of his actions that night. This was the first of several scrapes that Jake managed to wriggle out of, and I often wonder if he could have gotten help, had he told the truth about the accident in the first place. Although I didn't know it at the time, he was learning to become a master manipulator of both the truth and his own consequences.

Following Jake's car accident, we finally sat down and talked about some of our serious financial issues. I had opened the trunk of his car one day to look for something and found piles of unopened mail lying there. Most of it was bills, but some of the envelopes contained credit card statements, of which I had been totally unaware. It seemed that Jake had applied for several credit cards in his own name but had neglected to make payments on them for several months. The charges were all cash advances, and when I asked him what the money was used for, he told me he had used it to pay off other bills. I never did get a straight answer out of him. After adding it all up, I was horrified to discover that he had accumulated a grand total of almost $20,000 in credit card debt, and now it all needed to be repaid!

A few months prior to all of this, he had also talked me into agreeing to apply for a line of credit in order to buy the piece of land beside our house so that we could eventually build a garage. Of course, the garage had never been built, and now it was apparent that this money was also gone. That was another $10,000, so the total amount of our debt was close to $30,000—a huge fortune to us! The only bright spot was that we had no interest payments on our mortgage, since it was with his aunt and uncle. I was furious with him (and myself) and was completely panicked over the financial abyss we were now staring down. With only one of us working, we had no hope of paying the money back any time soon.

We decided to consolidate the debt into one loan, but in order to do this, Jake had to make a repayment of at least $3,000 within the next few days. Since we did not have any extra savings sitting around anywhere, I was forced to call Mom and ask her for a loan to see us through. Mom, much to her credit, did not ask any questions and immediately arranged to wire the money to me in Newfoundland. I was so grateful to her, as she reassured me that the money was not a loan but a gift, and I should not feel any pressure to repay her. It felt like my mother saved our lives that spring, and we would be forever in her debt for her generosity, understanding, and kindness.

Later that summer, Mom flew to St. John's to visit us for two weeks. As it happened, I was babysitting the two young children who had recently moved into the house next door. Sally had just lost her child care provider, and since she worked full-time, she was left in the lurch. I felt very badly for her because she was also having some marital difficulties, so when she asked me, I agreed to care for her children for seventy-five dollars a week. It soon turned into a full-time job for me, as Will and Mac were the same age, just six and three years old at the time. It seemed like I was running a small day care, and by the end of the week, I was exhausted and probably out almost as much money as I earned. I have always had a hard time saying no to people, and this was a classic example. I tried to make the best of it and included Sally's children in everything Mom and I did with my own kids during her stay with us.

After we stabilized our financial situation and started making the minimum payments required each month, things seemed to settle down with Jake. From then on, I took over the management of our finances, as obviously, I could not trust him to do it. He stopped staying out late at night, and although the drinking continued, he did not seem to be so out of control. In fact, he rarely drank alcohol in front of either me or the kids, but I assumed it never stopped. It was often hard to tell if he was drinking because he hid it well most of the time. If his parents or my mother noticed anything amiss, they never gave any indication of it.

I was so ashamed and embarrassed that I never told a single soul what had transpired during that terrible spring. One day, Amelia came to my door unexpectedly and caught me in the midst of one of my crying sessions. Almost immediately, she looked concerned and asked me what was wrong, but I could not confess the ugly truth about my marriage, no matter how desperately I wanted to confide in my caring and trustworthy friend.

Something very peculiar happened to me one day during a random visit from several of my neighbors. Rita, who lived directly across the street from us, had a sister who was a Christian, and for some reason or another, she accompanied the other ladies to my house. Shortly after they arrived, Rita's sister asked me if something bad was going on with me. Although I denied it, she was very persistent and asked me over and over if I was having problems with anything. I can only believe she had heard from the Holy Spirit that I desperately needed help, and I later wished I had confided in her. It was so hard carrying around such a big secret and an even bigger burden.

We did not regularly attend a church back then, and although we had gone to a small church in Topsail a few times, it seemed foreign to me, and the minister seemed more like a teacher than a preacher. I did not feel the presence of the Holy Spirit there and did not get much out of going. I had even taken Will to Sunday school a few times, but he had a hard time settling into class and acted out. As a result, we stopped going. Unfortunately, there was no evangelical church in Topsail or anywhere else near us at that time.

Although I was still unhappy about Jake's drinking, I felt powerless to stop it, and since I was not yet back at work, I was not able to leave him. Despite everything, I still loved him, and I was desperately hoping and praying that things would improve once our finances got straightened out for good. Unfortunately, I have since learned (the hard way) that things seldom improve when left alone by themselves. I knew the time had come for me to return to work, and since the children were a bit older now, it would be an easier transition for all of us. The problem was that more than five years had passed since I last worked full-time, so my RN license had expired, and I was now faced with writing the exams all over again! It was very important for me to be up to date with both my education and my practice, so I chose to do a refresher course and enrolled in a correspondence program that fall at Grant MacEwan University in Edmonton, Alberta.

Jake was thrilled that I would eventually be going back to work. In the meantime, I could study in the mornings, since William would enter grade one in September, and Mackenzie would also start preschool three mornings a week. This new endeavor was something meaningful that I could do not only for myself but also for my family, and I felt very excited to begin a new chapter in my work life. As a result, I delved into the textbooks with a fervor I may have lacked the first time I was in nursing school. I was now on a mission, and failure was not an option.

# CHAPTER 18

# Back to School

When people ask me, even today, when was I most happy, I say without hesitation that it was during the seven years I stayed at home to raise my children. Despite all the problems within my marriage, it was such a pleasure and a privilege to be able to spend those few precious years at home with them. Children grow up so fast, and once they enter school, things are never really the same again. However, once I made up my mind to go back to work, I never veered off course. I studied faithfully throughout the year, wrote twenty-one different exams, and completed my refresher course just shy of Christmas 1990. I received my recertification by mail in January 1991 with a grade point average of 4.0. My marks were even better than when I graduated from university twelve years before, and for the first time in a long time, I felt pride in my personal accomplishments.

My one break from studying was in August 1990, when Jake, Will, and I flew out to Vancouver and then on to Kelowna, British Columbia, to attend a National Campout. I attended as both a leader and a parent, while Jake went in his official work capacity, but Will probably had the most fun, just being a kid in the great outdoors! Mackenzie, who had just turned four, was now old enough to stay home with Nana and Papa, and she had a great staycation with them as well.

We still had our struggles though; Jake continued to binge drink off and on, and I now knew beyond a shadow of a doubt that he was a full-fledged alcoholic. Getting him to stop drinking was almost impossible, but at least he seemed to be a functional alcoholic while at work. As far as I knew, none of the staff had clued into the fact that he had a big problem.

Alcoholics are often good at hiding their secret lives, but at least there were no more incidents of violence toward either himself or me.

My health had also suffered over the course of the year, as I developed migraines, a chronic upset stomach, and an irregular heartbeat. After some investigation (and a referral to a cardiologist), it was confirmed by my family physician that almost all my symptoms were probably due to stress, and although Dr. Dixon pressed me to confide in him, I couldn't do it. I guess it was an issue of pride, but I also failed to see how he could help me. This would continue to be a pattern of mine throughout the years, as I felt very isolated and did not feel free to talk to anyone else about my problems. In the back of my mind, I wondered if it was only a matter of time before my make-believe world came crashing down around me. To quote Proverbs 21:4, "Pride goes before a fall."

Although I can't say I was truly happy during this time period, the children were doing well at school and preschool, even though we were starting to have some problems with Will's behavior. He could be rough when playing with Mackenzie, but since he never had any issues with other children, I initially put it down to sibling rivalry. I tried time-outs and even resorted to spanking, but his temper tantrums eventually became so bad that we took him to see a child psychologist at the children's hospital in St. John's. I had recently completed a pediatric practicum on a surgical unit there, so I was familiar with the hospital. I was concerned that Will might have ADHD (attention deficit hyperactivity disorder), as he was such an active little boy. After his assessment by the doctor, however, she was able to reassure us that he did not have ADHD or any other diagnosis and was just what he seemed to be—very active! He was a child who needed both structure and discipline in his life, so she gave us some strategies to use with him and his sister as well as a behavioral chart to help keep him motivated. I can't say it was a cure-all, but it did help a lot, and as Mackenzie got older, things gradually improved, since she learned how to better handle her big brother. Sometimes, I still wonder if the negative tension in our home may have influenced Will's behavior.

Mackenzie was by nature very shy, so I encouraged her to socialize with other children by putting her in activities she seemed to enjoy. She took swimming lessons and ballet with a genuine ballerina from France. Unfortunately, her main dance instructor was male and hailed from the

Czech Republic; although he was quiet and very patient with the young children, I sat in on all her dance lessons, since Mackenzie was nervous to be in the class by herself. She also now attended the same outdoor children's club as her brother, where I was usually in attendance as well. You could say that mother and daughter were joined at the hip! Will took swimming lessons and played hockey, and Jake often coached his hockey team. In the spring and summer, they both participated in soccer and baseball, like all the other children on the street. Between the two of us, we were trying very hard to give them both a happy, well-rounded childhood despite Jake's drinking problem.

In early 1991, I learned from another friend, Jodi, that a home health care organization, the Visiting Nurse (VN) program, was looking to hire an RN who would work exclusively on the weekends. Jodi's husband, Jon, worked with Jake, and she was a nurse who now stayed at home with her young son. She was also looking for a job but was reluctant to work every weekend. Since I was hoping to find employment in the community setting, I saw this position as a great opportunity to return to the workforce. I would be home with the kids all week, and Jake could look after them on the weekends. It seemed like the perfect solution for all of us and would not involve having to search for childcare.

I was very happy to get the tip from Jodi and was soon back at work. It was a casual position without any benefits, but it was all day shifts, and it did provide us with some much-needed money for all the extras. I used Dad's old car to get to my visits, but since my area consisted of a wide swathe in and around St. John's, I soon learned that the cost of gas was literally eating up most of my profits. Jake and I switched cars at some point, as we now had a new car, a Mazda, which his parents had generously bought for us when our old Jetta finally broke down. It was much smaller than mine and better on gas.

I loved working with VN, and my job description included a wide range of activities, such as administering insulin injections, taking blood, doing dressing changes, removing sutures, performing catheterizations, and doing foot care. My clients were adults of all ages, and I made only home visits, including going to nursing homes and a local convent, where I performed foot care on the seniors and the nuns. It was rewarding work, as my clients were usually appreciative of the care they received, but I did find the driving to be challenging, especially during the winter months. Jake usually took the kids over to visit with his parents on the weekends, so he had it relatively easy. They did enjoy lots of quality time with their grandparents, which they still reminisce about today. After my Sunday shift, I would usually drive over to Herring Bay to join them for dinner, and then our little family would return home to Topsail.

A wonderful event occurred in the summer of 1991 when my brother Gregg married a woman by the name of Jennifer, who was nineteen years younger than him. They met through our cousin Dale's wife, Elaine, who had worked with Jenny in the nursing home in Woodstock for several years. She had never been married and was a Christian who was not afraid to share her faith. Before they were married, Jennifer had worked for two doctors in Halifax as their nanny and housekeeper but planned to give up her job after the wedding and move to Fredericton to live with Gregg. I was very excited to meet her and see my family again, so Jake and I arranged to take a couple of weeks off work that September.

The four of us caught the ferry over to North Sydney, Nova Scotia, and then drove to Halifax, where they were getting married. We spent a few days visiting family and friends there and then traveled to Woodstock, following their small wedding in the Baptist church, which was just around the corner from David's house in Rockingham. Mom was having a hard time accepting Jenny into the family, as she and Gregg had become very close after his illness and divorce and Dad's death. Gregory had spent a lot of time with Mom on the weekends, and she knew their time together was now coming to an end. It would be a time of transition for her for sure. I was so happy for my brother, though, since he had been through so much turmoil, and I hoped and prayed this would be a new beginning for him and his new wife.

Jake and I suffered a big loss of our own that year when our good friends Cliff and Amelia moved back to Alberta. Cliff's job contract had ended, so they were now looking for new opportunities out west. I dearly missed my visits and outdoor time with Amelia, and since my friend Kelly had mysteriously stopped talking to me, I was lonesome for close female friendship. It seemed to me that all my friends eventually left me behind. I concentrated on my family and my work, and as the year ended, things became a bit better financially for us, but they still were not great. That

Christmas may have been a low point for me, when I opened my one and only gift from Jake, an electric can opener. I can't begin to express how unloved and undervalued his gift made me feel, especially since we opened our presents in front of Jake's parents as well as Debbie and Brad, who were visiting Newfoundland over the holidays. Eternally optimistic, I tried to focus on the positive, because the children had a good Christmas, and I earnestly hoped and prayed the new year would be a better one for all of us.

# CHAPTER 19

# Growing Pains

The next year, 1992, turned out to be a year of both challenges and transitions for all of us. Will was now in grade three, and Mackenzie was in kindergarten at grade school; fortunately, both children were good students, but two incidents with Will stand out razor sharp in my mind. One sunny spring day, a knock came at my door, late in the afternoon. When I opened it, a neighborhood man who worked at the glass works on the corner was holding Will in his arms. My son looked like he was sound asleep. Instantly alarmed, I asked him what had happened, and he sheepishly told me that Will had raced down the steep hill behind our home on his bike and slammed into the back of his parked pickup truck. Will had not been wearing a helmet, as they were not commonly used at the time, and immediately I was worried that he might have sustained a concussion, since he had a large goose egg on his forehead. The Good Samaritan came in and laid Will on the couch in our family room, and while I took his vital signs, Will woke up. Unbelievably, he seemed to be fine and did not even complain of a headache. I applied ice to his injury and watched him closely over the next few days, and thanks be to God, he never suffered any ill effects from his unfortunate accident.

Another day, around the same time of year, William went missing while playing outdoors with the other kids who lived in the neighborhood. I called his name over and over and searched high and low, up and down the street, but he never answered. I must have looked for him for over two hours, even venturing into the woodlot across the street from our house, but there was neither hide nor hair of him. It brought back terrible memories of when he was four years old and went missing while we were shopping in the Village Mall in St. John's. One minute, he was standing beside Mackenzie's stroller with Jake while I looked around the store, and the next minute, he'd disappeared entirely. Just as we began to search frantically for him, a man brought him back to the same store we had initially been in. It turned out that Will had followed this person into another store, since he'd believed he was his dad. I knew firsthand how easily accidents could happen and that children sometimes go missing.

Now in near panic mode, I called Jake to come home from work to help me look for Will. By the time Jake arrived at our house about forty-five minutes later, Will had turned up, emerging out of the woods with some of the other boys. They had been making a fort in there, and if he had heard me calling his name, he had deliberately ignored me. Most unfortunately, as Jake was rushing home, another car had run into his vehicle, T-boning the driver's side of the car. Unbelievably, Jake was uninjured, but our small Mazda was completely crushed on one side, and since it was not a high-end car to begin with, it was beyond repair. Jake was furious with me, as well as with Will, and we were now faced with the financial challenge of buying a new car. This time, we paid for it ourselves and bought a gently used cream-colored sedan that had been driven by a Chrysler executive. Over time, it turned out to be one of the best cars we ever owned, and Will never again hid out in the woods.

One day, that same year, Jake came to me and told me that he had applied for a job with the United Nations. In fact, he had already been accepted for a position in Ghana, West Africa, and would oversee all the forestry/engineering operations in western Africa. The salary was excellent and was all tax-free, and if he accepted it, we would be living in Accra, the capital of Ghana. Although Ghana was one of the poorest nations on earth at the time, we would have a nice home with servants, which was the way things were done over there. I was completely gob-smacked, as I thought he was happy with his current job and would not be eager to leave his parents, Aunt Bess and Uncle Harry, or his home province. After all, we had spent eight years putting down roots in Topsail, and my career was just starting to take off with the VN program. I was now making home visits to clients in Conception Bay South, since the organization was hoping to expand to areas farther around the bay.

Due to the terrible economic situation in Newfoundland, Jake told me he thought his job security was tenuous at best, and he might be made redundant. That certainly put a different spin on things, but I encouraged him to look for a position closer to home. AIDS was in the news a lot back then, and it seemed to be running rampant in Africa. Taking our precious children to such a dangerous place seemed reckless at best, and for once, I put my foot down about moving so far away from our family and friends.

Coincidentally, around the same time, a fairly large sum of money went missing from a volunteer fund in Jake's office. Only a few people had access to the safe, so it was puzzling as to who would do such a terrible thing. Jake was one of the few people who had access, and I felt I had to ask him if he had anything to do with the theft, which amounted to just over $3,000. He blankly denied taking the money and said he had no idea who took it. I was forced to take him at his word, but something about his expression left me wondering if he knew more than he was saying about the whole affair. Bitterly disappointed about not relocating to Africa, Jake started to look around for a new job elsewhere in Canada and soon had a job offer and visit set up for a position in The Pas, Manitoba.

Knowing next to nothing about The Pas, except that it was a long way away in northwestern Manitoba, my reaction was less than enthusiastic. The management position he had applied for was almost identical to the job he had done in Goose Bay, Labrador. Not only was he familiar with that type of work, but he was also very good at it, enjoying the combination of office and fieldwork. Already, it seemed like our days in Newfoundland were numbered.

In May, Jake and I flew by jet to Winnipeg and then on to The Pas by regional airline. His new boss, whose office was in Winnipeg, showed us around for a few days. It was a large town of over five thousand people, not including a large and prosperous First Nations reserve, Opaskwayak Cree Nation, just across the bridge over the Saskatchewan River. The Pas is known as the Gateway to the North, and a large figure of a trapper greets everyone who enters the town from the south. It is known for its long, cold winters and short, hot summers, as well as the aurora borealis or northern lights. A main attraction of the area is beautiful Clearwater Lake Provincial Park, which has one of the clearest blue lakes in the world, with several campgrounds, beaches, and caves to explore. There is also a large, flat agricultural area west of the town called Carrot Valley, which is known for its rich soil—good for growing a variety of crops and grains, including rice paddies. To the east of the town is Rahl's Island, a flat stretch of rural land parallel to the Saskatchewan River.

One of the biggest employers in the area is the pulp and lumber mill, which was called PAPYRUS during that era. Back then, there were a few storefronts, businesses, and restaurants along the main street of the town, a large RCMP office as well as the premier motel, the Wanderer's Inn, which is where we lodged during our short trip. The largest mall was located on the reserve; for variety, there was also another mall in the main town. There were several schools and churches; an old-fashioned movie theater, the Majestic (established in 1929); a midsized college, Aurora Community College; as well as a large hospital across the street from the Roman Catholic Archdiocese of Keewatin. The highlight of the long winter was, and remains, the weeklong Trappers' Festival, held in February, one of the coldest months of the year. This festival celebrates unique northern skills and activities, such as ice fishing, bannock baking, and wife carrying and hosts the World Championship Dog Race, a Pas tradition since 1916.

I knew if Jake accepted this position, it would be a huge change for all of us, although it would most likely be a stepping-stone for his career. I would certainly miss the shopping in St. John's as well as the beautiful scenery and family time with Jake's parents. Another negative (and it was a big one) was that the town of The Pas was isolated in the middle of the Manitoban wilderness. I soon discovered the drive from Winnipeg to The Pas was a long (and boring) seven-hour trip through nothing but a couple of small towns near Winnipeg, followed by lots of trees, a few lakes, and one Indian reserve, Easterville, located a couple of hours southeast of The Pas. When we flew back to Winnipeg and checked into our lavish hotel suite, I truly wished we would be living in that prosperous and multicultural prairie city, instead of yet another lonely, isolated northern community. I didn't know it at the time, but Jake had his own agenda and was trying to exile me from my family and friends on the east coast. Foolishly, he was also trying to run away from his own problems.

Back home in Topsail, the final decision was quickly made, and before we knew it, the movers were in our home and packing up our belongings once more. While we had been cleaning out the basement, prior to having the movers come in to pack, the kids had unearthed two disturbing items from a box. One was a signed photo of a scantily clad woman, obviously a stripper, and the other was a set of keys from a motel in St. John's. I never got a straight answer out of Jake about the photo, but he explained to me that the keys were from a work trip to St. John's that he had made over a decade before when we were living in Goose Bay. He had been forced to stay in a motel, as his parents' home had been flooded out, and I actually recalled that event happening.

Jake's parents were most unhappy about our decision to move so far away because they knew they would not see much of their grandchildren anymore. Air travel was expensive across Canada during that time, which made the distance seem even wider. I felt badly for them as well as for my own mom because we were going to be almost as far away from her. I also had to walk away from a job I loved, but since my salary was so much smaller than Jake's, there really was not much choice. By then, I was getting used to starting over.

We hired a local Realtor and put our beloved home up for sale, but we could not have chosen a worse time to sell if we had tried. For several reasons, the cod fishery closed in Newfoundland on July 2, 1992, and has pretty much remained the same to this day. As a result, the economy collapsed that year, which had a devastating impact on the real estate market for years to come. I cried bitter tears the day we left our home on Memorial Road, my dad's treasured car sitting abandoned in the driveway, as it was much too old to make the long journey west. Sadly, it was the last remaining link I had with my father. Once again, we were starting a new chapter in our lives, which was now anything but certain. I vowed to myself that this time, I would find a good church for us to attend, and I made this one of my top priorities.

# PART 3

# CHAPTER 20

# Back to the Future

At the end of June, we began our journey west. Full of sadness but also excited anticipation, we bid a fond farewell to Newfoundland and took the ferry from Argentia to North Sydney, Nova Scotia. Along the way, we once again visited with family and friends in Halifax, celebrating Mackenzie's sixth birthday with her cousins. We then drove to Woodstock and spent a week or so with Mom; afterward, we drove the long trek to Ottawa, Ontario, all in one day. We tried to make the trip enjoyable for the kids, but spending hours upon hours in a car with two young children can be challenging at the best of times! Will had a big stack of books, his Gameboy, and his pet turtle, Tubby, in attendance, while Mac had her dolls and stuffed animals to play with and her books to read. Every few days, we would have to find a grocery store to buy fresh, raw meat for Tubby to eat, which made things interesting, to say the least!

After exploring our nation's capital for a few days, we drove to Toronto, which was a highlight for all of us. We had guided tours of the CN Tower and the Skydome (now known as the Rogers Centre), where the Blue Jays play. One day, purely by coincidence, we happened to run into our family doctor, Dr. Dixon, with his family in the theater district on King Street West. Really, what was the chance of that happening? He knew we were relocating to Manitoba and wished us all well.

We then headed up through northern Ontario to Sault Ste. Marie. I remember driving through the main street of that small city, thinking this was a place I would enjoy living in and could call home. How I wished we could just stop driving and settle down in the Soo (the locals' nickname for Sault Ste. Marie), right then and there. Unfortunately, the timing was not right, so we had to press on. We then traveled through the northern United States, including the states of Michigan, Wisconsin, Minnesota, and North Dakota, with our compass directed due north to Winnipeg. We spent another few days in that sprawling, flat prairie city before setting out for our final destination, The Pas. By now, the kids were becoming very antsy, and we were all anxious to finally get there and settle into our motel.

The Wanderer's Inn was our home away from home for three long weeks, until we finally decided to lease a cottage at Clearwater Lake for another month. We were having a hard time finding a home to rent, as the options were very limited. I tried to keep the kids amused and busy during the long, hot days of summer by taking them to the library and putting them in a day camp run by the town. We somehow survived the month of August, and by September, they were both enrolled in Young Scholars Elementary School, which was in the center of town. I then became a chauffeur, driving them back and forth to school from the lake, which was about a twenty-minute ride each way. We eventually found a nice bungalow to rent, also in the middle of town, and moved in that October. It had been a long haul getting settled, but we finally had some stability in our lives. The best thing that happened by far that year was that Jake stopped drinking entirely, and our marriage flourished once more. He was happy with his new job, and now that both kids were in school full-time, I decided to start looking for employment opportunities for myself.

Since I had always been interested in public health nursing, I got up early one morning and walked into the local office of the Provincial Building, hoping to get a job application. It must have been God's favor at work in my life because I literally ran into the top regional manager for public health in the hallway! After excusing ourselves, Christine and I made our introductions, and I gave her a brief summary of my professional background. As it turned out, they were looking for casual nursing staff that fall, so my timing was good.

Within a week or two, I had an interview with Sue, a supervisor in The Pas, for a casual position working in the nursing stations of Cormorant and Moose Lake. They wanted a nurse with a nursing degree and experience working independently, since the job entailed driving several hours a day through the wilderness of northern Manitoba to work in the two small

First Nations communities. I would be assessing and treating walk-in patients with ailments and injuries as well as performing home visits and holding child health clinics for babies and young children. I would receive training around immunizations and already had extensive knowledge around growth and development. As a community health nurse, I would be working under the orders of the regional medical officer of health (MOH) and able to prescribe antibiotics and some pain medications, as needed.

I was excited and more than a little apprehensive to be spreading my wings, so to speak, while I waited to hear back from Sue. I was soon put out of my misery when I learned a few days later that I had the position and would be mainly working in Cormorant, two to three days a week. She wanted me to start immediately, so the next week, I was introduced to the staff in The Pas, where I participated in a child health clinic with one or two of the nurses there. I also accompanied Ellen, another nurse, on several postpartum visits to assess, educate, and support brand-new moms and babies.

Right from the start, I loved my new job and enjoyed working alongside my colleagues, learning new things while relearning others. Navigating my way to Cormorant proved to be a little more daunting, however, as instead of using a trusty GPS, I had only a map of the area to guide me and a very basic car from the provincial carpool to get me there. For communication and safety, I had no cell phone; instead, there was a gigantic and ungainly satellite phone that employees could book out; it had to be placed on top of the hood of the car and activated, prior to getting any reception. I could never envision myself using it, so I never bothered to take it with me!

For the next year and a half, I drove an hour and a half, twice a day, two to three days a week, to and from Cormorant. It was mostly over a gravel road, so I had to be careful, but only once did I break down with a flat tire. Fortunately, it was during the summer, and a natural resources officer (NRO) came along behind me and heroically changed it for me. During my travels, I saw all manner of wildlife alongside the road, including fox, bear, wolf, and even once a wildcat of some kind. One day, a huge moose emerged out of the woods and started running beside my car, frightening the living daylights out of me! I was too afraid to stop, so I just kept on driving, and it eventually turned back into the forest. I must have had my guardian angel sitting on my shoulder that day for sure!

Anne, the community health worker who worked in the Cormorant nursing station most days, was a competent, cheerful lady, and being Métis, she knew all the people in the community and could usually anticipate their wants and needs. She could also identify the troublemakers and helped me deescalate a few tricky situations. She was simply the best to work with! Thankfully, we didn't have a lot of emergencies, although I once had to call for an ambulance to come take an elder to the hospital in The Pas for a suspected heart attack. I usually visited people with chronic health issues, such as heart disease and diabetes, and in the clinic, I treated people with throat infections, ear infections, and minor injuries. The postpartum visits and immunization clinics soon became my favorite part of the job, and I knew I wanted to work as a public health nurse more than ever.

During the winter of 1994, my dream job suddenly materialized when a position to fill a maternity leave opened in The Pas office. I stopped traveling to Cormorant and instead started working full-time hours, five days a week, at the provincial office in town. It was a five-minute drive from our home and was very convenient for both Jake and me. His office was upstairs, while mine was downstairs in the same building. I was once again working beside Ellen, Claire, and Candy, the nurses who had provided me with my training in immunizations, but now I also worked in the area of communicable diseases and assisted with the case management, contact tracing, and treatment of STDs. I continued to make postpartum visits to new moms and babies, participated in child health clinics, and worked occasionally in travel health.

I took my turn teaching prenatal classes at night in the library and was the designated school nurse for one of the elementary schools. We nurses also performed all the school immunizations, adult immunizations, and influenza clinics in the fall and winter. It was a busy job, requiring a lot of independent practice, but I loved being part of a team and conferring back and forth with other professionals. Occasionally, we would even travel to one of the four nursing stations in our region to help with school immunizations or flu clinics.

Over the years, we dealt with everything from dog bites to bed bugs, head lice, and chicken pox as well as more serious diseases, such as rubella

(German measles), shigella, hepatitis A, hepatitis B, pertussis (whooping cough), and tuberculosis. A lot of the work in public health focuses on health promotion and disease prevention, and we also provided ongoing education in schools, day cares, the hospital, and the community at large. The Opaskwayak Cree Nation (OCN) Reserve across the river had its own federally funded health unit and was separate from us; however, in the areas of communicable diseases and STDs, we sometimes overlapped. I often felt like a detective, trying to get all the pertinent information from a client and then putting the pieces of the puzzle together. We also worked closely with our other community partners, such as the local doctors, social workers, public health inspectors, the hospital, and the schools.

When a brand-new program was introduced in 1999, we started making home visits to the families of babies and young children who were at risk for poor child development, due to health and/or socioeconomic factors. The program, aimed at improving child health outcomes for children up to the age of five, was both confidential and completely voluntary, and although it could be rewarding work, it was stressful as well.

Unfortunately, there was a fair bit of neglect and domestic violence in both The Pas as well as in the surrounding First Nations communities. It could be extremely challenging when trying to deal with angry, hostile parents, especially if Child and Family Services (CFS) was involved. We also saw our fair share of poverty, mental health issues, and alcohol and drug abuse, all of which put babies and children that much more at risk. The degree of lack of care could be severe and contributed to the misery that was part of their everyday lives.

What should have been straightforward cases could also be difficult to know how to manage. I stepped into a permanent full-time position in 1994, and during the next seven years, I faced everything from vicious dogs and bush fires to having a client's husband pull out a shotgun and proceed to clean it in front of me. One of our biggest ongoing problems was dealing with head lice. Back then, if there was an identified case, public health nurses went into the schools and proceeded to check each child's head in the classroom for nits and bugs. It was an endless job because the next day, another child could come into the classroom with a new infection.

As well, I must have spent countless hours checking the heads of people who walked in off the street, desperately seeking help to get rid of the pesky creatures. I even came home one evening and found a plastic baggie with head lice sitting on my front step! A friend from church had dropped it off, after she had found bugs crawling through her teenage daughter's head. Poor Donna had been working with young kids at a summer day camp and had been infected when a child hugged her. Donna's mom was unsure if this was indeed the dreaded bug, and despite having to give her bad news, I reassured her that head lice do not actually carry disease.

As we began to settle into our new life in The Pas, we eventually found a great church to attend. It turned out to be an evangelical congregation with a loving and supportive church family. Since we now had no family support of any kind, we soon became close with many of the members and families in our new church. The Pas had a small-town feel, where everyone knew almost everyone, and although many people were related, there were also a lot of transplants like us. Almost all the doctors were foreign-born, with several originating from the United Kingdom and South Africa. We also became close friends with many of the couples whose husbands worked with Jake, and our kids also played together and went to the same school. Right away, we developed a good support system, which was very important to me now that we were so far away from our own family and friends. Little did we know it, but our need for real friendship would soon be put to the test.

# CHAPTER 21

# A Devastating Blow

Toward the end of 1992, tragedy struck our family once again. We were relaxing at home on Boxing Day with a couple from Jake's work when I got a phone call from Mom. She told me Gregg had once again been admitted into hospital, this time to the ICU in Fredericton. Just before Christmas, he had begun to have problems with swallowing and eating, and his doctor was getting ready to send him to Toronto for further investigation. Experiencing déjà vu, I was very alarmed by this sudden turn of events and was frightened that his thyroid cancer had returned or metastasized elsewhere.

In early January, I flew to Toronto to be with my brother and sister-in-law, Jennifer, while Gregg's doctors prepared for surgery. It seemed my worst fears were realized, as they needed to remove a cancerous tumor from Gregg's esophagus and then stretch his throat and attach it to his stomach. He would permanently lose his larynx, or voice box, and would breathe through a stoma, only able to speak with an artificial device held to his throat. Obviously, this scenario was not ideal, but it would offer Gregg a somewhat normal life going forward.

Gregory's daughter, Jessica, was living and working near Toronto by then, so she and her husband came by each evening to visit Gregg and keep us company. On the day of the surgery, Jenny and I waited on pins and needles as Gregg went off to the operating room. Prior to and during the surgery, Jenny and I prayed fervently that all would go as planned. We did not have to wait very long for Gregg to come back from the OR. Afterward, the surgeon told us that once he began the surgery, he realized the tumor was not only huge in size but was also lethal looking, and we now had to wait for the results of the biopsy before he could proceed with the tricky operation. It was a devastating blow for all of us, especially for Gregg and Jennifer, who had been married for only a little over a year. They placed Gregg on a morphine drip for pain that he could control himself; he also had a tracheotomy in order to breathe and, since he could no longer eat solid food, a feeding tube in his stomach for liquid nutrition.

Perhaps to his credit, Gregory remained stoic throughout his terrible ordeal, probably for the rest of us, since we had a difficult time holding back our tears. I roomed with Jennifer in a residence beside the hospital for a week or so, while we waited impatiently for the biopsy results to come back. Meanwhile, the seconds seemed to tick by agonizingly slowly. The day we met with the doctor for the results was a dark, dark day for all of us. Although we already feared the worst, he confirmed that due to the nature of the tumor, there was nothing more that could be done for my brother, except to offer him comfort and supportive measures. He would be sent home to die and would never again enjoy the satisfaction of eating solid food.

I was left reeling by this dire news, but since I had now been away from home for two weeks, I had to think about going back. As I said a tearful last goodbye to my big brother, I knew I would never again have the chance to talk to him in person or simply give him a hug. I flew directly to Halifax to share the news with David, Barbara, and Mom, who were all waiting expectantly to receive a full report. The four of us sat in their living room, Mom and I crying, as Dave and Barb looked on in shocked silence. Ironically, I later learned from Jennifer that the secondary tumor was most likely caused by the radiation treatments that Gregg had been given following his first surgery seven years earlier. She had been told this by her former employer, who was a radiologist in Halifax. It is very true that sometimes the cure is worse than the disease, although it did give Gregg a few more precious years with his family and friends.

After I returned to The Pas, I spoke only a handful of times to Gregg on the phone, as he was often just not up to talking. His last wish was to spend his time with Mom in Woodstock, so he and Jennifer moved in with her, and with the assistance of Mom's family doctor, they set up nursing home care services to visit Gregg daily. Jennifer was a real trooper and learned how to do a lot of the nursing care he required, such as tracheotomy care, gastrointestinal (GI) feedings, and administering the supplemental oxygen he eventually needed. Gregg was able to receive visits from family and friends during the few weeks that he lived, which gave him and his loved ones valuable time to say goodbye. One of the hardest things for Gregg, other than dealing with the discomfort and pain, was being able to smell Mom's delicious home-cooked meals but not being able to enjoy or taste any of it. On Saturday nights, she always made baked beans, which was one of his favorites. Mom eventually stopped making this dish, as it was just too painful an experience for everyone.

On Saturday, March 20, 1993, Jake and I spent the morning at the local high school judging the annual science fair. We had been asked to be judges by the principal, who knew us both and had twisted our arms. When we arrived home in the early afternoon, a message was waiting for me on our answering machine. It was Mom, telling me that Gregg had passed away early that morning. Sometime during the previous evening, they had called for an ambulance to come and take him to the local hospital because his breathing had become labored, and Jennifer could not handle his care anymore. Once again, I was devastated by the news, but this time, I was not surprised. I immediately booked a flight to Fredericton and flew out the next day. Jake had to stay home with the children, as back then, the flights were terribly expensive, and we just couldn't afford to have all of us travel so far away.

Although it was comforting to be surrounded by our family and friends at the visitation and the funeral, it was also heartbreaking. I could not stop crying, and the nicer people were to me, the worse it was. Jessica, only twenty-nine, was especially bereft, sobbing over her father's open casket at the funeral home. It all seemed so unfair because Gregg never really got the chance to enjoy his life with Jennifer and never even had the opportunity to retire. He was certainly loved and admired by many people, as there was standing room only on the day of the funeral.

My one consolation was that I knew he was saved because he had given his heart and life to the Lord when he was first diagnosed with cancer. Although I could not understand why God had chosen to take him home at the relatively young age of fifty-nine, I knew beyond a shadow of a doubt that I would see him again one day. My poor mother had suffered another huge loss after losing my dad, and she was never really the same afterward. It doesn't matter how old the child is when they die, parents are not meant to outlive their children. She once asked me why I thought God took Gregory away from us so prematurely, and the only thing I could think of was that He must have had an important assignment for him in heaven. As they say in folklore, "Only the good die young."

Three short days after Gregg passed, Jake's father, Tom, also died at home in Herring Bay of liver cancer. Oddly enough, he had been ill at the same time as Gregg in 1986, only in his case, it had been with stomach cancer. Back then, he had had surgery to remove the tumor and seemed healthy until Gregg had his own recurrence of cancer. Jake had to go home immediately, and this time, we had to ask friends of ours to look after Will and Mackenzie until one of us returned home. Thankfully, two couples from Jake's work offered to take our orphan children; Mackenzie went to stay in the home of friends with a little girl her age, while Will went to the home of a different family who had a boy of the same age. Our kids had become friends, which made it much easier on all of us. I could once again see God's loving provision in the sadness and anguish we were going through.

Most unfortunately, a few months after his father died, Jake once again started drinking. During the summer of 1994, hoping for a positive diversion as well as some much-needed family fun, I planned a two-week vacation for all four of us through the Rockies. We left in early August and drove to Saskatoon, Saskatchewan—our first stop along the way. Right from the start, things did not go well. Unable to drink and drive, Jake was extremely miserable and agitated, especially with me, because he viewed this trip as being all my fault. He got so angry at one point that he turned the car around, but eventually he calmed down, and we finally made it to our destination. Once we got there, the kids had a great time, as there was a city fair going on. I had a charming caricature of the two of them drawn by a street artist, which I still have hanging on my wall to this day. From Saskatoon, we continued to Lloydminster, a city split between two provinces—Saskatchewan and Alberta. Next, Edmonton, Alberta, was a highlight for Will, as we visited the arena where his favorite hockey player, Wayne Gretzky, had played for many years. We also explored the West Edmonton Mall (which was the largest mall in North America at the time), where the kids went swimming in the wave pool with the artificial beach!

One night, while we were staying in Edmonton, I received an unexpected phone call from David. I had given him our itinerary, and he was calling to tell me that he and Barbara were with Mom, who had been admitted to the hospital in Woodstock for a bleeding stomach ulcer. They expected her to make a full recovery, but she was also feeling depressed over losing Gregg, which complicated matters. She would be treated with several medications for the ulcer and monitored for a few weeks, but it would take much longer for her to work through and process her deep-seated grief. From that point on, I worried about her and wondered if I should fly back home once again.

Trying to complete our vacation, we carried on to Hinton, Alberta, drove through Jasper, and went as far west as Golden, British Columbia. We then drove back to Alberta and spent a day exploring the Columbia Ice Fields, which sit astride the Continental Divide. While trudging up the side of the ice-covered glacier, both kids got "booters," and Mackenzie cried big tears from having cold, wet feet. After getting dried off and warmed up, we had lunch at the beautiful Chateau Lake Louise, and then we went on to spend a few days in Banff National Park. There was a lot to see and do in Banff, including strolling through the shops, visiting the famous Banff hot springs, and riding the gondola up through the picturesque mountains. Although we did not stay there, the Fairmont Banff Springs Hotel, famous for its history and spectacular views, was a favorite stop of mine.

As we approached Calgary, which is nestled in the foothills of the Rockies, we were awestruck by the beauty and majesty of the mountains, and we stopped many times to take photos of the wildlife, including bears, deer, and wild mountain goats. The last town we visited, Drumheller, is known as the Dinosaur Capital of the World and soon became another favorite of Will's. We toured through the Royal Tyrrell Museum of Palaeontology and took many pictures of the Badlands. We then drove back through Saskatoon, eventually arriving home in The Pas late at night. Coming back home was such a letdown, but we would always have wonderful memories and photos of this special family vacation.

# CHAPTER 22

# A Mixed Bag

During the summer of 1993, we received the unwelcome news from our landlord that we would have to move out of our rental home. The owners had sold it to an RCMP family who had just moved to The Pas, and because our lease was up, we were given only one month to vacate. Jake scrambled to find a suitable family home for the four of us to live in, but there was virtually nothing available. Since our beautiful home in Newfoundland still had not sold, we decided to lease it out for the short term. In the meantime, we had no option but to continue renting, which was not our first choice.

With the help of a Realtor, Jake finally found an older four-bedroom home, situated on a long street that ran right through the center of town. The owner was a minister, a woman who had lived there with her father; unfortunately, he had recently passed away in that home. It was in bad need of deep cleaning and painting, so we rolled up our sleeves and dug in. I was sad to leave the home we had been living in, since it was much newer and on a quieter street. Unfortunately, I saw this unnecessary move as a big step backward. We had little choice in the matter, though, as we packed up our possessions, by ourselves this time, and made the big move one street over.

The midnineties were a mixed bag for our family, at best. I loved my job working with public health, and Jake also seemed happy in his position at work, but his continued heavy drinking had a negative impact on our family life. I ended up hiring a lady from church, Rose, to clean our house every two weeks, which helped me maintain my sanity. Rose was a middle-aged, single Christian woman; she had several jobs and was a hard worker. She ultimately turned out to be a positive influence on our children; the kids were getting older now and started to notice that all was not right with their father. They once found porn magazines in the rafters of the garage and empty liquor bottles in the crawl space of the basement. They never directly asked me about their father's problems, but as their mother, I felt it was my job to normalize their lives as much as possible. I wanted them to have the happy and carefree childhood I had experienced growing up in New Brunswick.

By now, they were both attending Sunday school and church each week; in fact, I taught a Sunday school class. Our kids were also enrolled in a Bible-based group for young children, although neither one of them was great at memorizing Bible verses! Mackenzie joined Brownies (unlike her mom), while Will continued to play hockey. When he turned twelve, Will joined Army Cadets, which changed his life for the better. It seemed to give him both the structure and discipline he needed as well as personal confidence and a solid peer group to belong to. Both children were musical; Will played several instruments in the Army Cadet band as well as the baritone in the school band, and when he was in high school, he learned how to play the bagpipes. Mackenzie played the flute in the school band and became a strong swimmer with the local swim team. She loved movement and music and always took dance lessons of some kind through our local recreational center. In school, they continued to do well, and their teachers could always identify them as brother and sister. Both children were tall and slim with my blonde hair and their father's chocolate-brown eyes.

In the summers, they attended day camp for several weeks, and Mackenzie had a babysitter stay with her until she turned twelve. After that, she took the babysitting course and started to babysit on her own. Each August, we would drive both kids up to Simon House Bible Camp, northeast of The Pas, where one summer, both children miraculously gave their lives to Christ. They were nine and twelve years old then, young but still old enough to know what they were doing. I could not have been happier with their decision, and I earnestly thanked God for answering my prayers. I still worried about them, though, as Jake's behavior could be erratic at times, especially when he was drinking. He was never violent with the kids, but he sometimes lost his temper and could be very mean.

In a fit of rage, he once threatened to kill Mackenzie's docile and lovable cat, Ernie, by taking him out into the back garden and shooting him. Mackenzie was in hysterics while I pleaded with him for mercy, trying to calm him down. He eventually relented, and the latest crisis had passed. The thing is, I don't even remember why he became so upset.

My friend Lydia came to visit us one summer, and during her stay, I finally broke down and confessed to her about Jake's drinking and his behavior toward the kids and me. While she was with us, she and I took a brief road trip to Edmonton, Alberta, to visit her girlfriend. One day, while we were having lunch in a restaurant, I started to cry, and once the tears began, they would not stop. It was literally a watershed moment for me. If she was surprised by my desperate admission, she never let on, and although she listened, she had no advice to give me.

Mom also visited us that same summer of 1995, when she observed firsthand what was going on, right in front of her own eyes. Jake tried not to drink while she was there, and when he didn't drink, he could also be nasty and mean to both me and the kids. He marched downstairs one day and, for no apparent reason, picked up the laundry basket full of clothes and threw it right at me in front of Mom. At that moment, although she never said anything to me directly, I *knew* that she *knew*. How I wish that I had taken the opportunity, then and there, to confide in my mother, but I never wanted to burden her with my problems. She just looked at me rather sadly and said, "You work really hard, Becky."

By then, at the age of eighty-four, she was getting older; although her mind was as sharp as ever, she was becoming increasingly frail of body. She had fully recovered from the gastric ulcer she had been diagnosed with a year earlier, but she started to suffer from CHF (congestive heart failure), due to having been ill with rheumatic fever when she was a young woman. Without the treatment of antibiotics, the infection had damaged the mitral valve of her heart, which eventually started to affect her health. I noticed she would sometimes get short of breath when going up the stairs, and she did not have the same amount of energy she once did. Mom never complained, though, and true to form, she struck up a long conversation with the wife of the premier of Manitoba, who was sitting beside her on her flight home. Even in illness, Mom really was unstoppable!

Despite all the darkness that seemed to fill our lives, there were many times when God's goodness and mercy shone through. During that same summer while Mom was visiting us, Jake sat up alone at the kitchen table, night after night. He was drunk, crying, and reading the Bible while listening to the music of Steve Bell, a popular Christian recording artist from Winnipeg. I knew that deep down, God was convicting him of his sins and his desperate need for salvation. One night, as we prayed together, Jake invited Jesus into his heart. Once again, I was thrilled by his decision. I naively believed that finally all our problems would miraculously disappear. I could not have been more mistaken; his drinking continued and even worsened after that night. After years of reflection, I now know that a big spiritual battle was going on around us at the time. A person must also turn away from sin, and that can be a very difficult thing to do.

Around the same time that Jake was saved, some very eerie things started happening in our house. As I mentioned earlier, I don't believe in ghosts, but evil spirits can sometimes surround and even indwell certain people. They always try to deceive and terrorize us, negatively impacting our lives. I truly believe there were evil spirits both in that house and around Jake, trying to disrupt our lives in the worst way imaginable.

One day during late summer, I was sitting at the kitchen table, all alone in the house. Our calico cat, CJ, crept over to the dining room entrance beside me and slowly started to howl. I had never ever heard sounds like that coming from a cat, and as she stood there, every hair on her body started to stand on end. Even her long tail stood straight up in the air, and indeed, she looked like she was being electrocuted! Her strange behavior continued on like that for at least ten or fifteen minutes.

A short while after this bizarre occurrence, our boom box, which sat on the kitchen table and was plugged in, turned on to the radio all by itself. While I sat there trying to figure out what was going on, the top of a mason jam jar flew off across the kitchen and landed onto the floor. I had hand-washed and dried the lid and metal ring the previous evening and left them by the kitchen sink; now both were lying on the floor by the basement door. Frightened by all this paranormal activity, but trying not to feel intimidated, I knew what I had to do. I immediately got up and started walking through the house, praying out loud in the name of Jesus Christ, commanding the evil spirits to depart at once. I knew that evil had invaded our home, and I wanted it gone for good. As Christians, we have authority over the powers of darkness when we pray in Christ's name. My heaven-sent prayers must have worked, as no spooky phenomena ever occurred in that home again while we lived there.

When God is at work in our lives, the devil is sure to be in hot pursuit, trying to ruin God's plans. The more pain and sorrow I experienced with Jake, the more I turned to God, and as my faith grew, I could also feel the love and warmth of the Holy Spirit grow inside of me. That was a new experience for me; I started to become a more mature Christian and was not a baby anymore. I am still walking on that journey today, and I now know I will never reach complete adulthood until I am in heaven. Sadly, none of us can reach perfection while we live in this world, so we can only try to live a life of truth and excellence. Having said that, we are meant to do good works, but we are not meant to work our way into heaven. In John 14:6, Jesus answered, "I am the way and the truth and the life. No one comes to the Father except through me." As believers, we will one day be made perfect through Jesus Christ, our Lord.

# CHAPTER 23

# Mom's Lasting Legacy

As 1996 came to a close, Mom's health suddenly took a turn for the worse. In early November, David called and asked me to come home; Mom had been admitted to Carleton Memorial Hospital in Woodstock with complications of congestive heart failure. Barbara was planning to go to Woodstock to visit Mom and would pick me up at the Fredericton airport. I was thankful Barb would be with me because I knew how serious things had now become. Following my flight from Winnipeg to Halifax and from Halifax to Fredericton, we drove together to Woodstock. I quickly dropped off my luggage at Mom's house, and we headed over to the hospital.

When I walked into her hospital room, she was sleeping, but she eventually woke up and realized I was with her. She did not seem at all surprised to see me, but it was difficult for her to talk, as she was so short of breath. She was receiving oxygen and looked very tired and weak. I was able to speak with her doctor the next day, and he reassured me that he was doing everything possible to get Mom back home, at least for a few weeks. She was on several medications, including a diuretic, and only time would tell how she would respond.

As one week turned into two, I could see her slowly begin to rally, thanks to the rest, medication, and oxygen therapy she was receiving. I spent most of each day with Mom, sometimes with Barb in tow, but often it was just the two of us. Barb was enjoying spending time with her own family, who lived farther out in the country. As Mom became stronger, I was able to help her shower, and I could begin to see glimpses of my old mom coming back to me. We started planning her discharge back home with the assistance of the hospital's social worker; she arranged to have home care workers come to Mom's home daily to help her with bathing, cooking, and light housekeeping. Sadly, at the end of the two weeks, I had to return home, as my family and my job were waiting for me. Not for the first time, I regretted living so far away from my mother. It was very hard to leave Mom, but I felt good about the supports we had put into place, and as a bonus, her sister Ruth planned to spend every weekend with her. Toward the end of November, I left her while she was still in hospital, unsure if I would ever see my mom again. It was a heartrending goodbye for both of us.

Mom's return to modest good health was short-lived, which was not uncommon in patients with end-stage CHF. The second week of February, I got a phone call from one of the home care workers, telling me it was time for me to come home. The doctor had just informed her that Mom's organs were beginning to shut down, and her time was short; Dr. Grant had requested that the family be informed immediately of this dire news.

Back at work, I was preparing to go into my school to do yearly catch-up immunizations; however, since I had everything ready to go, one of the other nurses, Candy, kindly volunteered to take my place. Since time was of the essence, I asked Jake to drive me to the nearest bus depot in Swan River, which was about two and a half hours southwest by car. I then had another seven hours by bus to think about what I was going to face when I got home. I flew out from Winnipeg the next morning, on Valentine's Day, but during the middle of the flight, an elderly Black lady sitting a few rows ahead of me had a medical emergency. I had noticed her when she boarded the plane because she looked very unwell, so I was not at all surprised when she collapsed in the bathroom. The flight crew made an announcement, asking for any doctors or nurses to come forward to assist. Since no one else responded to the request, I went to the front of the plane, where they now had her lying in the middle of the aisle and were administering oxygen to her. Thankfully, although she was unconscious, she was still breathing, and I only had to monitor her vital signs while the flight attendants did an outstanding job of assisting her. They carried her off the plane by stretcher when we landed in Toronto, while I continued on to Fredericton. It certainly seemed to me that my life was never lacking for excitement!

Once again, Dave and Barb picked me up at the airport. We drove in almost complete silence but with a growing sense of urgency to Mom's house up on the hill. When we arrived, my cousin Dale and his wife, Elaine, were with her, trying to calm her down. I believe Mom was in the middle of an anxiety attack but could not verbalize her feelings. Aunt Ruth and one of her support workers were also with her. I walked Mom into her bedroom, got her to sit down on the edge of the bed, and put my arms around her. As she started to breathe more slowly, she calmed down, and we eventually got her settled into a recliner in her large country kitchen. She could see everyone there and was not as isolated as she would have been in her bedroom. She also needed to sit up in order to breathe more easily. She knew all of us, but because she was so short of breath, it was difficult for her to talk.

We tried to make her as comfortable as possible while family members quietly came and went. My sister-in-law Jennifer also arrived and spent the next few days with us. I think I took shifts sleeping on the sofa in the living room, as all the bedrooms were now full. It was so good to be close to Mom, though, since I knew this would be my last chance to spend time with her and my final opportunity to do everything I could to help her transition into the next life. Mom now had a female doctor who visited her as much as she needed. Dr. Suzanne provided morphine for her, which I carefully administered through a small butterfly IV in her chest. It helped to control her discomfort and allowed her to rest more easily.

On the afternoon of February 17, 1997, we knew the end was near. Mom slept a lot, but when she woke up, she had moments of lucidity when she would tell us that she hoped we girls never had to go through what she was now enduring. Mom could not open her eyes but was a living testimonial, as at times, she would randomly call out, "Heaven, heaven," and "Glory," and plead, "Please, oh please, let me come in." She repeated these phrases over and over, and I am convinced she had a vision of the life that was to come. After supper, while my brother was at the pharmacy picking up more morphine for Mom, I was in her bedroom, talking and crying on the phone with my mother-in-law, Joan, who had phoned me from Newfoundland. Suddenly, I heard Barb frantically shouting, "Rebecca, come quick!" It was too late. By the time I made it back into the kitchen, Mom was gone. My sister-in-law told me that just a few seconds before this, Mom had suddenly sat straight up in her chair, opened her eyes, and looked up toward the ceiling at an invisible presence. With a look of amazement on her face, she then closed her eyes peacefully, sank back down into her chair, and passed away. There is no doubt in my mind that Mom saw an angel, ready to escort her through the pearly gates of heaven that day.

At Mom's funeral, I asked her pastor to read Proverbs 31:10–31, Epilogue: The Wife of Noble Character:

> A wife of noble character who can find?
> She is worth far more than rubies.
> Her husband has full confidence in her
> and lacks nothing of value.
> She brings him good, not harm,
> all the days of her life.
> She selects wool and flax
> and works with eager hands.
> She is like the merchant ships,
> bringing her food from afar.
> She gets up while it is still dark;
> she provides food for her family
> and portions for her servant girls.
> She considers a field and buys it;
> out of her earnings she plants a vineyard.
> She sets about her work vigorously;
> her arms are strong for her tasks.
> She sees that her trading is profitable,
> and her lamp does not go out at night.
> In her hand she holds the distaff
> and grasps the spindle with her fingers.
> She opens her arms to the poor
> and extends her hands to the needy.
> When it snows, she has no fear for her household;
> for all of them are clothed in scarlet.
> She makes coverings for her bed;
> she is clothed in fine linen and purple.

Her husband is respected at the city gate,
where he takes his seat among the elders of the
land.
She makes linen garments and sells them,
and supplies the merchants with sashes.
She is clothed with strength and dignity;
she can laugh at the days to come.
She speaks with wisdom,
and faithful instruction is on her tongue.
She watches over the affairs of her household
and does not eat the bread of idleness.
Her children arise and call her blessed;
her husband also, and he praises her:
"Many women do noble things,
but you surpass them all."
Charm is deceptive and beauty is fleeting;
but a woman who fears the Lord is to be praised.
Give her the reward she has earned,
and let her works bring her praise at the city gate.

The day my mom passed was one of the saddest days of my life. But like I'd known of my father and brother before her, I knew Mom was with God and was now reunited with many of her loved ones in a much better place than this present world. My mom's death left a big hole in my life, which exists even to this day. Although no one can ever replace her, God must have known how much I would miss her because on February 17, 2017, twenty years to the day Mom died, He sent me a beautiful little bundle of joy, my first grandchild, Jeremy. He was born ten weeks premature and only weighed a little over three pounds, but six years on, he is a healthy, happy, and thriving little boy, a blessing to all of us who know him and love him. As I have often shared with my daughter, Mackenzie, and son-in-law, Rob, his blessed parents, God really has His hand on Jeremy's life. When we honored my mother's life that day, I knew I would pick up the pieces of my own life, and although things would be different going forward, they would eventually turn out to be okay.

That spring, I traveled back to Woodstock once more, this time to help my brother and his wife clean out Mom's home to get it ready to sell. Mom had been so careful and thoughtful, leaving us a letter regarding her last wishes as well as putting our names on items she wanted us to have. In her letter, she encouraged David and me to "Be close to each other, always." She tried to make things as easy for us as possible, although it was not easy to say goodbye. She left me all her living room furniture, including her cherished colonial wall clock and oil paintings done by a renowned New Brunswick artist. She also gave me all her dishes and crystal, personal belongings, photographs, family heirlooms, and recorded genealogy on both sides of the family. She never had much jewelry, but she left me all that she had.

Any valuable pieces, such as her engagement ring, family ring, and her mother's locket, had been stolen years before during a home invasion at their old house in Grafton. I still have most of Mom's belongings, and although I value them greatly, the most precious things she gave me cannot be seen or touched. Like the wife of noble character, they are the faith, love, and morals she and Dad left to all of us children, grandchildren, and great-grandchildren, and they are priceless beyond compare.

# CHAPTER 24

# Laying New Foundations

After her house sold, I shipped Mom's furniture and belongings to The Pas. Once everything arrived, I put the larger items into storage, since we didn't have room for them in our current home. Because I also inherited some money from the sale of Mom's home, Jake and I started to think about buying a home of our own again, this time in The Pas. Some might call it serendipity (I would call it God's favor), but after sitting for five years on the market, our home in Topsail finally sold that summer. Although we ended up losing some money, we were finally able to pay back Jake's aunt and uncle and the remainder of our debt and still had enough money left over for a good down payment on a new home.

Back in 1993, Jake had inherited a piece of property from his father, which he eventually sold; we subsequently purchased an acre of land on Rahl's Island, hoping to someday build a new home on it. That August 1997, we thought the time to build had finally arrived, so we asked our good friend Darren, who was also a carpenter and builder, to look at our house plans. After studying the architectural drawings, Darren reluctantly told us that it was too late in the year to start building a home with such high rooflines. Since winter arrived early in the north, it would be too treacherous to work on the home that late into the fall. We were disappointed, as that nixed our plans to build, and instead, we started to look for a home to buy. There were a few good options, but we finally settled upon a large, modern, multilevel home a few streets over from where we currently lived. It was on the corner of a cul-de-sac and was still close enough for both kids to walk back and forth to school each day. By that time, Will was in high school, in grade nine, while Mackenzie was in middle school, in grade six.

That November, I took a couple of weeks off work to move and unpack all our things. This would be our third and final move while living in The Pas. Right away, I loved our new home and took great pleasure in cleaning and decorating it. I filled the dining room with our solid oak furniture, and we moved Mom's dark floral furniture into the living room, along with a beautiful old player piano we were storing for Grace, a close family friend. She worked with child and family services, while her husband, Dean, worked with Jake. They had three children, and their youngest son, Josh, was a good friend of Will and Mitchell's (Darren and Kathy's son). All three boys were the same age and were enthusiastic members of Army Cadets.

We arranged our leather furniture in the family room (a few steps down from our kitchen), which also had a large patio door leading off it into the fenced-in backyard. I loved the open plan of the home, including a rec room, an extra bedroom, and a huge unfinished room in the basement. The third floor of the home had three bedrooms and two bathrooms, ample space for a family of four. By now, we also had two cats, Ernie (a large gray tabby cat belonging to Mackenzie) and Sandy (a small orange tabby belonging to Will). Our other cat, CJ, had been struck by a car and left to die on the street in front of our last home. Tragically, the kids had found her lying there one day in early fall, when they arrived home from school.

It is a fact that we carry our problems around with us wherever we go. Back when we were thinking about building a new house, God kept reminding me of the passage in Matthew 7:24–27, the parable of the wise and the foolish builders. Jesus cautions us to be wise about building our house on rock and not on sand. In this story, after the rain fell, the floods came, and the wind blew and beat on the two houses; the house on the rock was left standing, while the house built on sand collapsed. I did not understand what God was trying to tell me at the time, but in hindsight, I now realize I should have been much less focused on finding a new house and much more focused on the crumbling foundations of my own marriage.

Although our fortunes had finally changed for the better, Jake's drinking continued and even worsened in our new home. As the children got older and had their friends over to visit, I am sure Jake's behavior was embarrassing to them at times. He rarely drank alcohol in front of any of us, and he always tried to appear normal when he was acting anything *but* normal. He could also badly embarrass me when we were out socially if there was alcohol being served. I know that some of the people around us must have finally put two and two together and figured out he had a big problem.

One day, as I was working in my office, Sam came in to see me. He was one of the managers who worked for Jake, and he was also a friend. He seemed rather uncomfortable, but after a few minutes, with a look of compassion on his face, he asked me what he could do to help Jake with his drinking. By then, I was exploring all options for help that I could find, including accompanying Jake to see his doctor for symptoms of depression. Dr. Johnson had prescribed Jake an antidepressant, but it did nothing for him and may have even made him feel worse because he still drank alcohol while taking it. I reassured Sam that we were working on a solution, although I was anything but certain that Jake could stop drinking. At times, it seemed all but hopeless. Drinking was an everyday occurrence for him now, and his behavior was rapidly spinning out of control.

Just as disturbing was the fact that Jake had issues with pornography. One night, I woke up alone in bed and went to look for him. I found him passed out and slumped over our family computer in the basement with the image of a naked woman on the screen. I turned the computer off and left him as he was. Another time, I found an autographed photo of a stripper, so I knew he must have been going to strip clubs somewhere in town or when he traveled to Winnipeg. His behavior was disgusting and beyond disappointing, but once again, I felt powerless to stop it. I was also dealing with my own health issues once again, including heart arrhythmias and another abnormal Pap test result. Thankfully, both concerns resolved on their own over time, although I was followed by a gynecologist in Winnipeg for several years afterward.

While all this was going on, I tried to make our lives as normal as possible, keeping the kids busy with school and other activities. Mackenzie began piano lessons in addition to her other interests, and Will continued to participate in Army Cadets and band. When William got older, he spent one summer delivering newspapers and another one working at the new burger joint in town; he quickly discovered, though, that working in a fast-food restaurant was not for him! He cooked the french fries, and most evenings, he came home reeking of kitchen grease. Each summer, he went away for several weeks to an Army Cadet camp, which was always held at different bases in the west.

Jake once accompanied Will on a bus trip to Edmonton with the Cadets as a supervising parent but—ironically—spent most of his time away drunk. Will confided this to me many years later; no one ever mentioned it to me at the time. Several other parents and Cadet leaders were also on that trip, but once again, many people tried to turn a blind eye. It is human nature not to want to get involved in other people's problems, since we often feel we already have enough problems of our own to deal with. As my mother used to say, "Don't borrow trouble!"

Mackenzie especially loved spending time with her many friends. She often had babysitting jobs as well as a permanent gig cleaning a home day care for my friend Stacy, who lived at the end of our street. The summer she turned ten, she had surgery at our local hospital to have her tonsils removed. Another summer, she flew to Newfoundland to visit Nana and her new boyfriend, Howie. Mackenzie was my little social butterfly, while Will was the strong, silent type, although he had his fair share of friends too.

In the summer of 1998, Joan finally came for a visit to see us. It was her first time in The Pas, as she had been very angry with us after we left Newfoundland, for many years. She even rejected an arrangement of flowers we had sent her for Mother's Day one year because she was so bitter about us leaving her and Tom. By 1998, Jake's father had been deceased for several years, and she was dating once again. This visit was my golden opportunity to turn to her for help with her son, but when I finally got up the courage to tell her about his drinking, she just looked at me dejectedly and repeated, "What can *I* do?" over and over. She never did confront Jake about it, and for the rest of her trip, all she could talk about was her new relationship with Howie, who had been an old beau before she met Tom. Deep down, I knew she truly cared about her son's welfare, but it seemed her approach to dealing with life's big problems was avoidance and denial, probably a lifelong pattern and coping mechanism. In the meantime, the kids and I were silently drowning.

I had a much more captive audience with Dave and Barb when I flew back to Halifax for a brief visit, later that same year. Once again, I managed to summon up the courage to tell them what was going on, as I knew things were coming to a head. Although neither one of them appeared shocked, they were both extremely concerned and made me promise to leave with the kids if things got out of control. I assured them I would, as I continued to try to place a safety net around the kids and myself. That net included my church family, so when I returned home, I made a point of visiting our pastor, Walter, and his wife, Penny, to fill them in on what was going on. Like Barb and Dave, if they were surprised, they never let on. They were also supportive but did not offer any advice. Walter freely admitted that he had limited experience in dealing with alcoholics and addictive behavior in general, but he promised to do everything within his power to help Jake stop drinking and to support our long-suffering family.

# CHAPTER 25

# A Way of Escape

April 1999 is a month I will never forget. Following my frank talk with Walter the previous fall, he was as good as his word; all that winter, he proceeded to take Jake under his wing at church and started meeting with him for counselling each week, teaching Jake about God's mercy (not giving us the punishment that we, as sinners, deserve) and His saving grace (freely giving us the unmerited favor and love of God). He explained God's redemption for the world through Jesus Christ, God's only Son, who died on the cross for our sins but rose again on the third day. Wally was aware that Jake had prayed with me several years before, asking for forgiveness of his sins and giving his life to Christ.

Saying and doing are different things, though, and Jake's behavior did not match the commitment he made that night in 1995 when he invited Jesus into his heart. The Gospel of Matthew tells us that the Christian walk can be challenging, and the gate is small, and the road is narrow, and not many will enter in. Like Christ, we often seem to suffer along the way. The upside of this truth is that as we are going through our worst trials, temptations, and tribulations, God's protection and favor strengthens and sustains us, molding our character like a potter with clay.

From what I could see, Jake was not walking the Christian walk. It surprised me then when Jake made the decision to be baptized (which is a step of obedience in itself), and a date was set for the church service. The actual baptism would happen in the swimming pool at the local high school, and afterward, Jake and I both planned to join the church on the following Sunday.

On the morning of April 11, we stood side by side at the front of the church with all eyes upon us while Jake gave his personal testimony. Just a few days before, he had unexpectedly smacked me across the face, sending me reeling onto the floor of the bathroom. There was no explanation (or apology) for his behavior, except that he was drunk, as usual. Now, standing behind the pulpit in our church, he did not admit to his struggles with drinking, but he gave a stirring talk about his life anyway. I stood as his witness and support person and gave part of my own testimony. Our children looked on and listened in complete silence, as did the rest of our church family. After the service, a small group of people went over to the swimming pool to watch Wally baptize a handful of people, both young and old. I was hoping and praying this would be a brand-new start for Jake as well as for our family. Sadly, it was not to be.

During the week following his baptism, Jake continued to drink, and on Sunday, April 18, he was still intoxicated from the night before. The kids and I got ready and went to church just the same, and for some reason, Jake followed along behind us. Right up to the moment before I went to the front of the church with several other people, Jake threatened not to join me. Totally fed up with him by then, I turned around and told him to do whatever he wanted, and then I slowly walked up the aisle by myself. When I looked back, however, there he was, as if driven by something he could not control. I believe it was the power of the Holy Spirit, convicting him to go. We did indeed join the church that day, and even now, all these years later, I have never belonged to a more sincere, loving, and caring church family.

The following week, things at home continued on a downward spiral. On Monday evening, Jake came home from work after the kids had already gone to bed. I had found a bottle of rum that day and drained it down the kitchen sink; when he discovered what I had done, he was incensed with me. Already intoxicated, he didn't say much, but I knew from the dark look in his eyes that I had crossed a line. As they had many times before, his eyes appeared glazed over and unfocused, and I wondered if he was also possessed by an evil spirit. I knew there was most definitely a spiritual battle going on inside him.

He followed me into the dining room, slowly circling me around the long dining room table. His behavior was intentional, threatening, and mean. Not for the first time, I felt frightened for my life, but I could not reach our landline in the kitchen. After what seemed liked hours but was probably just a matter of minutes, he left the house, and as he did, I ran behind him, quickly locking all the doors. There was a dead bolt on the back door, off the garage, which I made sure to turn. I also turned the dead bolt on the front door off the living room and secured the patio doors off our family room.

Feeling a little bit safer, I called Lydia in Halifax to tell her what had just happened. My hands were shaking so badly I could hardly hold onto the phone. As I recounted my tale to her, she sounded frightened for the kids and me and begged me to call the police before Jake returned. Deep down, I knew she was right, but I was still reluctant to do so, as I knew this action would greatly affect his reputation, both at work and around town. There would be no turning back, and I felt frozen to the spot with indecision and fear. As far as I knew, there was no handbook on how to deal with this type of situation. She was very insistent, however, and suggested I should also call David to inform him of what was going on. Furthermore, she wanted me to come to Halifax with the kids as soon as possible; to me, that seemed like a giant step I was still not ready to take. She even offered to fly to The Pas to help me drive back east, and I finally started to think of leaving as a real possibility.

I had no sooner hung up the phone with Lydia when I heard someone pounding on the back door. I knew it was Jake, returning to finish the job he had started. There was a small glass window in the door, and since he could not get into the house any other way, he took off his shoe and used it to break the glass. Suddenly aware that he was back inside the house, I quickly ran up the stairs to our bedroom and locked the door behind me. I noticed both kids still had their bedroom doors shut, and I hoped and prayed he would leave them alone, since there were no locks on their doors. I had an extension phone in my bedroom that I could use if I had to.

Sure enough, he followed me up the stairs and proceeded to stand outside our bedroom door for what seemed like an eternity. I could hear intermittent knocking, but otherwise, all was silent. "Go away," I pleaded. "If you don't, I'll call the police!" It seemed like a long standoff, but he finally left. After a few minutes, I took a deep breath and slowly opened the door. I then took the opportunity to check on both kids, who had not made a peep throughout the whole episode. Thankfully, they both seemed to be sound asleep. I quickly ran back downstairs to inspect the damage to our back door, which now hosted a broken window; there were also large shards of glass and a trail of blood on the floor. Aware that I now had literally no way to keep him out of the house, I made the tough decision to call the local detachment of the police.

Once again, it seemed like forever before a patrol car rolled up at our front door, and when it did, the officer just sat there. I eventually went outdoors and gestured for him to come into the house. It was my guess that he was not accustomed to responding to calls from our area of town, or perhaps he knew who lived in our house. When he finally came in, somewhat reluctantly, I gave him a brief synopsis of my evening and showed him the broken window in the back door. For some strange reason, he seemed to doubt my story. In the middle of all this, Jake showed up for a third time, acting as if everything was just hunky-dory. Always charming, butter would not melt in his mouth. He flat-out denied everything I had related to the cop, but by now, I felt almost frantic and was desperate to be taken seriously, so I strongly contradicted his outrageous lies. I told the officer just how frightened of Jake's behavior I really was and that there were also two vulnerable children living in the house. He must have finally realized the terrible state Jake was in and eventually believed me, taking Jake away in the squad car. Once again, I hoped and prayed that the kids had slept through the whole ordeal because they never came out of their rooms. Now, many years later, I know for sure that they overheard the whole sorry scenario.

I finally called Dave and Barb and filled them in on the events of the evening. Unfortunately, I woke them both up from a deep sleep, as the hour was late, and the time in Nova Scotia was two hours ahead of Manitoba. They were both shocked and angry at what Jake had done and wanted me to fly back to Halifax with the kids as soon as possible. Although it seemed like a drastic move, I knew I was truly at the end of my rope with Jake, and the children and I needed a safe place to land, in order to get a fresh perspective on our lives. It's funny how things must often come to a crisis before we wake up and smell the coffee.

I also knew, deep down, that Jake would never leave me alone if I stayed in The Pas. Both Dave and Barb went on to tell me that the three of us could live with them for as long as we needed to, and they even extended the invitation to our two cats. Their ancient cat, Tiger, had recently died (at the age of twenty), and they both had a soft spot for the furry creatures. Barb also asked me if I needed any money to tide me over, and knowing I would have to repair the broken window as well as prepare for our trip, I gratefully accepted her kind and generous offer.

Since I knew we would need a vehicle while we lived in Halifax, it was decided that David would fly to Winnipeg, where we would meet him, and then we would all drive back east together. I knew I would feel confident driving from The Pas to Winnipeg because we had made the trip as a family so many times before, but I was not yet ready to take on a cross-country tour by myself. After I hung up the phone, I felt relieved to have finally made the decision to leave Jake and was so grateful I had such good family and friend support. I knew I would never be able to begin to thank them for all their loving kindness, especially their nonjudgmental attitude.

At the end of my frightful and interminable evening, I called Lydia back to fill her in on what had just transpired. After she digested all that I told her, she also seemed relieved that I was finally leaving Jake. Whether it was permanent or not, I did not know; I would have to make a lot of big decisions in the coming weeks and months. I was not at all sure how I would support the three of us, and I felt torn about leaving my job so suddenly. I also felt badly about taking the kids out of school, so close to the end of the year, and had no idea how they would handle the news. I was still in shock and totally overwhelmed, as there was just so much to think about and do; David planned to arrive in Winnipeg that Saturday, which was only five days away. Already, time was running out, but thankfully, God was making a way of escape.

# CHAPTER 26

# Playing James Bond

I slept very little that night, and the next morning, a Tuesday, I called in sick at work. It wasn't a lie, as I was literally sick to my stomach with anxiety. I still had to face telling the kids what had gone on between their father and me the night before as well as my decision to leave The Pas and go to Halifax. I was dreading it. In the meantime, I called my boss, Chris, and told her what had happened. I am sure she was shocked, but when I asked her for a leave of absence from work, she was very supportive and advised me to use up all my sick time first. The only requirement was a note from my doctor, stating that I needed time off for medical reasons.

Feeling tremendously relieved, I wasted no time in going to see Dr. Johnson that very day, explaining the situation to him. Again, he was very supportive, especially since he had seen Jake and me together earlier in the winter when Jake had sought help for depression. It turned out that I had over three months of sick leave coming to me, and I figured if I needed more than that, I could use up my vacation days as well.

While Jake was still locked up in our local jail, I knew I had to act quickly, so I called Pastor Walter and informed him of the previous evening's events. Immediately, he suggested I file a restraining order against Jake, and he even offered to go with me to the provincial courthouse to start the ball rolling. Once we got there, however, he changed his mind because he was concerned that doing so might incite Jake to further violence. We both knew the act of filing a restraining order was no guarantee of safety or security. One of the social workers I knew and sometimes worked with was at the courthouse that day and obviously figured out that something strange was going on with me. Although we didn't talk, I wondered if he would tell his boss Grace (my close friend) that he had seen me with Walter.

In the late afternoon, after school was over, I had a heart-to-heart talk with both Will and Mackenzie. It soon became clear that I would have a big fight on my hands in convincing them to leave home and accompany me to Halifax. Although they seemed to understand why *I* needed to leave, neither one of them wanted to be separated from their friends, schools, or after-school activities. As their mother, however, I knew there was no alternative, since I could never leave them with their father. Will was now fifteen, and Mackenzie was only twelve; they would both have birthdays in July. I could not trust Jake to be around them anymore, as his drinking had descended back into violence. Lots of tears were shed that day and in the days to come, but once again, God came to our rescue.

Later that evening, not entirely unexpectedly, I got a phone call from Grace. She knew some of what had happened to me, probably because Dan had told her about seeing me with Walter earlier that day. She also must have discovered that Jake was now in jail. The Pas was a small town, and everyone knew everyone.

By this time, I didn't care *who* knew *what*, as I was finally starting to figure out that things never really improve until they are brought out into the light of day. Still, I had to be careful, because I had decided not to file charges against Jake, and he would soon be released. I was having the window in the back door repaired the next day, and I could not take the chance of having him find out about my plans before they were executed. There was no telling what he might do next! Desperate people do desperate things, and as I had discovered, after years of working with abused women and children, the most dangerous time for a victim of domestic violence is when they are preparing to leave their abuser.

Right then and there, I decided to confide in Grace, whom I trusted implicitly, and I proceeded to tell her everything. Shocked and horrified, she asked me how I could possibly take William out of high school and Army Cadets, so close to the end of the school year. I'm sure I was defensive with her, as I told her I felt I really had no choice in the matter. I was completely taken aback when she very generously invited Will to move in with her, Dean, and their family, until things improved with Jake. I needed some time to think carefully about her offer, since it was certainly not my first choice to leave Will behind. I wanted what was best for him, though, and after sleeping on the idea (or, rather, sitting up all night and thinking about it), I called her back on Wednesday morning and told her he could stay with them. After discussing our plans with Will, he was also on board and was happy and relieved to be staying with his friend Josh.

Mackenzie was another matter entirely. She was still miserable about being uprooted from her life and was especially sad about leaving her many friends. Trying to soften the blow, I allowed her to share the news with a couple of her closest girlfriends; I also visited her middle school to inform the principal of what was going on. He gave me a transcript of her marks, and I assured him that I planned to enroll her in school once we arrived in Halifax and got settled. I also visited my office one evening to ensure that all my paperwork was up to date. Because he was now out of jail, I was terrified that I might accidentally run into Jake, and I took great pains to get into and out of the building as quickly as I could. Most incredibly, I saw no one that night, not even the cleaning crew!

By this time, I was feeling a little bit like James Bond, but as careful as I was, I could not avoid Jake entirely. He came by the house later that week during the daytime, very unexpectedly. He used his house key and entered nonchalantly, like nothing had ever happened. Seemingly sober, he went on to tell me that he was now sleeping at the bunkhouse in The Pas and was attending outpatient sessions at True North Haven, a treatment center for addictions in town. Looking down at me, he admitted that he regretted what had happened earlier that week and eventually wanted to return home.

When he sauntered into our bedroom, I was sitting on the bed, trying to decide which clothes to take away with me. I silently thanked God that I had not yet brought out our suitcases or started packing. I could hardly bear to look at him and said nothing to him as he grabbed some clothes of his own to take. Heaving a huge sigh of relief when he finally left, I quickly ran behind him, this time double-checking all the doors. I could only hope and pray that he would not return before we left The Pas on Saturday morning. That could be catastrophic for all of us.

I spent the remainder of the week packing. I would have to take extra clothing for Mackenzie and myself, including our summer wear.

155

My cleaning lady and friend from church, Rose, was a godsend to me that week. She promised to keep an eye on the house and even took Mackenzie's dwarf hamster, Coffee Bean, home with her. Rose was a devout Christian and promised to pray fervently for all of us. It was so reassuring to have her in our corner!

One of the last things I did before we left was to drive out to the airport to put our two cats, Ernie and Sandy, on a plane to Halifax. I felt so sorry for them because they were very anxious in their crate, but after I administered the sedation provided by our local vet, they seemed to calm down. I talked gently and soothingly to them, telling them both that we would soon be reunited.

It was a cold but sunny Saturday morning when I drove our new Ford Windstar out to Carrot Valley to Dean and Grace's home. Penny, Walter's wife, had persuaded me to take the newer vehicle, since she didn't think it was safe for us to drive our old car on such a long journey (and Jake already had the Chrysler anyway). On Sunday morning, Wally, along with some of the other men in the church, planned to tell Jake that we had already left The Pas. But for now, Will sat beside me in the front seat, while Mackenzie sat behind me in the back seat, trying desperately to hold back her tears. By the time we arrived at their house, I think we were all crying, including Grace and Dean.

Leaving Will behind was one of the hardest things I have ever had to do, especially since I did not know when, or even if, we would ever see him again. Mackenzie and I each gave him a big hug as I told him I loved him very much and handed him some spending money. I thanked my wonderful friends once again, telling them I would soon be in touch. I knew there was no way I could ever repay them for their kindness, caring, and generosity of spirit. Despite our physical separation, I knew for sure that Will was in safe hands and that God was watching over all of us, both that day and in the days to come.

# CHAPTER 27

# Life in the Wilderness

Mackenzie and I had an uneventful trip to Winnipeg that day, albeit an emotional one, and as darkness fell over the city, we checked into the New International Inn near the airport. David arrived later that evening, a sight for sore eyes, while we watched him slowly descend on the escalator to the baggage area, where we were expectantly waiting. There were more hugs all around as my daughter got reacquainted with her uncle. The next morning, after a good night's sleep, we continued our journey and took our time driving back east with several overnight stops along the route. We spent one memorable evening in Sault Ste. Marie, where the three of us had lots of fun bowling in the alley attached to our motel. It was a much-needed emotional and physical release as we stretched our cramped arms and legs after long days of sitting in the van.

Dave was our designated driver for the trip, and it turned out that he loved driving our van. Mackenzie kept herself amused by practicing her flute, and David, good-natured as always, never complained if some of the notes were a bit off-key! Like David in the Bible, he was a man of true humility but also of quiet strength. He insisted on paying for everything, which I felt badly about, but it made things much easier on me. As we drove through our hometown of Woodstock, I began to breathe a bit easier because I was now back in familiar territory, and I knew it was far too late for Jake to follow us.

When we finally arrived in Halifax and walked into Dave and Barb's large bungalow, poor Barb was busy filling up her new fridge, since the old one had just died. She greeted us warmly, as did our two cats that she had picked up from the airport a few days earlier. They were so excited to see us, and we were equally happy to see them! That evening, Barb prepared one of her delicious, home-cooked meals, and we started to adjust to our new home away from home. Dave and Barb decided to live at their cottage in Mount Uniacke, about a forty-five-minute drive away, while we stayed at their house. This would give all of us more space and privacy as Mackenzie and I tried to heal and started to put the pieces of our lives back together again. I was so grateful to both David and Barbara for their kindness and generosity, and I told them so.

After we got settled into our new bedroom and unpacked all our things, I made an appointment to take Mackenzie over to meet the principal of her new school. Unlike her middle school in The Pas, it was a junior high school in Clayton Park, which was close to where we now lived in Rockingham. She still needed to complete grade seven, and although her grades were excellent, I knew that attending a new school for just two months would be difficult for her. I could only imagine how nervous she must have been, but thankfully, she made friends quickly with two girls who lived close by. Their friendship as well as the love and support of our family and friends in Halifax helped to see us both through what seemed like a long and excruciating spring and summer.

Right from the start, the weather was unusually hot and humid that year, and with no air-conditioning, we resorted to using fans. It helped move the hot air around but was no substitute for the real thing. Our days began to fall into a rhythm with me driving Mackenzie back and forth to school and then trying to fill up the rest of my day. My friends were all working, so I was often on my own during the week, but it gave me lots of time to think about my situation and what I was going to do next. I would often walk up to the nearest shopping center and go to Tim Hortons for coffee and a doughnut, sometimes stopping in a store or two to window-shop. I tried not to spend much money, since we were now living on one paycheck and had to make it last.

On the weekends, we would visit with my friends Olivia, Lydia, and Kurt and make plans to do something fun. Each Sunday, Mackenzie and I would accompany my other sister-in-law, Jenny, who was now back living in Halifax, to her Baptist church in Sackville. We often brought Lydia and Olivia along as well; afterward, we would all go out for brunch. Being back in church provided me with a lot of comfort, as I drew on my faith to sustain me through all the upheaval going on in my life. Although I tried not to let it control me, the fear of the unknown loomed large on the horizon.

I often corresponded with friends in The Pas or spoke with them on the phone, and I talked with Will several times a week. After three weeks of living with Dean and Grace, he moved back home with his father, as Jake had completed his rehab program and was doing much better by all accounts. I wasn't too sure how I felt about this because Jake had reacted very badly at church that first Sunday after he was told we had left him. I heard later from Walter that some of the men in the church had to physically restrain him until he finally calmed down. As well, when I first arrived in Halifax, Jake had called me on the phone and threatened to take Will away from me for good. I remember sitting in Barbara's kitchen, crying hysterically while Jenny tried to comfort me, as I feared I would never see my beloved son again. My emotions were totally out of control, ranging from anger to extreme sorrow and despair, all in a matter of moments.

I would sit up late at night reading my Bible, trying to make sense out of all that had happened to me. Two passages always came to mind. The first is in Daniel 3:8–25, the story of the fiery furnace. Daniel's three Jewish friends, Shadrach, Meshach, and Abednego, were thrown into the fiery furnace by King Nebuchadnezzar of Babylon because they would not bow down to the king's golden image. They would only worship Yahweh, their one true God. Although the king ordered the furnace to be heated up seven times hotter than usual, when the young men were thrown in, they were not touched by the fire, nor was there any smell of smoke on them. When the king looked in through the open door of the furnace, he could see four men walking in the flames, and one looked like "the son of God."

Not only were Daniel's friends miraculously saved that day, but Jesus Christ was with them. If we trust and obey Him, Almighty God—the Trinity—consisting of God the Father, God the Son, and God the Holy Spirit, will ultimately bring us through our trials and sufferings, either by courage and perseverance or through death, to the other side. Sometimes He takes us out of our trials altogether. I was hoping for the latter, and although we had escaped a terrible situation, it looked like I was going to have to persevere and find a permanent solution to my problems. Courage was most definitely called for.

The second passage that really spoke to me was Zephaniah 3:14–20, especially verse 17, "The Lord your God is with you, He is mighty to save. He will take great delight in you, he will quiet you with his love, he will rejoice over you with singing." Verse 20 reads, "At that time I will gather you; at that time I will bring you home. I will give you honor and praise among all the peoples of the earth when I restore your fortunes before your very eyes, says the Lord." Hadn't God done exactly that for me? Indeed, He had saved me (and my children) and brought me home. Although the final chapter of my life was not yet written, God had already fulfilled many of His promises to me.

In the middle of all my anguish, God performed another miracle; Will unexpectedly got word that his Army Cadet summer camp would be in CFB Greenwood, deep in the heart of the beautiful Annapolis Valley of Nova Scotia. All his previous camps (and all those going forward) were out west, so I could only assume once again that God was in control! He knew how much I missed my son, and I am sure Will also missed his sister and me too. I so looked forward to opening the sweet cards and letters I received from Will in the mail, and I made sure to send him care packages each week to cheer him up. I knew life could not be easy for him now; living in a small town was much like living in a fishbowl.

When school finished at the end of June, I searched for a day camp for Mackenzie to help keep her occupied during the summer. She had successfully completed her school year, and because she had a big interest in dance and music, I enrolled her in summer theater in Halifax. It ran for the month of July and would keep her busy most days during the week. Once again, I drove her back and forth, this time to Argyle Street, in the downtown core. At the end of July, Lydia, Kurt, and I watched with pride as she sang and danced in an adaptation of *Rent* along with the other young performers.

In the meantime, I kept myself busy, helping Lydia clean out her basement (a gigantic task), while on Friday afternoons, Mackenzie and I would drive two hours to Greenwood to pick up Will and bring him home for the weekend. He was always filthy dirty, and long before we made it back to Rockingham, he was usually sound asleep as well! On Sunday afternoons, we would drop him off at the base once again. It kept us all going through a very difficult time. We celebrated both kids' birthdays in July with our friends; Mackenzie turned thirteen, and Will turned sixteen. It seemed they were growing up all too quickly. At the end of July, we even invited Jake's sister, husband, and family over to celebrate her birthday. It felt good to be able to mend some fences with his family. I had also spoken with his mom on the phone a few times over the summer, and although she was initially angry that I had left Jake so suddenly, she soon calmed down when she heard the whole story. I often thought to myself how sad it was that she hadn't taken me seriously the summer before when I had desperately asked for her help. She obviously felt powerless to help her own son.

The one thing I did for myself was to attend an Al-Anon group at a nearby church. It helped to meet others who also had loved ones with addiction issues, but honestly, I sometimes left feeling more depressed than when I had arrived. I can't say the group helped me a lot with healing or in making any permanent decisions about my life, but the people there made me feel more normal and less alone. Meanwhile, still in The Pas, Jake had completed his time at True North Haven and had been working all summer. We talked occasionally on the phone, where he clearly indicated that he badly wanted the kids and me to return home.

I thought and prayed about what I should do almost constantly, asking God to give me direction. My friends and family left the decision up to me, knowing a lot was at stake. The kids were very forgiving and wanted to be reunited with their father. By the end of July, with my sick time depleted and my vacation days dwindling, I decided to give Jake another chance. Not only were my marriage and family life very important to me, but my work was also. We finally agreed that Jake would fly to Halifax in early August, and then he, Mackenzie, and I would drive back to The Pas together. Will would be back home by then and would once again stay with friends until we arrived.

After Jake rang the doorbell, one day during the first week of August, I opened the door slowly but was still shocked by the change in his appearance. He had lost a lot of weight and looked much older than I remembered. Similar to our first date, his manner was serious, and he seemed very quiet. There was a big, happy reunion between him and

Mackenzie, but it was much more subdued between the two of us. He also seemed to harbor an underlying anger and resentment toward me, and immediately, I wondered if I had made a big mistake. To be honest, I was still a little afraid of him, especially since I had not seen him since April. Just as I had had doubts at the altar, I experienced them again now; but once again, it felt much too late to change my mind.

Following an emotional goodbye with our family and friends, the three of us started back on the road home. As a pleasant diversion, we took the ferry from Nova Scotia over to Prince Edward Island and spent the day visiting both Cavendish and Charlottetown. We enjoyed several fun-filled hours at the amusement park in Cavendish, riding the roller coaster over and over, and then toured the Anne of Green Gables house. In late afternoon, we went to the playhouse in Charlottetown and watched the play by the same name. Mackenzie and I had both read the book and knew the story well. To end our busy day, we feasted on mouthwatering lobster at one of the many seaside restaurants in Cavendish, before driving across the Confederation Bridge to New Brunswick. We left late at night, and I still recall the beauty of the full moon shining over the dark waters of Northumberland Strait, guiding us as we went. It had been a magical day, one we all desperately wanted and needed.

We drove through Canada, like we had with David when returning to the Maritimes. I don't remember much about the trip home, so it must have been uneventful, which was good. It was great to be back in my own home again and to be reunited with Will. Barb, God bless her, said farewell to Ernie and Sandy and put them on a plane back to The Pas a few days later. I am sure that our two cats were as happy to be home as Mackenzie and I were. The old adage is very true—there is no place like home. I returned to work the following week, and, thankfully, my work colleagues were supportive and unassuming about my absence. I must have filled them in on a few of the details, but by then, everyone knew the whole sordid story. I was especially grateful to our wonderful friends Grace and Dean, who had taken Will in when he needed a safe and happy place to land.

It was very hard for me to face people again, even my own friends, since there was a huge element of shame to the entire ordeal. The things that happened to our family don't happen to people like us; only they do, all the time. Unfortunately, though, like me, a lot of people try to hide the truth and pretend everything is normal. We want to be in control of our own lives, and as a professional and a natural caregiver, I did not want to admit that I also needed taking care of, even temporarily. In trying to carry my burden alone, I was being weak; I now know that everyone needs help at some point in their lives, some of us more often than others. No one is immune from trouble, and no one is perfect, which is hard for a perfectionist to accept. The most important lesson I learned during my separation from Jake is that no person can change another person's behavior; they themselves need to want to change and do their own work. It took me a long time to learn this, and unfortunately, I learned it the hard way.

# CHAPTER 28

# Goodbye, Yellow Brick Road

December 31, 1999, came and went, and the year 2000 was ushered in. Despite all the dire predictions, the world did not end! We saw the new year in at a house party with some church friends, including both adults and kids. It was the start of a new millennium, and it felt like a new beginning for Jake and me as well. Things were slowly improving between us, now that he was not drinking. Later that same year, I applied for a brand-new part-time position within our public health region and was thrilled when I was the successful applicant. My job was to plan and implement the immunization programs and clinics, such as the influenza clinics we held each fall and winter. It was a chance to carve out a new role for myself while I still participated in child health clinics and sat on several regional and provincial committees. I was also responsible for providing informational and educational releases to the media around immunizations.

That fall, I had the opportunity to attend the National Immunization Conference in Halifax with Lori, another public health nurse from Cranberry Portage. The two of us had a great time, especially since I also had the chance to make a brief visit to see my family and friends. I loved my new job and was so excited about it! Jake seemed to be content with his job as well, and both kids had settled back into another new school year, with Will in grade twelve and Mackenzie in grade nine. Will would graduate the following June, and I wanted him to make the most of his last year in high school. This was also Mackenzie's first year of high school, so it was another big year of transition for her. Poor kid ... she thrived that year, though, and loved being around all her many friends.

When 2001 rolled around, I was presented with a unique opportunity to help my friend Lydia, who lived in Halifax. She was still working at the children's hospital, but I knew she wanted a change of scenery and was interested in working outside of the hospital setting. When a friend who worked at Aurora Community College called me up one day, looking for a nurse to teach the Personal Support Worker program for the First Nations communities, I told him I might have someone in mind.

When I arrived home from work that day, I talked to Jake about the idea, and he was supportive of having Lydia come to live with us for a few months. I knew teaching was out of her comfort zone, but knowing that she was resilient and a person who was always up for a new challenge, I called her that night and pitched the job to her. Although she was hesitant at first, she eventually decided it would be a big boost to her nursing career, and she made plans to fly to The Pas in early February, one of the coldest months of the year.

Lydia stayed with us from February through June, and for the most part, things went well. She had some challenges with her class, an understatement for sure, since there were huge cultural differences to overcome. Most of her small class did end up graduating, however, and I attended the graduation ceremony with her at the end of June. Our family also had a big celebration that month when Will graduated from grade twelve. He did well with his marks, and in early June, he traveled to Winnipeg with his international studies teacher, Mrs. Beatty, and another classmate to participate in a model United Nations debate. They ended up tying for the win with North Carolina, which was no small feat. Of course, I knew firsthand how much Will loved to argue, and he often won the debate!

We were all so proud of his accomplishments, and after he and I sat down one day to review his options, he made the decision to study journalism at the University of Ottawa. Although I had anticipated he would be leaving The Pas, Ottawa still seemed very far away, and I knew I would miss him dearly. Nana was also visiting us during this time, since she had arrived for Will's graduation. We had a full house, to be sure, but life was sweet once again.

Wise people say we should never get too complacent with our lives, and that saying turned out to be all too true for our family. One evening in early summer, Jake came home from work and landed a bombshell on me. Nervously perched on the edge of the bed, he confessed that he was being transferred to a bigger office in Winnipeg later that August because two managerial positions in two different departments were being merged into one position. Since the other manager had seniority over Jake, he was offered the new expanded role, whereas Jake would now take on a new job description. It was not a demotion in terms of salary or pension, but it really seemed like a step backward to him. Deep down, I had to wonder if his history of drinking had played a role in the decision-making process.

To say that he was extremely unhappy about the move would not be a lie. I was quite literally gobsmacked and was also disappointed, as I was just starting to get my own feet wet in my new job. We now had so many decisions to make once again, and it would mean more upheaval for our family. I was thankful that Will's plans, at least, would not be affected by our move. Living in Winnipeg, we would be a little bit closer to our son, who would be residing in Ottawa, come September. Like last time, Mackenzie would be the most affected, and I knew she would not be a happy camper. I also had to break the news to my boss and colleagues at work, who had all been so kind and supportive of me over the past few years. I was dreading telling them.

When we told the kids about our upcoming move, as expected, Will was largely unconcerned. Mackenzie, on the other hand, was devastated to be once again leaving her school, friends, and activities. We tried to make the best of it and told her that her friends could come visit her in her new home, and she could also return to The Pas to see them now and again. That softened the blow a little bit. Toward the middle of July, Jake and I made the familiar trek to Winnipeg to look for another house. We found one we loved and put in an offer on it, which was conditionally accepted. We believed our home in The Pas would be purchased by an employee of Jake's, whose wife had fallen in love with the home and was intent on buying it.

Despite everything, it did seem like things were working out for us in the end because many doors opened at the same time. The sale of our home went through smoothly, and we did quite well on it. My good friend and fellow public health nurse, Wendy, along with her husband, Liam (who was also our kids' pediatrician), held a work party for us in their beautiful home. Our friends from church also threw a huge barbecue for us at one of their homes, and Jake's office staff held a farewell luncheon for us at a popular restaurant. It was so sad to say a final goodbye to friends we had known and loved for close to a decade.

When the movers had finished packing up our furniture and belongings and we were finally on our way to Winnipeg, it was with mixed emotions. I remember Jake was in a particularly foul mood that day and stopped the car at one point to throw our vacuum cleaner out of the trunk and into the ditch. Obviously, his immaturity and bad temper had not completely disappeared when he stopped drinking. Secretly, I was worried that he might start drinking once again, so it was with trepidation and an impending sense of doom that I traveled to our new home that day.

# CHAPTER 29

# Gateway to the West

Winnipeg is called the Gateway to the West, but for our family, it meant moving to a more southernly climate. This was one of the more positive outcomes to our move. The summers in this flat, urban prairie city are usually very hot, with hordes of blackflies in the spring and mosquitoes in the summer, due to an abundance of freshwater lakes and rivers. In 2001, the city routinely sent fogging trucks out to get rid of these bloodsucking flies, and I believe the practice continues to this day.

Other than that, it was a big treat to live in a city once again, and after we were settled into our new home, which was large and finished off quite nicely, we started to enjoy the many amenities Winnipeg had to offer. The shopping and restaurants were wonderful, and we especially enjoyed going to The Forks, which was (and still is) a popular historical, cultural, and retail attraction, located at the confluence of the Red and Assiniboine Rivers. It comprises an indoor food market with artisan shops and boasts a high tower overlooking an expansive outdoor vista. The outside space hosts both summer and winter festivals, and in the winter months, there is also a picturesque skating rink for outdoor enthusiasts. Winnipeg or "Winterpeg," as the locals call it, is the capital of Manitoba and is also home to the Royal Winnipeg Ballet, the Royal Canadian Mint, the Winnipeg Blue Bombers, the Winnipeg Jets, and the Assiniboine Park Zoo. The zoo soon became one of our favorite places to visit during the short period of time we lived there, and it was always enjoyable, every time we went.

We lived in a leafy suburb of the city in the southwest part of Winnipeg, close to the University of Manitoba. Jake started work right away, while I once again unpacked and put things away. Meanwhile, Will prepared for university, and Mackenzie looked forward to starting grade ten. She would be taking the city bus back and forth to her high school, which was also located close by.

Shortly after we moved in, an acquaintance from The Pas dropped by; her husband had once worked for Jake, and she now worked in management for the city of Winnipeg in public health. She was aware of my work background and completely surprised me by telling me there were two positions within public health that would soon come open. Sandra asked me if I was interested in applying for one of them. God was certainly smiling down on me that day; I told her that I was most definitely interested and subsequently forwarded my résumé over to her.

Following a formal interview process, I was ultimately offered the part-time job, which was my preference. It was a job share that involved working two days one week and three days the next week, as well as some weekends. It would mean a thirty-minute commute in the morning and an hourlong drive home in the late afternoon, across the city through Portage and Main. This intersection was infamous for being both the windiest and coldest corner in North America, and my trek took me across two major rivers. Right away, I bought a good map and started to learn the routes around the city. I was all set to begin my new job in mid-September, after Will had moved to Ottawa and Mackenzie was settled into her new high school.

During the first week of September 2001, Jake and William left for Ottawa, driving our Ford Windstar. The van was packed to the rafters with everything Will might need for his upcoming school year. He was planning to live in a dorm, as most first-year students do, at the University of Ottawa. There were lots of hugs to go around and a very tearful goodbye (on my part anyway), before I sadly watched them pull out of our driveway. I knew things had changed forever in our lives, and we would never again be the same nuclear family we had once been. Mackenzie also started school that week, which was a good distraction for me. I wanted to ensure that she was happy and well settled into yet another new school.

Since our backyard was endowed with several fruit trees, producing an overabundance of juicy plums and tart apples, I spent the remainder of my week and weekend picking apples and preparing them for the freezer. On the morning of Tuesday, September 11, I took a break from cutting up apples and sat down in front of the TV with a cup of coffee. Along with the rest of the world, I was mesmerized with horror and disbelief as I watched the second plane fly into the south tower of the World Trade Center in New York City. I couldn't fathom the reality of the situation and sat transfixed for most of the rest of the day. Back then, we had no cell phones, so I had to wait for Jake to contact me on a landline. He finally called later that evening and said he had just left Halifax, where he had gone to visit his sister and his mother after dropping Will off at school a few days before. Although he had originally planned to drive back through the States, he now had to travel through Canada, since the borders were all closed. I was thankful that he did not get trapped in another country, because we had no idea how long this disaster would continue to play out. Jake eventually arrived home safe and sound, but our world changed, irreparably and forever, on that fateful day.

I started my new job later that month and enjoyed getting back into the swing of things. It gave me something positive to focus on, as I became part of a team once again. I shared an office with Kim, who worked opposite days from me, and I spent my time making postpartum visits to new moms, performing case management and contact tracing of reportable communicable diseases, and doing school immunizations in the spring and influenza clinics in the fall and winter. I continued to carry a caseload of high-risk families with our home-visiting program, and on the weekends, I worked alone, doing postpartum visits and answering a breastfeeding hotline. Several times a year, I taught prenatal classes one evening a week with Kim, which was one of my favorite parts of the job.

The work was more narrowly defined than what I was used to, but it was extremely busy. Since Winnipeg is a culturally diverse city, the language and customs could also be a challenge. It was a bit daunting in the beginning, but as I became increasingly familiar with the city and its ways, I enjoyed it more and more. The public health nurses and support staff were friendly and helpful, as was my boss, who was male. There was also more money in the pot for continuing education, and we were allowed to attend conferences within the city. That was a big bonus for me, since most of the time I had worked in the north, due to budget constraints, we were not allowed to travel outside of our region.

Jake also excelled in his job that year as he traveled back and forth to the United States for work. I remember he was away from home a fair bit, but that Christmas, Will flew home from Ottawa, and Joan came for a visit from Newfoundland. It was wonderful to be together as a family once again, so we splurged on some special treats, such as going to brunch on Boxing Day at the Fort Garry Hotel in downtown Winnipeg. Nana, Mackenzie, her best friend, and I also attended a special performance of *The Nutcracker* by the Royal Winnipeg Ballet, just prior to Christmas. Mackenzie still had a deep love for ballet, and this outing was a special gift for her.

Both kids did quite well in school, and having completed Army Cadets, Will decided to join the Army Reserves and became a member of a prominent regiment in Ottawa. Unfortunately, though, Mackenzie struggled with math and had to retake it in summer school at the end of the school year. On the plus side, she joined the high school hockey and basketball teams and made a new best friend, Chloé. The two of them soon became inseparable, to say the least! When Mackenzie turned sixteen in early July, she and Chloé went to the zoo for the day; when they arrived back home, tired and very sunburnt, all of Mackenzie's school friends were waiting to surprise her with a sweet sixteen birthday party. Chloé became my young partner in crime that day!

Despite all these positives about Winnipeg, we didn't feel settled living there, so Jake started looking around for another job. After living in the west for ten years, I could feel my heartstrings pulling me closer to my homeland in the east. Simply put, I missed the rest of my family and wanted to be closer to them so that we could visit each other more often. Jake agreed with me and hired a headhunter, who found three potential jobs for him right away. One was in Victoria, British Columbia; one was in Whitehorse, the Yukon; and the third was in Sault Ste. Marie, Ontario.

Although we both loved Victoria, we knew it was expensive to live there, and it was west of Winnipeg, not east. For me, Whitehorse was just too far away on the map, although it was Jake's favorite pick of the three. They had flown him there for an interview, where he took a side trip to Alaska, and, of course, he loved it. It seemed he really had a thing for the north! Me, not so much. This time, I firmly put my foot down, knowing we would be very isolated living there, which would not be a good situation for either Mackenzie or me. In the end, he was offered all three jobs, but for once, *I* made the final decision about where we would live, and, perhaps surprisingly, I chose Sault Ste. Marie.

We had driven through there several times, and despite its reputation as a steel town, I always thought the rolling hills and valleys around Lake Superior and Lake Huron were extremely beautiful. It was also a border city, with Sault Ste. Marie, Michigan, just across the international bridge. I could envision us all living there one day, and I think God gave me a glimpse of the life we would eventually have there. Mackenzie was vehemently opposed to yet another move, which I completely understood, but I knew the longer we stayed in Winnipeg, the harder it would be to leave.

In the end, Jake accepted a managerial position in the Soo, which is what the locals call Sault Ste. Marie. In the spring of 2002, the three of us flew there to look at homes and do a bit of sightseeing. Once again, Mackenzie was not impressed, and I felt terrible about moving her away from a place she so obviously loved. This time, however, I hoped and prayed we could stay put until she finished high school, at least. During that trip, we were very blessed to find a great house in a beautiful subdivision on the outskirts of the city. It was perfect for us, although it would mean driving Mackenzie back and forth to school each day.

Once we were back in Winnipeg, we quickly put our home up for sale, and on the very first day, we had three competing offers over the asking price! This was a stark contrast to the terrible experience we had endured in Newfoundland for over five years. It was confirmation to me that we had made the right decision, as it seemed like several doors opened for us all at once. By now, I firmly believed God's timing was always perfect. My work colleagues threw me a party at the home of one of the nurses, and I said adieu to a great group of people. Unlike our previous exit from The Pas, I was excited about this move and felt that we were in control of our own destiny for the first time in a long time.

# PART 4

# CHAPTER 30

# Homeward Bound

Right from the start, moving to the Soo felt like coming home. Unfortunately, I was so sick and tired of moving by then and Mackenzie was initially so unhappy that I had second thoughts about our decision. It was a difficult transition for her, and I felt very guilty about moving her around so much. Things had worked out well for Will, however, as he was now in his second year of university. That summer, in addition to settling into our new home and new life in the Soo, we had to make the long trip to Ottawa to help Will find a new place to live for the upcoming school year. Students were only allowed to stay in residence for one year, and Will had somehow managed to overlook this fact!

We scrambled to find him a decent place to live, but by the beginning of August, we finally secured a one-bedroom apartment a few streets over from the university. It was a bit of a walk for him, but as the old proverb says, beggars can't be choosers. As a mother, I was thankful he had a safe roof over his head, although it was not cheap. We would have to go back to Ottawa at the end of August to move him in, which was a nine-hour drive each way, along a two-lane highway. It was a long, monotonous journey, to say the least!

I eventually decided to take a year off work to concentrate on moving into and decorating our new home, and most importantly, to be there for Mackenzie. Her high school was a few miles away from our home, and since she was not eligible to take the school bus, I drove her back and forth each day. Eventually, we carpooled with another family in our subdivision, who had two daughters attending the same school. The first semester was probably the hardest for Mackenzie, as she had no established friends, and by grade eleven, most kids already had their own peer group to hang out with.

One evening, after overhearing quiet sobbing in her bedroom, I realized that the situation with Mackenzie had become much more serious. She desperately wanted to go back to Winnipeg to attend the same school her best friend, Chloé, was now attending. After talking with her that night, I reluctantly agreed to accompany her in the spring to tour the school, which was in downtown Winnipeg. In the meantime, after I spent some time praying about it, I suggested she try to make friends with some of the girls whom she ate her lunch with. The following day, she connected with a small handful of girls at lunch hour, and by the end of the semester, she had a core group of close girlfriends. Once again, God had answered my SOS for help! As the year progressed, things continued to improve, as Mac joined the girls' basketball and hockey teams, ran track and field in the spring and fall, and played the flute in the high school band.

The next May, true to my word, the two of us flew to Winnipeg, where we visited with Chloé and her family and finally met with the principal of her prospective school. Mackenzie still wanted to go there the next fall, but once again, after praying about it, I made the decision that she would be better off at home with us for her last year of school. I felt that otherwise, she would not have the adult supervision she still needed at such a tender age. She was quite angry with me for a few weeks, but eventually, she calmed down and moved on. Chloé came to visit us later that same year and got to meet Mackenzie's new friends from school. To this day, the two girls are great comrades and stood up for each other in their respective weddings.

The other concession we considered for Mackenzie was getting a dog. We already had two cats, but owning a dog was going to another level entirely. Dogs were a huge commitment, and I knew I would most certainly inherit the animal once she left school and went away to university. Despite my qualms, in the fall of 2002, Jake, Mackenzie, and I made a trip to our local animal shelter and came home with Ellie. She was a rescue dog, part German shepherd and part Labrador retriever mix. She was just a puppy when we first brought her home, but she quickly grew into a large, goofy, affectionate pooch that we all came to know and love.

True to expectations, Ellie turned out to be a whole lot of work for me, as her white-blonde hair shed a lot, demanding daily brushing and grooming as well as daily vacuuming of the hardwood floors in our great room. One positive was that due to her large size, she required a good walk twice a day, which turned out to be beneficial for me as well! Both Jake and I had not owned a dog since we were children, so this was a new experience for the whole family. I could easily understand how dogs come to mean so much to people, and Ellie soon became an integral part of our family and our home. She was good company for me when I was all alone and was also a very good guard dog, as we lived in the countryside. She brought love and laughter into our lives and was always there when we needed her. I never regretted bringing her home for more than just a few minutes, usually when I was vacuuming the floors or trying to chase her down in our community!

Jake seemed to enjoy his new job and found it challenging because he oversaw many learned people, including several scientists. His work also involved some travel, usually to Toronto, which he always seemed to look forward to. But just as our lives started to fall into a natural rhythm, disaster struck once again, this time with his family. The first summer we lived in Sault Ste. Marie, Jake's aunt Bess, who still lived in Newfoundland, suddenly became ill. Most unfortunately, she had a deep-seated fear of all things medical and refused to have any tests done or even be admitted into hospital when she became extremely sick. As a result, she died within a few weeks, most likely from cancer. Three weeks after her death, her husband, Uncle Harry, also passed away. He had had a series of small strokes, and without his loving wife by his side, he had simply given up on life. We had been very close to them both when we lived in Newfoundland, and they were like second parents to Jake and Debbie.

We flew back to St. John's for their joint funeral in late summer and discovered they had left each of us a sizeable inheritance as well as a generous educational trust for each of our children. We were aware of the latter, since Will was already away at university, but not the former. Once we were back home, reality set in, as it slowly dawned on us that our lives would never be quite the same again. We wasted no time in paying off our mortgage, and that winter, I splurged on a new car for myself, a spiffy black sports car. We could finally retire our aging Chrysler, which was by then eleven years old! We felt so grateful to Jake's aunt and uncle for such an unexpected blessing upon our lives.

Just before Christmas, I flew back to New Brunswick on a mercy mission for two weeks to support my aunt Ruth, who was having surgery for breast cancer. She was well into her eighties by then and was a lifelong heavy smoker, so naturally, I was worried she would not survive the surgery. She turned out to be a lot tougher than even I realized, since she not only endured the mastectomy, but she lived for over another decade, and we made many more trips back home to visit her.

That same winter, Jake, Mackenzie, and I flew to Puerto Vallarta, Mexico, for a two-week vacation. It was the first luxury holiday we had taken since our Caribbean cruise in 1982, so it was long overdue! Because it was also March break, Mackenzie missed only one week of school, and she took her textbooks with her to prepare for her upcoming exams. Although I picked up a stomach bug and became ill for a couple of days, we all loved Mexico, especially the parasailing and ziplining, and hoped to return one day. We even attended a local bullfight, which I rather enjoyed, but Jake and Mackenzie had no appetite for it at all!

A bizarre event happened to me during the late winter of 2003. Since Mackenzie was in school and Jake was at work, I spent most of my days alone in our large house, which was situated on a heavily treed, one-acre lot. A person could feel very isolated and lonely there, and it was rather spooky at times. One day, when I was alone in my bedroom upstairs, reading my Bible and praying, I was suddenly and sharply jolted by a strong electrical current. It started at the base of my neck and traveled down to the tip of my spine, startling me enough to make me jump up off the bed. A few days afterward, I started experiencing weird symptoms in my feet, legs, hands, and face, which included warmth, tingling, numbness, and the sensation that something was crawling all over me.

Aware that these symptoms were neurological in nature and could be early warning signs of multiple sclerosis (MS) or something similar, I was very frightened! When I went in to see my family physician, he agreed with me and quickly referred me to a neurologist for follow-up. The itinerant neurologist from Toronto ordered two MRI scans a month apart and eventually informed me (thankfully) that they were both normal. He went on to explain that he had seen this occurrence once before in another of his female patients, who was Japanese. He called it a benign form of multiple sclerosis; it mimicked the disease but was not real, nor did it cause any damage to the body. I would just have to put up with it, and hopefully, over time, my symptoms would subside.

Extremely relieved, I tried to forget about it, and over the course of a few years, my symptoms faded and finally disappeared entirely. I have since read that an attack of this kind can be spiritual in nature. It made me realize once again that even as Christians, we are not immune to the powers of darkness, as the devil is the enemy of our soul. To further summarize Ephesians 6:10–18, each day we need to "put on the full armor of God: the belt of truth, the breastplate of righteousness, the sandals of peace, the shield of faith, the helmet of salvation, and the sword of the Spirit." Most interestingly, the "sword of the Spirit" represents the Bible or the Word of God and is the only offensive weapon in our arsenal—the rest are all defensive. That is just how important the Bible really is—still as relevant today as it was when it was first written thousands of years ago.

# CHAPTER 31

# Empty Nesters

By the summer of 2003, ready to return to work, I applied for another job within public health. Once again, I felt truly blessed when I quickly secured a permanent full-time position in child health with the local health authority and started working in early August. I soon discovered just how much the job entailed, as I worked in many different areas. I made numerous postpartum visits and home visits with the high-risk program, answered a parenting hotline, worked at a drop-in center for new mothers and babies, and assisted with the breastfeeding clinic. I also helped teach a parenting class for new moms and babies, while I worked with two other nurses on a special project, developing a brand-new parenting program for teens and young adults. There were always the seasonal influenza clinics to staff, and for a change of pace, I sat on the Health and Safety Committee for several years. It sometimes seemed like I had a finger in every pie!

My work life wasn't the only thing keeping me busy. One advantage of coming into some extra money was finally being able to travel. We did just that over the next few years, enjoying cruises around the Hawaiian Islands (for our silver wedding anniversary), through the Panama Canal, and around the Mediterranean, as well as flying to Hong Kong with my niece and her husband and then cruising down the coast of New Zealand and up along Australia's Gold Coast. We also took a Caribbean cruise with Will and his then girlfriend, as well as some family trips to Cuba and the Dominican Republic. It was great to reconnect with Jessica, who still lived outside of Toronto, and with my aunt Alice, who joined us for Christmas one year in the Dominican Republic. She was living in southern

Ontario once again and was all alone, having broken up with her American boyfriend a few years before we relocated to Ontario.

In June 2004, Mackenzie graduated with honors from high school. Nana came for her graduation, and together we celebrated all her accomplishments as well as her plans to attend the University of Guelph in the fall. Most of her friends were also going there, and she was excited to be moving into the next stage of her young life. I was less than thrilled, knowing that the last baby bird was leaving the nest, so I tried to savor each moment I had with her.

She had worked for two summers at a large indigenous craft store, which was located about forty-five minutes away, north of Sault Ste. Marie on majestic Lake Superior. Fortunately, the company bused her back and forth each day, which made for long hours but gave Mackenzie some extra spending money for school. In early September, the three of us made the long journey to Guelph and got her settled into her dorm room, which turned out to be hers alone, since her roommate never did show up. After we left her that day, I cried the whole way home. The next spring when we picked her up to bring her back to the Soo, it was *Mackenzie* who was shedding the tears as she bid her new boyfriend, Rob, a sad goodbye in the pouring rain.

The year 2006 heralded many changes for our family. In May, Will graduated with his hard-earned bachelor's degree in journalism. Once again, Nana was on hand with Jake and me to proudly watch his convocation ceremony from the University of Ottawa. Two weeks after Will's graduation, still active in the armed forces, he and his best friend from university, Pierre, went to serve in Afghanistan for a six-month tour of duty. Most unfortunately, the two young men witnessed many horrendous things involving military and civilians alike; at the time, our brave soldiers were dodging land mines and searching caves for Osama bin Laden.

It was common for Al-Qaeda to shoot missiles over and onto the base, and one evening, several of them hit their mark. One of Will's best friends from Ottawa was struck by shrapnel around his heart and lungs as he was eating dinner in the mess tent. He had to be airlifted to Germany for emergency surgery and spent several more weeks recuperating there. Thankfully, he recovered fully and made additional tours to Afghanistan following his close call. During that time, I never stopped thinking about and praying for the troops who were stationed over there serving our country.

Work was a good distraction for me, but at the end of the day, I would race home to turn on the twenty-four-hour news channel to get the latest update on the fighting. The period that Will was stationed over there was one of the worst in terms of combat and casualties, for both our Canadian soldiers and our allies. Unfortunately, I knew only too well that my anxiety and worry were not misplaced. Once again, though, God answered my prayers because Will and his friends all came home safe and sound just before Christmas that year. Jake, Mackenzie, and I met him when he got off the plane in Sault Ste. Marie, and that evening, which was Christmas Eve, we all went to midnight Mass at a little church we had just started attending. As a mother, I could not have been more thankful for Will's life that night, and although I was very proud of him, I earnestly prayed that he would never go back to Afghanistan, and he never did.

During the fall of 2006, I decided a change was in order for my own work life. I once again went part-time, dividing my time and energy between working on the prenatal team and overseeing a new developmental program for preschoolers. I also continued working with our high-risk program as well as some of our other initiatives. The next summer, I took three weeks of vacation and stayed close to home, relaxing and reflecting on my life in general. For some strange reason, I could not stop thinking about retiring from work all together, although there was really no reason for me to do so. I still loved my job (most of the time) and now had ample spare time as well, but my thoughts of packing it all in became almost obsessive in nature. When I finally talked to Jake about it, he was not a big fan of the idea, although financially, we were doing very well just on his salary alone. After much more reflection and a lot of prayer, I ultimately decided to put in my notice at work, and almost immediately, I felt a big sense of relief over my decision. I still could not understand why my thoughts had become so focused on staying at home, but over the next few years, I came to believe God was preparing me for what was to come.

In October 2007, the girls from work took me out to dinner at one of the many Italian restaurants in the city, where we all said a fond farewell. This time, though, I could keep in touch with my nearest and dearest friends there, since I was not moving away. Jake completely surprised me by secretly arranging to have both kids come home with their partners for the weekend to celebrate my early retirement. Once again, we feasted on delicious cuisine at yet another Italian restaurant. I was so touched by his thoughtfulness! I truly believed that this period of our lives would be a new start for us, with both kids now out of the house and Jake doing so well with his recovery. He had now been eight years sober, and things were looking up for all of us.

I tried to spend my newfound freedom well. I decided to volunteer, both with my church, teaching Sunday school to the kindergarten class with my good friend Rachel, as well as with the local pregnancy center where my close friend Anna worked. It seemed that I still loved to help struggling young parents and children whether I was getting paid or not! I have always been naturally drawn to young mothers, fathers, and children and put my experience with public health to good use. I also sought out spiritual growth and friendship with other women by attending a weekly ladies' Bible study at church. Jake accompanied me to church each week, and together, we attended a series of small groups in the homes of our church friends.

My next-door neighbor and good friend Laura wanted to start a book club in our neighborhood, so one fall, we went door-to-door with flyers, inviting others to our group. The book club helped me get to know many of our female neighbors whom I had never met before. I continued to walk Ellie faithfully twice a day, and I also continued to attend the gym, which helped me lose over forty pounds the first winter I was at home. During the past two stressful decades, the weight had slowly crept onto my small frame, but I now looked and felt so much better, having gotten back to my normal weight. Like my mom before me, I was proud of my big accomplishment; I enjoyed buying clothes once more, and for fun, Jake and I took ballroom dancing classes for a couple of years.

In May 2008, Mackenzie graduated from the University of Guelph with her bachelor's degree in sociology, but sadly, she chose not to attend her ceremony. Always goal oriented and driven, she joined her childhood friends in northern Manitoba for tree planting that spring and summer so that she and her steady boyfriend, Rob, could spend the fall touring Europe. Mackenzie and Rob returned home exhausted but jubilant from their travels, just prior to Christmas, and in January 2009, Mackenzie flew to Australia with a girlfriend to continue her university education. Most unfortunately, while she was enjoying her year abroad, a string of tragic events occurred back home, each worse than the one before it.

# CHAPTER 32

# Storm Clouds

During the fall of 2008 and the winter of 2009, we lost both of our beloved cats. They were getting older, each one of them close to fifteen years of age, so it shouldn't have come as a big shock. One frosty day in November, I woke up and could not find Ernie anywhere in the house. After calling his name over and over and looking frantically for him, I finally found him under a desk in our basement, where he had died of either a stroke or a heart attack. He had been in renal failure for some time, but it was still devastating to lose our old friend.

The next January, Sandy developed type 2 diabetes, so being a nurse, I started giving him insulin injections twice a day. He seemed to rally for a few weeks, but toward the beginning of spring, he took a turn for the worse. Jake's aunt and uncle were visiting us at the time, as was Joan, so it was Aunt Julia who accompanied me to the vet's office just up the road. Sandy had been a great little cat, and I knew that Will especially would be very sad to hear the news of his death. Jake buried both cats on the big hill in front of our house, where we placed a small, flat granite stone left over from our recent home renovations, with both of their names engraved on it. I sometimes wonder if the stone remains there still and whether the new homeowners have any idea of its significance.

One Sunday in May 2009, I got an early-morning phone call from David and Barbara. They both sounded extremely upset, telling me that David's blood sugar had been exceedingly high for the past few days, and he had also been losing weight recently for no known reason. I was aware he had type 2 diabetes, which was supposedly being controlled by his diet, but the numbers were so high that I knew at once something must be terribly wrong. His unexplained weight loss also alarmed me, and I immediately thought of cancer, although I knew it could also be a sign of uncontrolled diabetes. I advised him to see his doctor as soon as possible and asked them to call me back when they had a better idea of what was going on.

After Dave had completed some bloodwork and received a full-body MRI, which he paid for out of his own pocket, he and Barb called me back with dire news. He had been given a diagnosis of primary liver cancer (probably due to fatty liver disease), which was inoperable due to its location. He had also been referred to a hepatologist, Dr. Pelly, who had once worked with Olivia on the GI unit of the King George Hospital. It turned out that David was not a good candidate for a liver transplant either, so there was very little they could do for him except to offer comfort and supportive measures with a prognosis of a few short weeks or months to live.

To say that the whole family was blindsided would be a serious understatement. Dave, Barb, and their two sons, Jamie and Brent, were totally heartbroken by the news, and I knew that once more I needed to travel back home to be with my brother and his family. I spent the entire month of June with them, going to doctors' appointments, picking up groceries and medications, and cooking the odd meal, but often just lending an ear (and shedding many tears along the way) to their worries and concerns. It was helpful to have some medical background of my own, and Olivia was a good advocate for us with Dr. Pelly. On June 24, Barb made David his last birthday cake, honoring seventy-three years of a life well lived. That was a bittersweet celebration, to be sure.

I spent as much time as I could with David, where I also had an opportunity to share with him how Jesus had become my best friend and how He could be David's best friend too. I am sure that my brother gave his life to Christ at some point during his terrible suffering and ordeal, as I personally witnessed the "peace that surpasses all understanding" (Philippians 4:6–7) come upon him. He and Barb carefully planned out his funeral arrangements and made important decisions for their business going forward without David at the helm. He made one final trip to his original tire store, where he was still working when he became ill, to say a last goodbye to some of the many employees and friends who had worked for him over the years.

At the beginning of July, needing to return home, I sorrowfully left David and Barbara, unsure if I would ever see my wonderful big brother again. I had been back home in the Soo for only a month when I got a phone call from Barb, telling me to come back to Halifax as soon as possible. Since Jake was working, I quickly packed a bag and flew back to Halifax by myself. Jamie's son, Mark, picked me up at the airport in the early afternoon of August 4, as the rest of the immediate family were at the hospital with David. He had remained at home for as long as Barb could manage his care, but the weekend before, it had become too much for her, and he had been transferred to the KGH. The team caring for him felt his death was imminent and had called for all the family to be there. Jamie and Brent, along with Barb and Jamie's wife, Emma, were still in his room with him when I arrived with Mark. They were all exhausted, so they took the opportunity to go home for a short rest and to get something to eat while I stayed with my brother.

He seemed to be resting comfortably and was in a deep sleep due to being heavily sedated with morphine for the pain. I was bitterly disappointed because I desperately wanted him to know that I was there with him at the very end. Nevertheless, I felt a deep sense of peace and calm descend upon us as I sat there in the chair next to David's bed, and I knew beyond a shadow of a doubt that God was with us.

Suddenly, while I was bending over him, he woke up, opened his eyes wide, and stared up at me with a look of surprised recognition on his face. "I love you, David," I quickly told him before he closed his eyes once again and went back to sleep. I truly believe God gave my brother and me that brief but all-important time together at the end of his life. In hindsight, I think he was waiting to see me before he departed this world for the next. David passed peacefully away later that evening with his son Brent by his bedside. We all traveled back to the hospital that night to say our final goodbyes to a man we all greatly loved and admired and who could never be replaced in our hearts. Larger than life, David was genuinely one of a kind.

A few days later, there was standing room only for the many mourners at his funeral. David had been a prominent businessman in Halifax as well as a big patron of the local hockey team. He and Barb had a lot of family and friends who wanted to pay their last respects. One of the hymns they had chosen together was "In the Garden"; as we all sang together, I had a beautiful image in my mind of David walking with Jesus in heaven. It was so reassuring for me to know where my brother had gone and whom he was with.

With Jake standing by my side, I was honored to give the eulogy that day, which was challenging for me to get through but an important part of my own journey. Due to the lateness of the season and David's own wishes, he was cremated and would be buried the next spring in the Lower Brighton Cemetery beside the rest of our family. I flew back home to the Soo with a heavy heart, starkly aware that nothing would be the same for me, ever again. I had now lost both of my parents as well as both of my brothers, and at the age of fifty-three, I was the last surviving member of my birth family. It was a very lonely feeling indeed.

That fall, I had a chance to kill two birds with one stone. Joan was now dealing with vascular dementia, like what my own father had suffered with many years before. She had spent several winters with us in our home and would afterward travel back to Halifax to spend the rest of the year with her daughter Debbie. As a result, her home in Herring Bay sat vacant and unloved, and she was very homesick for the Rock. Feeling badly for her, I offered to take her back to Newfoundland for a visit and to help her complete some long-overdue medical appointments. After talking to him on the phone, Will shared with me that he was eager to return to his home province as well and to have a good visit with his grandmother and me. With our plans finally settled, we all agreed to meet up in St. John's for Thanksgiving.

In early October, I flew to Halifax and connected with Joan in the departure lounge of the airport; the two of us then traveled on to St. John's. Joan's first comment to me earlier had been, "Now, I'm in charge," which made me wonder what I had in store. We picked William up from the St. John's airport later that same day, after he had flown in from Ottawa. The three of us had a great week together, with Nana cooking a small turkey with all the trimmings. We made sure to have at least one meal of the traditional fish and chips as we toured around St. John's and its surrounding area. Most importantly, Joan was able to visit with her sisters and other extended family members from both sides of the family. It turned out to be a wonderful homecoming for her!

The week was not without its problems, however, since Joan, greatly relishing her freedom, was determined to drive her small SUV around both town and country. I knew from Jake's cousin, Sheila, that she had had many close calls in the past and was not well enough to drive. She and I had it out one day in her optometrist's parking lot, where I finally called her bluff. I reluctantly passed the car keys over to her as she sat stewing in the passenger seat, and I courageously asked her to switch spots with me. I guess it came down to a matter of choice, because she immediately backed down and returned the keys to me without further complaint. I know for a fact that God does indeed have a sense of humor and finds a way to work out even the smallest details of our lives! The following year, Jake and Debbie put their family home up for sale, and the next time Joan went there for a visit, it was her final one.

The spring and summer of 2010 were a particularly bleak time for me, following the heartbreak of the previous year. When I think back upon it even now, it all seems like a bad dream. April started off well, with Jake and I taking a beautiful cruise around the coast of Brazil. Afterward, his mom came to visit us for a few weeks, and then we all planned to fly back east together on the Victoria Day long weekend in May. We would drop Joan off at Debbie's home in Halifax, and then the two of us would drive up to New Brunswick to attend my brother's burial in Woodstock. Unfortunately, several fateful events occurred leading up to our trip, which were most certainly a foreshadowing of what was to come.

Jake was acting strangely and seemed distracted in general. He had recently become preoccupied with his appearance; he was now wearing contact lenses, regularly going to tanning beds, working out at the gym, and growing out his sideburns. He also started splashing on large amounts of aftershave and cologne each day. He seemed obsessed with his oral hygiene, and when I looked under the sink in the second bathroom upstairs, I found at least eight large bottles of mouthwash, which he told me he had purchased on sale. I wondered if he had started drinking it, although I had no evidence of that. Instead, I chose to believe that he was simply going through a midlife crisis.

One day, when I was unpacking his overnight bag after a trip to

Toronto, I was horrified to discover a packaged condom in the inside zippered pocket. When I confronted him about it later that evening, he denied it was his and said it belonged to another male coworker he had shared a room with. I had a hard time believing him because he never shared a room with anyone else when he traveled, and as far as I knew, he usually traveled alone. As I started looking around for more incriminating evidence, I discovered porn on our home computer after I completed a search history. His secretive and disgusting pastime was especially disturbing, since his mother slept in the bedroom across the hall.

My thoughts slowly drifted back to Labour Day weekend in 2007, when my niece's first marriage had broken up, and she had flown up to the Soo to spend the long weekend with us. One morning, while Jessica was still there, Jake had a terrible meltdown in our driveway, admitting that he had recently lost his wedding band. He seemed frantic, almost ranting and raving, so the three of us started searching for it until I finally found it on the floor of the back seat of his truck. It seemed like a strange place to lose a wedding ring, and Jessica later told me that she thought I should hire a private investigator to follow Jake because she did not trust him. At the time, I dismissed her suggestion, as I never once imagined he would cheat on me. This time, however, unlike losing his wedding band, he acted like having a condom in his luggage was no big deal at all. Since I had no proof of any actual cheating, I put my ever-growing suspicions on the back burner and prepared for the difficult journey home to bury my brother. Unbeknownst to me, ominous, dark storm clouds were gathering on the horizon, and a deluge of rain was about to begin.

# CHAPTER 33

# The Worst of Betrayals

It was very early in the morning on a beautiful day in mid-May when Jake, Joan, and I set off for Toronto. Since we were also delivering furniture to Mackenzie in Oakville on our return trip home, we ended up taking Jake's small red truck. During the few times we stopped to take a break, Jake was constantly texting on his cell phone. I wanted to believe that he was preoccupied with work-related matters, but his strange behavior certainly caught my eye.

Unfortunately, since his elderly mother was with us, I had to sit on the jump seat in the back of the truck, all the way from Sault Ste. Marie to Newmarket, where his aunt and uncle lived. It was a seven-hour trip over a two-lane highway, and my poor back felt like it could give out at any moment. Jake's driving had never been good at the best of times, but now it was downright reckless. I offered up a silent prayer of thanks after we flew through a red light near his relatives' address. Indeed, it was a miracle we weren't all killed that day. We finally arrived at their home and had a brief visit with Aunt Julia and Uncle Ron, parking our truck in their driveway. We then got a limo to the airport in Toronto and arrived in Halifax late in the day.

Jake's sister Debbie picked us all up at the airport and drove us to her house just outside the city. We had eaten an early dinner at Pearson airport, so when Jake announced that he wanted to take his mom's SUV out for a short drive to get a coffee, I was not all that surprised. But after our lengthy trip, I was played out and planned to go to bed early that night, since we were driving up to Woodstock the next morning. I told

190

him I was not interested in going out with him, and off he went on his own, seemingly undeterred.

As the evening ended and Jake had not yet returned home, I became more and more worried about him, as did his family. I tried calling him on his cell phone, but it automatically went to voice mail, so I assumed he had it turned off, on airplane mode, or it had finally died. Keenly aware of his poor driving habits, I had visions of him lying dead or being badly injured by the side of the road. Finally, when it was approaching midnight and we had still not heard back from him, Debbie's longtime boyfriend, Andy, went out to look for Jake with her teenage son. Andy worked for the city and knew every inch of it. If he could not find Jake, he could not be found. Surprisingly, the pair returned home about an hour later with no sightings of either Jake or the SUV anywhere, and I sensed the situation had suddenly turned much more serious.

Finally, searching for any possible clues to his whereabouts, Andy and I went upstairs to look through Jake's backpack, and what we discovered was disturbing, to say the least. Inside one of the inner pouches was a leather cardholder full of seven or eight credit cards, none of which I was aware of. I knew, then and there, that he was up to his old tricks of hiding both his illicit spending and the lifestyle that went with it. I experienced a terrible sinking feeling inside my stomach, and it felt like my whole world was once again crashing down upon me. Later, as we all sat around the kitchen table still waiting for any news of Jake, we decided to start calling the local hospitals and police stations to see if we could find him. Once again, he was nowhere to be found.

Around 3:00 a.m., just as I was about to give up all hope, Jake pulled up into the driveway and waltzed in through the back door, acting as if nothing had ever happened. Miraculously, he did not have even one scratch on him. Right away, he started regaling us with a far-fetched story about how his mother's SUV (which was always in good working order) had broken down, and he had been left stranded by the side of the road all this time. He also told us that he had lost his cell phone, which was why he had not answered my calls. Not one of us believed his tall tale. When we finally went up to bed, I decided to have it out with him once and for all. I showed him what Andy and I had found in his backpack, and I told him no sane person would believe his ridiculous story.

After about twenty minutes of evading my questions, he must have realized the jig was up. With a pained expression on his face, he finally blurted out that he had been caught red-handed in a sting operation by the Halifax police, involving prostitutes at a fleabag motel along Bedford Basin. They had arrested him, confiscated his phone, and escorted him downtown to the main station, where he was charged with solicitation of prostitution and then released on bail. He had been texting with an undercover cop earlier in the day instead of the "happy hooker" he had been hoping to meet up with.

Stunned beyond belief, I was completely speechless for several moments, as the terrible truth started to sink in. I remember slapping him across the face and asking him, over and over, "How could you?" He had no answer for me, and when I finally crawled into bed, exhausted but too full of adrenaline to sleep, I could not turn off the thoughts of self-recrimination in my mind and feelings of self-loathing in my heart. Totally blindsided, I blamed myself for being so trusting that I had not seen what was going on behind my back. (It really is true that the wife is usually the last to know.) I have since learned that many people also tend to blame the victim instead of placing the blame where it rightly belongs. That night was only the first of many sleepless nights for me. My mind was racing as I tried to piece everything together, eventually realizing that his double life of cheating and crime must have been going on for some time. Our marriage felt so tainted, and I was so disgusted with his behavior that I never wanted to have anything to do with him ever again.

Unfortunately, when I arose on Friday morning, I knew I would have to somehow get through the coming week with Jake by my side. I had tried calling my nephew Brent to see if I could catch a ride up to New Brunswick with him, but he was not answering his phone. In fact, I could not get hold of anyone in my family, so I knew I would have no choice but to share a car for seven long hours with the man who had become a monster to me overnight. I would just have to try to survive the long weekend.

The burial service for David was set for Sunday morning, with a reception and family dinner scheduled afterward. On Monday, I planned to visit Susan, my good friend since grade school; she now lived with her husband in Nackawic, a small pulp-and-paper town just below Woodstock. I had not seen Susan since shortly after her wedding many years before, but we had recently reconnected. I was hoping and praying I would make it through until Monday.

I forced Jake to tell his sister everything about the previous night's activities before we left for Woodstock. I have no idea how that conversation went down, as I couldn't get out of the house fast enough. It was not lost upon me that Jake's underhanded dealings had also been revealed in front of his whole family. Obviously, God wanted them to know the truth about their son and brother. On the road to Woodstock, driving in Joan's vehicle, I was still totally in shock and incredulous. I repeated my question from the night before over and over, and shouted at him intermittently, "How could you?" He never once answered me.

It is no small wonder that we didn't have an accident that day or in the days to follow. When we finally checked into the New International Inn in Woodstock, I was surprised and relieved to discover that Jamie and Emma were directly across the hall from us. What were the odds of that happening? It was comforting to know that I had family members who loved me and cared about me so close by, and I could call upon them if I got into trouble. During our three-night stay, I think I once threw a toothbrush at Jake, but other than that, no violence was incurred there that weekend.

During those dark, dark days, it seemed I could not stop crying, but of course, Sunday morning was the hardest. In addition to feeling tremendous sadness and loss over losing my beloved brother, I felt compelled to play the charade of being in a happy, loving marriage in front of all my family. I did not want to burden them even more when they were already mourning the loss of their husband, father, and grandfather. The burial service was a large one, but the spring weather was perfect, and some of the mourners spotted several deer grazing in a nearby field. It truly felt like my brother was with me in spirit that day while I accepted the heartfelt condolences of old neighbors, extended family, and friends. Later that day, we picked up my frail and elderly aunt Ruth from her retirement home and took her with us to the family dinner; she walked with a cane and was ninety-six years of age by then. That was the last time I ever saw her because she died rather suddenly the next year from complications related to a fractured hip.

We ended up spending most of Monday with Susan and her husband at their home, where once again, I tried to act like everything was normal.

It felt like God was surrounding me with people who genuinely cared about me, and it was comforting to know that I was not alone in my misery. Despite everything, we had a nice visit with them, and when we arrived in Halifax at the end of the next day, I dropped in to see my friend Olivia to tell her what had happened. She was completely dumbfounded and blown away; when I confessed to her that I blamed myself for not knowing what was going on, she consoled me by saying that I had trusted him not to cheat because I would never cheat on him. That was all too true.

For some reason, despite all the anger and fury I was feeling toward him, I still tried to help Jake. I shared with Olivia that he would eventually have to face court in Halifax for charges of solicitation, and I asked her if she knew of a good criminal lawyer who could represent him. In fact, she did, and she proceeded to give me the name of a top attorney in the city who "always gets all of the worst crooks off."

After flying back to Toronto, we spent the final leg of our journey in Oakville, Ontario, where we stayed a few days with Mackenzie and her boyfriend, Rob. Mackenzie was now working with an organization as a therapist for young children, while Rob worked with technology. She and Rob had just moved into their first apartment together and were in bad need of some furniture. We retrieved Jake's truck from his aunt's home and delivered our used furniture to their new home. It was impossible for me to act like things were normal around my inquisitive and intuitive daughter, as she knew me all too well, and in fact she did ask me what was wrong on more than one occasion. I couldn't bear to tell her anything at the time because the naked truth was just too awful and too ugly to share with my children.

Looking back, I can say with total honesty and clarity that the whole experience of that week was probably the worst in my entire life, and as Jake and I drove back home to the Soo, our future was anything but certain. For reasons of his own, Jake acted very angrily toward me, and his emotions were so unstable I feared that he might drive into the rock cliffs along the Canadian Shield more than once. In fact, he threatened to do just that. My guardian angel must have been with me for sure, as we finally arrived home safe in body, though not sound in mind. All I could think of over and over was, *How could he do this to me, especially on the weekend of my brother's burial?* If there were any easy answers, they were not forthcoming.

# CHAPTER 34

# How Do You Mend a Broken Heart?

For the first few days after we arrived back home in Sault Ste. Marie, I felt and acted like a zombie. I was almost paralyzed with fear. I had so many decisions to make about my marriage, but the most immediate one involved getting Jake to move out of the house. There was no way I was going to be the one to move out this time around, given what I had just discovered about him. As he returned to work and tried to pretend that nothing had changed in our relationship, I gradually began to reveal the truth to my family and close friends about what had happened. This included Barbara and Jessica as well as my close friends Lydia, Rachel, and Anna. They were all shocked by my story, and in fact, none of them could believe it. Barb was especially surprised, and her comment to me years afterward was "You could have knocked me over with a feather." Unfortunately, it was all too true, and Rachel and her husband, Lucas, our close friends from church, agreed with me that Jake *had* to move out of the house.

Together, we came up with a plan. One afternoon the following week, Rachel came over to my house and was waiting with me when Jake arrived home from work. This time, it was he who was shocked when he walked in and saw his welcoming party! Lucas's brother Gary was parked along the road near our house in case we had any problems with Jake. Gary's wife, Sarah, was a trained therapist as well as a friend from church, and she had kindly offered to help me work through my thoughts and feelings, informally, over several luncheon dates. It seemed that God was surrounding me with His best people, all ready to lend both an ear and a helping hand.

When I finally confronted Jake that day and told him that what he had done to me was completely unacceptable and we could not live under the same roof anymore, he became very indignant with me and immediately lost his temper. As his countenance turned red with rage, he got right in my face and started yelling at me, while Rachel looked on in stunned disbelief. Used to dealing with emergencies at work, I stood my ground with him until (thankfully) Lucas arrived and demanded that Jake back off and stop his threatening behavior. Like the true bully he was, he backed down right away. I thank God I was not alone with him that day because I really don't know what he might have done or how far he would have gone to get his own way.

Emboldened by the support of my friends, I instructed Jake to get a suitcase and pack up his belongings right away; when he reluctantly went to the basement and brought up a tiny overnight bag, I told him to go back down and get a larger suitcase, as he would be gone for a long time. He did just that, packing up his clothes and personal items, and left without further complaint or incident. I heaved a huge sigh of relief, as did Rachel and Lucas, and this time, I had the foresight to ask Jake for his house keys as well.

A day or so after Jake left, Mackenzie called to ask me a question about how to cook chicken. Unfortunately, I was not doing well at that point, and I broke down completely, telling her what her father had done. She immediately started to cry and said she wanted to come home. I knew her father's betrayal would be especially hard on her because she had always been close to him. Both kids ended up flying home for the weekend, and we spent our time together talking and crying. I knew they loved me very much, and I so appreciated their caring attitude and support. I was bereft when they left again on Monday, but I knew life had to go on.

Instead, I concentrated on trying to put the pieces of my life back together again. I made sure I met with my friends each week, and I also saw a counsellor through my workplace insurance. She was an impeccably dressed older lady, probably in her midseventies, who was also the organist at her church. I am sure she was shocked over the revelations about my marriage, and at one point she laughed nervously, saying that she thought she would prefer her husband to have an affair with a man rather than with a woman. I don't know how she thought her declaration would be helpful to me in any way, shape, or form, and after a few more sessions with her, I never went back. I was getting far more emotional support from meeting Sarah for lunch, when she listened to me in confidence as a friend.

There was no concrete help from my pastor, either, as he never once acknowledged that he was aware of any problem within my marriage; Rachel, however, shared with me that he knew what had transpired with Jake. He had learned that my church friends were helping me, and I guess he thought that let him off the hook. It seems that many pastors are not comfortable or even properly trained to assist their church members who are going through a crisis, especially that of a sexual nature. Nevertheless, I continued to go to church each week and often sat with Rachel, since Lucas sang in the choir and was the worship leader. Even though it was a large church with a big congregation, I felt self-conscious, but if anyone noticed that I came to church without Jake, they didn't say anything to me about it.

I never told any of my neighbors that Jake had moved out, as I was so ashamed of what he had done, and I dreaded telling people the awful truth. For several years, we had been included in hosting and attending occasional dinners with a large group of our neighbors, so this was very hard for me. I also quit my volunteer job with the local pregnancy center, since I just couldn't face it anymore. It was an extremely lonely time for me despite being able to lean on my family and closest friends for support. Now I finally understood why I had felt so compelled to quit my job almost three years earlier; there was no way I would have been able to pull myself together enough to get up and go out to work each day.

I spent a lot of time in prayer, and one morning, quite miraculously, I woke up feeling like a huge weight had physically been lifted off my shoulders. I had been carrying around a huge spiritual burden and was not even aware of it until God took it away. I felt about ten pounds lighter—what a wonderful friend and Savior we have in Jesus, just like the old hymn says! As Christians, we are so privileged to be able to carry all our burdens to Him in prayer. In Matthew 11:30, Jesus tells us, "For my yoke is easy and my burden is light."

I also tried to keep myself physically active at home by cleaning the house, walking Ellie, continuing to work out, and painting our huge back deck. One day when I was outdoors on the patio, a thunderous sound erupted from the small forest beside our house. Shortly afterward, a black bear cub emerged from within the trees and came galloping across the lawn toward me, followed closely behind by the mother bear! Ellie and I wasted no time in getting back inside the house. Overall, though, I still had way too much time on my hands for my own good.

There were some practical and unpleasant issues that needed to be dealt with as well. One of the first things I did after I returned home from the Maritimes was to visit the nurse practitioner in my family doctor's office to have blood tests taken and a physical examination completed. I was terrified that I may have been exposed to a sexually transmitted infection, although Jake had tried to reassure me that we were both fine, as he "always used a condom." After working for years in this area, I knew just how unreliable that notion was, and I could not rest easy until I had been thoroughly checked out. Thankfully, all was normal, and I knew I had dodged another bullet. God had performed another miracle for me, but I wondered, not for the first time, what may have caused all the abnormal Pap test results I had received over the years. Our bodies naturally try to clear out invading organisms, such as HPV (human papillomavirus), and this may have been my saving grace.

The icing on the cake was that I also had a colossal financial mess to clean up. After grilling him about it, I discovered that Jake had rented a secret post office box at a local store, where his new credit card statements were quickly piling up. I slowly collected them and was horrified to discover that he owed close to $70,000. There was no other option but to take that money out of our joint investments to pay off his spiraling debt; afterward, I wasted no time in cancelling all his credit cards. I was furious with him for placing us both in such a precarious financial position yet again, but what else could I do but try to make things right? I certainly could not trust him to fix the problems of his own making.

Throughout the remainder of the spring and summer, Jake continued to work and lived in the basement apartment of a bungalow in a subdivision a few streets over from our house. He had the audacity to show up one day, the week after he moved out, with a bouquet of red roses for me. He knew how much I loved flowers, and I guess he thought that would do the trick. I took his flowers, but I never allowed him back inside the house.

After much pleading on his part, I finally agreed to meet him once a week for coffee, usually at a local cafe. Our meetings were strained at best, and I really did not see much point to them. He continued to show up at church as well, where I just tried to ignore him. I knew he was desperate to reconcile with me, but I had no idea how I would ever trust him or forgive him again. I was just too trusting and too loyal; those were two of my biggest problems.

# CHAPTER 35

# Something Old, Something New

That August, Jessica was preparing to get married once again, and she had kindly asked me to stand up with her. I was very excited to fly down to southern Ontario early in the month to visit her and her fiancé, Matt, and help them prepare for their wedding at the end of the month. One day, Jess and I decided to drop by to visit our aunt Alice, who lived about a twenty-minute drive away from Jessica's home in Newmarket.

Right away, we realized she was not doing well. She now lived alone on a rural property in Uxbridge and was too far away from SSM for me to be able to help her out in any meaningful way. The house was literally falling down around her ears, but worse still, she herself was in bad physical condition. It appeared that she had become a hoarder, as there were multiple garbage bags full of used tissues and other junk in one of the bedrooms as well as soiled linens on her bed and layers upon layers of dirt in her home. The kitchen sink was full of black, inky water of some kind. Nothing had been thrown out, replaced, or upgraded in a very long time by the looks of things, and although she was in her right mind, she was not making sound decisions about her own welfare. To top it off, she had a habit of fainting, often when she was standing in line at the checkout of the supermarket; each time, the poor manager would have to call an ambulance to transport her to the nearest hospital. She obviously had some serious health as well as public health issues, not the least of which were the animals that had taken up residence in her attic and inside her home.

As both a public health nurse and her niece, it felt awful to see her living like this, but no amount of persuading or reasoning would get her to move out of her beloved home or even begin to consider the idea of going to a retirement home. She had more than enough money to pay for assisted living, so means was not the issue. She had been married to my father's youngest brother, Uncle Carl, and because he had passed away from cancer many years before and they had no children, there was no one to step in and take charge. Her own family were all deceased, and her only relatives were distant cousins who lived in the United Kingdom and the United States.

Simply put, like my aunt Ruth in New Brunswick, Aunt Alice was a particularly strong-willed and independent woman of a certain age (she was in her early eighties by then) who was not interested in listening to advice from anyone. I was especially concerned about her physical and social isolation, since she only seemed to have one neighbor whom she kept in touch with. We exchanged phone numbers before I returned to the Soo, and I asked her to please let me know if my aunt took another turn for the worse or ended up in the ER once again. Jill promised to do just that.

Following Jess and Matt's beautiful outdoor wedding, I flew back home, where I started to worry incessantly about Aunt Alice's predicament. Like my fixation on quitting work a few years before this, I went over and over her numerous and complex issues in my mind, trying to problem-solve the situation. I called everyone I could think of who might have been able to help me with my aunt. This included the social worker (SW) at the local hospital, the community mental health worker, the public health inspector, the police, and even a long-term care coordinator to determine what the process would be to get Aunt Alice on the waitlist for a nursing home. In addition to all of this, I researched some of the nicer retirement homes nearest to her, but really, I was just spinning my wheels without her cooperation. There was not much else I could do because she was legally of sound mind. The whole affair was extremely upsetting and frustrating for me, and it kept me awake at night. I was worried that she would die all alone in that horrible old house and not be found by anyone for days on end. It was a gruesome thought.

Thankfully, providence intervened. When I phoned her neighbor Jill a week or so later, she told me the ambulance had been called to my aunt's home that very morning to take her to the hospital. When I phoned the hospital, the social worker whom I had previously talked with remembered our recent conversation and was aware of just how dire my aunt's situation really was. Fortunately, Aunt Alice was still in the ER, but as usual, she was not being truthful about her circumstances. Once again, she would be discharged back home later that day if they found no reason to admit her to the hospital.

Aware that she was frail and underweight, I asked the SW if the hospital could at least run some bloodwork and other tests on her before they discharged her. Fortunately, my tenacious aunt agreed to this, and the hospital was able to keep her for a little while longer. The social worker was sympathetic to her plight and told me about one newer retirement home located in the countryside that might have a current opening. She would call them right away and get back to me before they discharged Aunt Alice back home.

Amazingly, the SW managed to talk her into going over to check out the retirement home, which was in the same region she lived in. It turned out to be a huge, sprawling bungalow in a private and rural setting, where deer often came to graze on the wide-open, meandering lawn. It was run by the couple who owned the home, so it was more like a real home than an institution, which better suited my aunt. Right then and there, she agreed to stay, and I was ready to shout hallelujah! I heaved a huge sigh of relief that she would finally have a clean, safe home to live in. She would also receive some much-needed medical attention and home care for her personal needs. It seemed like the perfect solution to a horrible dilemma. I knew that, once again, God was in the mix.

Now we just had to decide what to do with her old ramshackle house, which was not an easy task! Jess and Matt stood up to the plate and did the heavy lifting on that one for me. As luck would have it, Matt worked in the construction industry and was able to rent two huge containers to hold the junk and garbage while I hired a company to clean up the house so that it was safe enough to enter. They specialized in sanitizing murder scenes in Toronto, and I imagined they were more than up to the task. They also set up a huge trap on the roof of the house and caught a twenty-five-pound raccoon that had been living in her attic; there were also rats in the basement and a nest of mice living in the back of her favorite easy chair. There was not much worth saving, but Jess and Matt managed to salvage some photos, china, and glassware. We ended up throwing out most of her clothes, as they were not really fit to wear. The house and property were eventually sold, and Aunt Alice settled quite nicely into her new digs.

The next winter, I gave a talk about my experience with my aunt to the employees and volunteers who worked with patients and clients with dementia at an annual conference hosted by their organization. My good friend and next-door neighbor, Laura, was the executive director, and being familiar with my story, she asked me to provide a personal viewpoint. I did some research on the subject, and it turned out that my aunt was suffering from something called Diogenes syndrome, a behavioral disorder displaying the characteristics of hoarding, domestic squalor, extreme self-neglect, and a general lack of shame over the whole situation. I was more than happy to be able to shed some light on a rather rare condition that afflicts the elderly population who live alone.

On a brighter note, when I returned home from my niece's wedding in late August 2010, something had changed deep inside of me. I had been thinking a lot about Jake recently, and I was trying very hard to forgive him. I went to one last counselling session, and on the drive home, I turned on the radio and listened to a Carrie Underwood song, one about heartbreak and redemption. I felt that I wanted to give both Jake and our marriage one last chance despite still having some misgivings. If he let me down for the third time, like in baseball, he would be out.

That week, when we met for coffee, I tentatively broached the subject with him. He seemed conflicted about the idea for a few moments but then agreed that he was doing much better and was ready to move back home. He reassured me that he had been seeing a counsellor over the past few months as well as attending Alcoholics Anonymous meetings weekly and was working on overall self-improvement. Most importantly, he agreed to attend Christian counselling with me in southwestern Ontario later that year. I had heard about the ministry from Rachel, who had highly recommended it. The pastor specialized in helping individuals and couples overcome spiritual battles and strongholds while addressing their effect on one's mental and emotional health. Jake and I would each have to complete a personality profile, which we would then mail to the pastor (who was also a therapist). He would then assess our compatibility for the program and hopefully put us on the waitlist.

Jake moved back home in early September, but our kids were not supportive of our decision, to put it mildly. They still did not trust him, but I was careful enough this time around to not be totally stupid. Although he was physically back in the house, we had little physical contact, as I felt he still had to prove to me that he could be faithful. It was impossible to get the images of those women out of my mind, and I finally broke down one night and questioned him about them.

He confessed to me that the cheating had begun during the time when we had lived in that old rental house in The Pas. Unsatisfied with his vague answer, I asked him about his more recent activities, around the time of David's burial in May 2010. He admitted to me that during the months of March and April, he had probably slept with eighteen or more women, some of them as young as eighteen years of age. (The first part of April, we had been on our cruise, which made his confession that much worse.) I felt so disgusted by his admission—those girls were much younger than even his own daughter! That was typical behavior for him, apparently. He had obviously struggled not only with alcoholism but also a very severe sexual addiction throughout the years.

It was just too awful to comprehend, and when I pressed him even further about ever having had an affair, he just looked at me miserably and said, "Who would have me?" My angry and hurt response to him was "What about me?" Right then and there, I wondered if I had made a terrible mistake by taking him back. Although he had an attitude of entitlement, he obviously had very low self-esteem and did not seem to value either himself or me, his faithful wife of thirty-one years. His unexpected candidness that day was a real eye-opener for me, but he also admitted, "None of my behavior is your fault," which gave me a small measure of comfort at least.

That October, I invited Olivia to fly to the Soo for a visit, which was a pleasant distraction from my ongoing problems and concerns. I also wanted to show her a bit of beautiful northern Michigan, so we drove across the border to the small city of Traverse to go shopping for a couple of days, stopping in several quaint seaside towns along the way. Most of our family and friends were rooting for me and Jake, although it was hard to know what people really thought. That Christmas, I spent the holidays with Mackenzie, Rob, and Will in Oakville, while Jake remained behind in the Soo. Our children had still not forgiven him for his transgressions and did not want to see him. After I flew back home for New Year's, we opened our gifts from each other and tried to celebrate the dawning of 2011. I could only hope and pray that this year would be much better than the previous one.

On Valentine's Day weekend in 2011, Jake and I celebrated six months back together as a couple by attending a relationship retreat at our church. At the end of the two days, we quietly sat on the hard wooden pews, repeating our renewed vows to each other. Unfortunately, we were still waiting to get a date for the in-depth counselling that I really felt we both needed. On the other hand, I finally believed we were both committed to making our marriage work, and although I was on the road to forgiveness, I could never quite forget his betrayal. Perhaps the passage of time would accomplish that.

# CHAPTER 36

# The Last Straw

Toward the end of March, a strange event occurred. Things were going well with Jake and me (or so I thought), and he had even talked me into taking a transatlantic cruise (and subsequent trip to Paris) with him that upcoming May. I had initially been very hesitant to commit to going on another trip because we still had not completed our counselling sessions, since the ministry was backlogged with people on the waitlist. I managed to put my reservations aside, however, and decided to take a chance on things working out.

One Friday night, Jake came home with some precooked lobster and offered to make dinner for me. There was nothing I loved more than lobster, so I sat down in anticipation of a delicious meal. For some reason, the lobster seemed rather tasteless, but the color and consistency appeared normal. Although he had lobster on his plate, Jake, who usually tolerated the delicacy, just sat there and watched me eat it all by myself. Finally, I asked him straight-out why he wasn't eating, but he evaded my question and continued to watch me closely with a funny look on his face. Ever so slowly, the hair on the nape of my neck started to tingle, and a sense of impending doom began to spread throughout my body. Something was not right.

Shortly after I went to bed that night, I became violently ill with horrendous abdominal cramps and nausea that did not subside until dawn was breaking. It felt like my insides were imploding, but the strange thing was I had no other symptoms of food poisoning. My groans of pain were so bad at one point during the night that Ellie, lying downstairs on her

206

doggie bed, started barking frantically, as if she knew there was something seriously wrong with me. I considered going to the hospital, which was newly built and just around the corner from us, but I toughed it out until the symptoms finally disappeared. Jake remained as silent as the tomb throughout my night of misery. In my mind, I wondered if Jake had deliberately tried to make me ill, although I could not imagine why he would do such a terrible thing. He was feeling fine and dandy, as he had not even had so much as one bite of the lobster meat! I tried to put the incident out of my mind, but a nagging suspicion lingered.

The next Monday evening, Jake announced he was going to the gym, which he usually did two or three times a week. I took no notice of him and instead tucked a cozy afghan around myself on the couch, settling down to watch TV. About a half hour after Jake left, our home phone rang, so I got up to answer it. When I said, "Hello," no one answered, although I could hear muffled talking in the background. I figured out right away that it was Jake, talking to a woman. There seemed to be a lot of banter between them, but the only thing I could clearly make out was Jake saying, "You've put in new flooring since I was here last." I thought about where he worked out and wondered if that was the place he was referring to. I continued to listen in as I slowly realized he had pocket-dialed our phone number by accident.

I must have remained on the phone for about twenty minutes until I finally clued into what was going on. He was not working out but was instead having sex with a woman! I felt completely revolted and sickened by what I was hearing, but honestly, it did not come as a complete surprise to me, even though it was shocking to hear it with my own ears. Unable to endure listening to any more heavy breathing, I hung up the phone and immediately called Jessica. Her first words to me were "I knew you should have hired a private investigator." When I also told her about the weird incident on Friday night, she agreed with me that I needed to get out of the house and away from Jake as soon as possible. I now wondered if my very life might be in danger because his deviant behavior seemed to be escalating. I literally felt sick to my stomach and very foolish to have given him one last chance.

Sitting on pins and needles, I waited for him to come home, which he did about an hour later. The strange thing was he looked just the same as when he had left the house. When he finally fell asleep in his easy chair, I tiptoed to the hall closet and went through all the pockets in his leather jacket as quietly as I could. Immediately, I found a money clip with five hundred dollars in it, a clear indication that he was once again up to his old tricks with the credit cards. I couldn't believe it! But as Dr. Phil used to say, "The best indicator of future behavior is past behavior," which was all too true with Jake. As far as I knew, he was not drinking again, but that paled in comparison to the sexually addictive behaviors he indulged in, including his issues with pornography, strip clubs, and prostitutes. Not for the first time, I wondered what else he could be caught up in; the Soo hosted a large casino downtown, and I began to think he may have become a compulsive gambler as well.

That night, I felt very frightened to be under the same roof as him, but I tried to act as if everything was normal. I don't think I slept a wink, but instead, I stared at the ceiling all night long, reciting Psalm 23 over and over in my mind. It begins, "The Lord is my shepherd, I shall not be in want ... Even though I walk through the valley of the shadow of death, I will fear no evil, for you are with me." I had memorized the whole passage when I was in Sunday school many years before and had to recite the last verse at the front of the church one Sunday: "Surely, goodness and love will follow me all the days of my life, and I will dwell in the house of the Lord forever." I knew God was with me in my darkest hours, as He always had been. God's divine attributes are omniscience (all-knowing), omnipotence (all-powerful), omnipresence (all-present), and omnibenevolence (all-loving). His character is eternally unchanging, and His Word (the Bible) is faithful and true.

The next morning, I flew into action; after Jake left for work, I started to go through our bills. Under a pile of papers in the den, I finally found his cell phone bill with scores of itemized calls to a business called Black Rose. I immediately went onto the internet and discovered that it was a "massage spa" in the city. If I had any remaining doubts about what I had overheard the night before, there were none left now. I knew what I had to do next, so I reluctantly phoned my daughter that afternoon and told her the latest news about her father. I asked if I could stay with her and Rob in Oakville for a few weeks until I landed on my feet. I could not stay with my niece, as I would have to bring Ellie, and Jessica's cat would not be very happy with a large dog in the house! Brokenhearted about her father once more, Mackenzie (and Rob) generously agreed to let the two of us stay with them temporarily until I could find a suitable place for us to live. I later phoned Will in Ottawa and broke the news to him as well. Although they were extremely disappointed, neither one of my children were terribly surprised by Jake's latest escapades. By that time, it was evident that Jake was a compulsive liar and risk-taker, struggled with multiple addictions, and displayed criminal behavior. It was not a pretty picture.

Once again, I wondered if he could possibly have bipolar disorder (BD); it seemed more than likely. I also considered that he may have developed antisocial personality disorder (ASPD)—not being an expert in mental health, I could not be sure, but I was aware that the two disorders often overlap. Not for the first time, I pondered how this could have possibly happened to me. I was one of the most cautious people I knew, but I had become trapped in a terrible marriage within a cycle of abuse, and once a person is in that situation, it can be very difficult to get out. I knew from my work with at-risk families in public health that many abused women return to their partner time and time again before they have the insight, courage, opportunity, and support system to get out for good. Most regrettably, many women never make it out alive. I was determined not to be one of them.

The same day I phoned my kids, a Tuesday, my next-door neighbor Bill dropped by to borrow a tool from our garage. Since I had already made the heart-wrenching decision to move to southern Ontario, where I had a caring and supportive family, I knew that I finally needed to tell Bill the truth. He and Laura had become good friends of ours over the past few years, and I wanted them to know what was going on. Since they had no prior knowledge of what had happened to me the previous year, Bill was completely shocked and astounded by my news. Everyone liked Jake, as he was a charmer and a very good liar most of the time. I knew that Bill was having a hard time believing my far-fetched story. He immediately went home and told Laura, who came over to see me before Jake arrived home from work that day. They both offered me only kindness and support and told me how sorry they would be to see me leave. I knew I would miss them too, as well as many of my other neighbors who had become good friends over the years.

I was acutely aware that I did not have very long to develop an escape plan, since Jake was flying to Halifax in two days' time to attend a "John" school, part of his plea agreement from the year before. As ironic as that was, the timing of Jake's trip seemed serendipitous; deep down, I knew it was heaven sent. He planned to stay with his sister and would be gone over a long weekend, which would barely give me enough time to pack up and move out. On Saturday, Ellie and I would drive together to Oakville, where Mackenzie and Rob would be waiting for us.

On Wednesday, the movers came to the house in the morning to get instructions regarding what I wanted to take with me. I planned to put everything into storage until I could find a place to live. I was terrified Jake might come home while they were still there, but thankfully, that didn't happen. I had walked around the house the evening before, taking an inventory of furniture and other belongings, but I planned to leave more than half of it behind. I wanted to include all my mother's furniture, artwork, and clocks, as well as a spare bed, bedside table, and bureau for myself. I also planned to take the dining room furniture, as Jake's mom had just shipped her dining room furniture to us, which was now sitting in our basement. I would let him keep our huge projection TV and leather furniture in the family room as well as the kitchen set and extra chairs around the island. This also left him with almost two complete bedroom sets, which I thought was more than generous, given the circumstances.

I decided to take the sofa bed at the last minute, thinking that I might need it in the future. I also planned to take most of the photos of the children but sadly knew I would have to leave other treasures behind. There was no time to sort through all the years of memories, now stored in the numerous containers and boxes in our basement. At one point during the evening, Jake became suspicious of my activities and asked me what I was doing. I quickly improvised and told him I was getting ready to start my spring cleaning.

I had cut a lot of my ties with the community the year before when my world first fell apart, and I could not face seeing people anymore. That would make it somewhat easier to leave now, although I was still going to miss the home I had come to love and all my wonderful friends. I had put down deep roots in SSM, where, like The Pas, I had lived for nine years. Rachel, Lucas, and Anna were also aware of what was going on and were in total agreement with my final decision to leave Jake. On Thursday evening, I hugged my husband goodbye for what I thought would be the last time ever. He responded that he had not had a big hug like that from me in a long time, and I thought to myself how sad it was for him to say that to me now.

As soon as Jake left for the airport, I put my plan into action. I pulled out items from the kitchen cupboards that I wanted to put into storage, and I packed several bags for both Ellie and me to take with us to Oakville. Rachel and Lucas showed up at the house around 8:30 p.m. and shared with me that although Jake's flight had been delayed due to fog, it eventually took off for Toronto. Unbeknownst to me, they had gone to the airport and watched the activity for themselves, concerned that Jake might return home unexpectedly. That would have most certainly ended in complete disaster for me. I was so thankful that I had been oblivious to it all. I was also thankful to have such loyal and faithful friends, who even offered to help me pack up the house, although the movers would do most of that for me the following day.

On Friday morning, the moving van showed up as planned, and late on Friday night, totally worn out, I finally sat down at the island in our kitchen and wrote Jake the "dear John" letter he so deserved. I told him about what I had discovered and overheard earlier that week on the telephone and that this time I was leaving him for good. I was so tired and overwhelmed by then, I really don't remember exactly what I wrote, but I could picture him walking into our half-empty house and spying the note on the counter. I knew his reaction would not be good, but at least I would not be there to see it, God willing. That night, alone in bed, I recited the Lord's Prayer over and over in my mind until I finally fell into a deep and dreamless slumber. I felt at peace with my decision at last. To quote the lyrics of the wonderful Christian song, "No Turning Back," "I made up my mind ... I leave it behind ... no turning back."

# PART 5

# CHAPTER 37

# My Exodus

The morning of Saturday, April 2, 2011, broke cold, clear, and sunny as I jumped out of bed with a sense of purpose and butterflies in my stomach. This was the first day of the rest of my life. I had a strong sense of déjà vu, remembering the time Mackenzie and I drove to Winnipeg in 1999, almost twelve years to the day. This time, however, it would be only Ellie and me making the trip. I was concerned about the drive, which was eight hours long (not including the rest stops), and how Ellie would make out in the back seat of my car. She was an oversized dog, to say the least, and my car was only midsized at best. I would also have the trunk filled with suitcases and other essentials we would need for the next few weeks, so there was no room to spare. We left around eight o'clock in the morning, with Bill and Laura there to see us off. It was so sad saying a last goodbye to my dear friends and bidding a final farewell to the house that had been my home for the past nine years. I still remember the two of them standing in the driveway, waving to Ellie and me. I consoled myself with the promise that we would all see each other again, someday soon.

Much like Moses, God parted the Red Sea for me that day. I ended up making several stops to allow Ellie to stretch, use the bathroom, and have some water. I ate my prepacked picnic lunch in the car with her. It was an uneventful drive, thank goodness, and I was very relieved to finally see Mackenzie and Rob waiting for us at our prearranged meeting spot just north of Toronto. They were surely a sight for sore eyes! We all embraced, trying to hold back our tears, as Mackenzie's lovable pooch recognized her old friend and bounded over to her, tail wagging frantically with her usual

215

energy, happiness, and enthusiasm. I was so grateful for my family that day because I knew many people were not nearly as fortunate as me. Not only did I have my children's loving support but also that of my niece and her husband, as well as a few established friends who lived in Oakville. That made all the difference.

I also knew I had a huge mountain to climb, as I was unemployed with no home and no income, and I faced an uncertain future at best. I was now almost fifty-five years old and was not a good candidate for job opportunities, although I did have a solid work background. At the time, though, I could not even contemplate looking for employment until I found a permanent place to live and tried to mend my broken heart for the second time in less than a year. I certainly had my work cut out for me.

I slowly began to settle into life in Oakville, sleeping on the futon in the spare bedroom of the kids' apartment, with my car parked in the hospital parking lot across the street. I was very concerned that Jake might come looking for me at my daughter's home, so I tried to hide my vehicle from easy view. On my first Sunday in Oakville, I had called Debbie to fill her in on what had happened. Debbie called her brother on the phone later that night, after he returned home from his trip to Halifax. She later told us that he had gone ballistic when he found me gone—he was even threatening suicide. There was very little she could do to help him, especially since she lived so far away. It was not the first time he had threatened to take his own life, and I knew by then that all such threats should be taken very seriously. Once Mackenzie also spoke with Debbie on the phone, she decided to call the police in the Soo to inform them of what was going on with her father.

They did a welfare check on him later that night and called her back to say he seemed to be all right and was refusing any help. Furthermore, they did not see any imminent threat of self-harm or danger to anyone else. It was an extremely upsetting time for all of us, and my emotions were mixed, at best. I was still furious with Jake, and at that point, I probably felt deep down that he deserved everything he got. I firmly believed he was not only a scoundrel but also a horrible husband and a terrible father / role model to my children.

He made a recovery of sorts and at some point, returned to his normal mode of operation. He decided to go on the transatlantic cruise by himself, where he had the nerve to wire me a tiny arrangement of pink roses for my birthday in May. I was so incensed with him that I marched them straight over to the hospital across the street and gave the delicate little bouquet of pink rosebuds away. I was still reeling from the pain of his dreadful deception and double life, and I walked around most of the time with what could only be called a huge hole in my heart. Like Anne of Green Gables, I felt like I was in the depths of despair, although I was still able to function normally each day and slowly started to plan for my future. Looking back, I would say my depression was situational and not clinical, but it sure hurt a lot just the same.

The mother of Mackenzie's best friend from university happened to be a real estate agent, so she graciously helped me find a rental home in northwest Oakville. It was a spacious two-bedroom brownstone on a street called Woodstock Trail, and on the day we went to look at it, Cindy did a big double take when she opened the lockbox on the front door. The code spelled out THE PAS, which I knew right away was a sign from God that this was the home for Ellie and me. The fact that it was located on Woodstock Trail only underlined that reality for me. I could now afford to pay the rent, as I had hired a lawyer to represent me in the divorce, and Jake had reluctantly agreed to cover the cost of my rental home for a few months until I could find a job (he really had no choice in the matter). The home also had a small backyard for Ellie, and although the house was in the city, there were lots of great walking trails nearby for both of us.

After living with Mackenzie and Rob for six weeks, Ellie and I moved into our new home in the middle of May. I was finally able to get my furniture and other belongings out of storage, and most of it fit well into the narrow, three-story home. Unfortunately, neither the extra-big bedroom bureau nor the bulky sofa bed would fit through the interior doors, so I asked the movers to put them both back onto the truck and return them to Jake in the Soo. He was more than happy to get them back.

I also bought a few items for my new home, including a box spring and mattress for my bedroom, a desk and chair for my office, two TV stands, and three kitchen island chairs. Will came from Ottawa to visit me that month and helped me pick out some of my new purchases. When summer arrived, I even splurged on a manual lawnmower, small barbecue, and patio set for the tiny backyard. I made do without a bedroom dresser, using storage containers for my clothing. Although it all worked, I was really hoping and praying that I could eventually find a good job and would not have to rent forever.

# CHAPTER 38

# Starting Over

I would never say the time I spent living in that home was happy because I was very lonely, despite receiving weekly visits from Mackenzie and Rob. Ellie was a great comfort to me, especially since my emotions were running rampant. Jake had started drinking once again, apparently during his cruise, so I had a really hard time getting any cooperation out of him. He would ignore my emails for days on end, and even his own lawyer had a difficult time getting hold of him. I despaired over ever being freed from his clutches.

I reached out to several different supports, including a divorce care group affiliated with a local church, where one evening a week, I would meet up with other poor souls going through the same thing I was. Most Sundays, I would attend a different church in the area, trying to find the right one for me. Overall, though, I found it impossible to make new friends and was alone most of the time. There were a few exceptions, as Cindy and I had become good friends, and we would usually meet for breakfast on Saturday mornings. My niece and her husband were kind to me as well and often invited me up to their home in Newmarket on the weekends. Occasionally, Jess and I would visit our aunt Alice in her retirement home or take her out for lunch in nearby Uxbridge. Since I had Ellie to look after back at home, I was usually gone just for the day, but with Jessica and Matt, I enjoyed good company and had family whom I could talk to and share my feelings with.

One Sunday, alone in my dining room, I sat down and wrote an email to the pastor of my church in Sault Ste. Marie. I was angry and very disappointed with him because he had never once tried to contact me—not when I was going through my ordeal with Jake or even after I left him and moved to Oakville. I knew both him and his wife personally, although not very well, but I still expected at least a phone call or an email of encouragement from him. I had attended and supported their church for years and could not believe I was now totally invisible to them. I heard back from him right away, apologizing to me for not getting in touch sooner. It was a case of too little, too late for me, but I hoped and prayed that my email would cause the church to sit up, open its eyes, and try to help the next person who was in trouble. By now, I had come to expect very little from the church as an entity, although my church friends had most certainly come through for me when I needed them most.

Emotionally, I was not doing well, and one day in a fit of rage directed toward Jake, I threw out our wedding albums as well as the many photo albums from our trips abroad. I could not bear to look at our happy, smiling faces ever again. The next day, I drove over to the local thrift store in bordering Mississauga and gave away my beautiful wedding dress, cap, and veil. I had lovingly kept the three items wrapped up in blue tissue paper in my cedar hope chest all these years, thinking Mackenzie might want to wear them one day. Now, however, I hoped that some lucky young girl could play dress-up in the outfit or even wear it for Halloween—how appropriate … trick or treat! I shed many tears that weekend and during the days and weeks that followed. It got so bad, in fact, that I remember lying in bed night after night, praying to God and pleading with Him to take me directly up into heaven. By that time, I was feeling so miserable that I could not see any purpose for my life down here on planet Earth anymore. As a last resort, I roamed the aisles of the bookstores in my neighborhood, looking for anything that I could read to help me try to understand why my husband of almost thirty-two years had so carelessly cast me aside and broken all his wedding vows. Tragically, there was no such book out there. My situation seemed hopeless, and I just wanted to die.

My caring, sensitive, and thoughtful daughter must have recognized the telltale signs of depression and suicide ideation in me, as she suggested, one day in late spring, that the two of us attend a one-day seminar on suicide prevention at the Holiday Inn. It was to be provided by the mental health team in our local public health unit. This information would help Mackenzie in her future job as a social worker and was also a tool I could use with my own clients, once I started working again. Somewhat reluctantly, I agreed to go with her, and as I read the list of warning signs and symptoms leading up to suicide on the overhead screen, I recognized many of the same red flags in myself. That day turned out to be a real eye-opener for me, as I realized that I had slowly sunk down into the rabbit hole of depression. How strange that we often cannot recognize what is going on in our own psyche. As a Christian, however, suicide had never been a real option for me, but I got a big wake-up call that day, just the same. Going forward, I vowed to try to ignore my own dark thoughts and feelings and instead turn my negative thoughts into positive ones.

After all, the source of most of our thoughts, feelings, and emotions begins in the mind. To paraphrase Hebrews 12:1–2, we need to run our race with perseverance, with God as the author and finisher of our faith. But as 1 Peter 5:8 tells us, "Be self-controlled and alert. Your enemy the devil prowls around like a roaring lion looking for someone to devour." As the "deceiver of our faith," I believe that although Satan cannot read our minds, he often plants thoughts and ideas there in order to destroy our very souls. Like in 1999, the practices of praying and reading my Bible every day must have worked, because I slowly entered the land of the living once again. It was a process, to be sure, and it took many weeks and even months for me to emerge from my own personal rock bottom and reach the other side.

I also suffered from many physical ailments following my separation from Jake, which were all related to anxiety and stress. I put up with symptoms of chronic yeast infections, indigestion, significant weight loss, and insomnia for months and months. I worked hard at improving my overall health, and with the assistance of Rob's mom, Crystal, a holistic health practitioner, I eventually started to feel better. She made several house calls to me during the spring and summer months, which helped lift my low spirits. Indeed, she and her husband, Malcolm, often included me in their own family events, such as a dinner at their home, a swim in their pool, or a trip to their cottage, with Ellie in tow!

In July, I finally felt strong enough to tackle the problem of looking for a job. I updated my résumé and dropped it over to the office of the regional public health authority. Amazingly, I heard back from them within a week or so, since they were hiring public health nurses at the time. I had an interview the following week, and in early August, I started working in a full-time casual position with their high-risk home-visiting program. My office was in a high-rise building about a twenty-minute drive from my house, which worked perfectly for me. I felt extremely relieved, if not ecstatic, about getting another chance at my nursing career. I also knew that I desperately needed to connect with work colleagues, and I hoped to make some good friends there.

Fortunately, I was very familiar with the nature of the work, so it would not be a difficult transition for me. I did have to learn the geography of the region, which covered a huge area, but with some assistance from my fellow nurses and our wonderful support staff, I felt I was up to the challenge. I remember how difficult it was for me to smile for the camera on the day Anita took my photo for my work ID. It seemed that not only had I forgotten how to be happy, I had even forgotten how to smile. My new job really was a lifesaver, as some of the girls from work eventually became good friends of mine, and I also joined another book club through work. My social circle quickly expanded, and I felt good about supporting myself once again. I was even able to join a local gym and could treat myself to a few extras every now and then. The money from Jake came to an abrupt end, but I was more than able to live within my means. Once again, I knew that God, "Jehovah Jireh," was my provider, and He was most certainly looking out for me.

# CHAPTER 39

# Scars Are a Sign of Healing

I would like to say that all went well in my life after that, but unfortunately, once again, strange events started to happen. One Saturday morning in August, as I was driving home from the food store with my groceries, my car suddenly started wobbling back and forth. I couldn't imagine what was wrong. It was very difficult to control both the steering and the wheels, but I kept going and managed to make it back home in one piece. I ended up taking my now ancient car back to the local dealership because they had just put new tires on it, and I wondered if they had somehow forgotten to tighten up the lug nuts properly. Right away, they put the car up on the hoist, and sure enough, all four of the wheels had loose lug nuts. The manager could hardly believe it, but he apologized and assured me that this kind of thing almost *never* happened.

That weekend, I talked on the phone with my nephew Jamie, who now helped run my brother's tire stores in Nova Scotia. He shared with me that an incident like this *could* happen but was extremely rare. It was considered a big no-no in the auto industry world, and there were safeguards in place to prevent this type of mistake from happening. I was extremely puzzled about how all the lug nuts could have been loose at the same time, but I still suspected the dealership. I soon changed my mind about that.

Three more similar incidents occurred, each about a week apart—twice when I was out shopping on the weekend and once when I was on my way to the hospital in Milton (as a regular part of my workday). The first time it happened, I once again managed to limp back home. Unbelievably, my Scottish next-door neighbor was a mechanic and had at one time worked at a tire shop installing tires, so I asked him to look at my wheels. After inspecting them, he shook his head and, with a grave look on his face, told me it was a miracle that I had not had a serious accident driving home. All four tires were extremely loose, especially the tire by the driver's side door! He tightened them up for me with a wrench, and I then drove over to Auto Tire to have them reinspected and tightened properly. The next time it happened, I went directly back there, where they diagnosed and fixed the same problem once again.

The last time it occurred, my good friends Bill and Laura arrived at my house from the Soo later that same day, and I asked Bill to look at them. Once again, he was astounded by just how loose all four tires were and promptly tightened them up for me. By now, I was worried that someone was either trying to kill me or seriously injure me in an accident. In both scenarios, I was most certainly being terrorized. It was still hard to comprehend, but I started to keep my eyes and ears open, both during the daytime and nighttime hours. I finally shared what was going on with Mackenzie and Rob, and we discussed the possibility of setting up a video camera by the front door to record all unseen and nefarious activity. Unfortunately, we never got around to actually doing it.

One hot and sunny Saturday morning in early September, I took Ellie out for a walk in the neighborhood. Even from a distance, I noticed the old derelict car parked at the very end of my street, on the wrong side of the road, facing my house. Feeling brave with the dog by my side, I started walking toward the suspicious-looking vehicle. As I got closer to it, I could clearly see a dark-skinned man, possibly Pakistani or Indian, sitting behind the wheel, watching me intently. When I was about thirty feet away from him, he suddenly started up the car and pulled out from the curb, squealing his tires as he made a quick getaway down the side street next to us. It was like watching something out of a movie, only I was in it! He went so fast I was unable to get a good look at the license plate, but there was no doubt in my mind that he had been staking out my home and watching my activities. I even wondered if he was planning a break-in. Shivering, I felt chilled to the bone, despite the heat of the day.

After my walk with Ellie, I went back into the house and finally called the police, explaining what had been going on with my car during the past few weeks as well as the incident that had occurred that morning. The female police sergeant I spoke with was very sympathetic to my situation and took my concerns seriously. She urged me to get extra locks put on my front and patio doors and to install security cameras and motion detector lights outside. Finally, she told me that the police would patrol my neighborhood regularly to be on the lookout for any suspicious activity. The sergeant went on to say that she had not heard of any car thefts or break-ins recently in my neck of the woods. In particular, she emphasized to me that they almost *never* got reports of tire thefts in the tony and very prosperous city of Oakville.

I felt rather discouraged after talking to her, since I knew it would be problematic as well as expensive to add extra locks and security equipment to my rental home. That was not really an option for me. I did, however, install blinds at the front door window. Surprisingly, the frightening incidents completely stopped after I confronted the man in the sketchy car and mentioned the events to Jake on the phone one evening. I still remember his sarcastic comment to me, "You think that I did that?" which was not really a denial. I informed him that the police were aware of the incidents and were now watching my house. Since I didn't have any known enemies and was in the middle of an acrimonious divorce, I could only guess who was behind the whole thing.

In November 2011, I finally got an appointment date for the in-depth Christian counselling I had signed Jake and myself up for the year before. I still wanted to complete the weeklong course, but because I was female and the pastor was male, I had to take a support person with me to their offices in southwestern Ontario. I asked my daughter to come along with me because I thought she might also benefit from some of the counselling. She was now back in university pursuing a master's degree and had some extra time on her hands, so she graciously agreed to accompany me. I was excited to finally complete the counselling, and the two of us set off for our mini getaway in early December.

Our destination was a small town located in Amish country, with not a lot to say about it except that it is the birthplace of the renowned Canadian author Alice Munro. There was only one small motel to lodge in, boasting two twin beds and a tiny kitchenette. I was there for one reason only—to complete my counselling and try to put a final period at the end of my marriage to Jake. After several months of working on myself, I was slowly starting to feel better and was painstakingly putting the pieces of my life back together again. The counselling took up only half of each day, so we had lots of spare time to spend on our own, talking and hanging out with each other. I am sure it was painful for Mackenzie to hear some of my admissions about her father and to relive some of the memories that still haunted us both.

I felt a lot of guilt over what my kids had witnessed and gone through, mostly when Jake had been drinking. I finally realized that I should have left him many years before I actually did. Children should never be exposed to an alcoholic parent, no matter what the circumstances are. I had felt it was my role to normalize our lives, and in so doing, I tried to cover up and fix all his shortcomings as a husband and a father. Some psychologists might call that enabling, but I prefer to think of it as endurance in the face of adversity. Others might call it survival or resilience. Whatever it had been, I mourned all the lost years, but I would never rewrite history; if it were not for my husband, I would never have had my beautiful children and grandchildren. For that alone, I will always be eternally grateful to God.

On our last morning there, Mackenzie woke up in a panic. She had several large red bite marks up and down her neck, which looked suspiciously like bedbug bites. Right away, we both knew what they were, as I had seen them years before with my clients in The Pas, and Mackenzie had been exposed to them when she and Rob had stayed in some of the hostels in Europe. They had slept in the same room but in different beds, and she had been the only one with bites; now the same thing had happened once again. I wasted no time in going to the management of the motel, informing them of the nasty infestation. I then ran out to the local drugstore and bought a package of large garbage bags, placing our remaining clothes and belongings in them and tying them securely. We left my large fabric suitcase in the room and quickly fled the scene of the crime.

After our final counselling session that morning, we both purchased new clothing at the local Jumbo Mart and spent the rest of the day at the Laundromat, washing and drying all our other clothes. I am sure we looked the worse for wear when we returned home later that night, but at least we felt clean. What we couldn't wash and dry, we put into bags, which we left out in my freezing-cold garage for several weeks. We eventually had our suede boots dry-cleaned, and the books we had been reading went into plastic bags in the freezer. Our quick actions must have done the trick, as there was no further evidence of any bedbugs. Looking back upon the whole episode now, it seems rather comical, but I could not help but think that this could only happen to Mackenzie and me!

# CHAPTER 40

# Joy Comes in the Morning!

The fall of 2012 and winter of 2013 were busy ones for me. My aunt Alice was not doing well, physically or mentally, and her days in the retirement home were numbered. I had researched all the LTC (long-term care) homes in Halton Region because I wanted her to be nearer to me and had selected my five favorite picks for the waitlist. One day, early in December, I got the call I had been waiting for, and although the home was not in Oakville, it was just across the border in the city of Mississauga. Even though I lived on the other side of Oakville, it was near enough for me to be able to visit her frequently and was also close to a major hospital.

The day of her move turned out to be a minor undercover operation. I drove Aunt Alice in my car, while Jessica followed closely behind with all her worldly possessions. I knew right away that she was very ill, as she became car sick during the trip, forcing me to pull off the busy highway into the parking lot of a restaurant. We eventually made it to the nursing home and got her settled into her semiprivate room. I knew that although it was an older institution, the nursing care there was excellent, and she would finally get the level of medical care and attention she so needed. Mackenzie and I were able to visit her together on Boxing Day and watched as she slowly opened the Christmas presents we brought her, with childlike anticipation. She still knew us at that point but did not have a lot to say, and I knew she was beginning to slip away from us even more.

About six weeks after she was admitted to her new home, she suffered a massive stroke, leaving her comatose and hospitalized for almost two weeks. Upon further investigation, the gerontologist determined she had a huge ovarian tumor; the only interventions that could be done for her now were a combination of supportive and comfort measures. One of her nurses turned out to be Rob's aunt, which was very comforting to me at the time. I knew she was getting the best care possible. Still, Jessica, Matthew, and I were all in shock, since we had not realized her condition was quite so dire. We were able to visit her a few more times in the hospital, where she woke up and appeared to know us. I spoke with the hospital chaplain and arranged to have volunteers come in to sit with her during the long days and evenings so that she was not all alone.

It was a sad day for me when she passed away at the age of eighty-seven, but I knew that both Jessica and I had tried to do our very best for her. Her final wish was to be cremated and buried beside her husband in the Lower Brighton Cemetery near Woodstock. That spring, once again on the Victoria Day long weekend, we all flew back to Woodstock for her burial service. My cousin Brian had once been close to Aunt Alice, and being an Anglican church minister, he was honored to perform the graveside ceremony. With our extended family also in attendance, I gave a short but heartfelt eulogy about her life.

By the spring of 2013, my divorce was almost finalized (after a lot of blood, sweat, and tears), and I had even told Jake that I had forgiven him. It was a work in progress, though, and sometimes I had to remind myself that I *had* actually forgiven him. It felt so good not to be carrying around anger and bitterness in my heart; closure was very important to me, as was tying up loose ends.

Jessica and I had flown back to the Soo in the summer of 2011 to sort through all the many dusty boxes and containers in the basement. Jake was visiting his family in Halifax that weekend and had allowed me to come back into the house. Poor Jess had come down with a terrible head cold a few days before we left Toronto, but after working together for two days straight, we had a good collection of stored-up memories to bring home. Hopeful for his ongoing cooperation, I left all the storage bins in the garage for Jake to bring down to me later. In early August, he kept his word, and after dropping off the containers at my house, he took Ellie out for a short walk. He then drove on to southwestern Ontario to complete the counselling that I went on to do later that same year. Most unfortunately, I knew he was secretly drinking, so I wondered how effective the counselling would be.

When he arrived back in Oakville at the end of the week, he called me, wanting to talk. Against my better judgment, we went out to eat that night at a nearby restaurant, where neither one of us ate much steak. Over dinner, Jake summoned up the courage to tell me that the crux of his problems had begun in his early teens and had nothing at all to do with me. He had suffered through a massive trauma, a malignant burden that he was still carrying around ... an albatross around his neck. He desperately wanted to reconcile with me, but there was no chance I could ever trust him again, and to be perfectly honest, I knew that I deserved much better. Thankfully, the evening ended without incident, and that was the last time I ever saw Jake.

Just when I thought I would never have anything to look forward to ever again, God intervened once more. Mackenzie and Rob had been encouraging me to go on a dating website to "get back out there." I was hesitant to do so because I had not dated anyone since my marriage to Jake nearly thirty-four years earlier, and as I often said to myself, "Once bitten, twice shy." I was very lonely though, and I still believed in true love. Now, after living alone for almost two years, I was ready to take a giant leap of faith and start dating once again.

I did not join a dating website per se, but my real estate friend, Cindy, was on one, and she had connected with someone she thought would be a perfect match for me. She knew that I was a genuine Christian, and this man described himself in the same way. Paul lived in Kitchener, Ontario, which was about an hour's drive away from Oakville. When Cindy and I looked at his online profile one evening, I was impressed by how handsome and youthful he appeared. He was a chartered accountant and a mortgage broker and had recently moved back to Canada from Dallas, Texas. I had been earnestly praying to God for several months that I would meet a Christian man—one who was honest, handsome, intelligent, funny, kind, and a truly nice person. For some strange reason, I also asked God to send me someone who could sing, and as it turned out, Paul has a beautiful tenor voice! That idea must have been heaven-sent, as I have no earthly notion where else it would have come from! I eventually learned that his dad had been a pastor, and he came from a large, extended Christian family.

On Valentine's Day, 2013, I sent him a long email about myself as well as a photo and waited to hear back from him. He responded to me the very next day, and despite a few bumps along the road, the rest, as they say, is history. Today, we have been together for ten years, happily married for six years, and we are still writing the story of our lives. It is never too late to start over!

Joy Comes in the Morning:

Sing to the Lord, you saints of his;
praise his holy name.
For his anger lasts only a moment,
but his favor lasts a lifetime;
weeping may remain for a night,
but rejoicing comes in the morning. (Psalm 30:4–5)

# EPILOGUE

It has been just over twelve years since my exodus from Sault Ste. Marie, and my life is completely different now. I retired from public health nursing at the end of 2016, and in 2017, I married my husband, Paul, a wonderful Christian man. My daughter, Mackenzie, has been happily married to her college sweetheart, Rob, for several years, and our joy was made complete when she gave birth to Jeremy, our sweet, beautiful grandson, also in 2017. During the global pandemic, at the end of 2020, we were doubly blessed by the addition of Charlotte, our adorable little granddaughter. In addition, my son, Will, completed his master's degree in 2016 and has a full and rewarding life living in Europe with his lovely partner, Tessa. He has also been blessed with the opportunity to work in a challenging and unique career.

Throughout our time together, Paul and I have endured many challenges. Our lives are not easy by any means, but they are genuine. As I reflect upon my first marriage, instead of considering it a complete failure, I prefer to think of all the good things that have come out of it. The best outcome by far from my marriage to Jake was my children and grandchildren and my career in public health, which I most likely would not have attained had we not moved to northern Manitoba. I also have many wonderful friends across Canada as a result of my travels. Now, like the prophet Job, I am praying that my latter days will be better than my former days (Job 8:7).

We all make decisions as we travel through life, some wise and some not so wise, and hopefully we learn from our mistakes. Although there were many red flags during my first marriage, I stayed with my husband through thick and thin, as I loved him, and I desperately wanted to keep our family together. I never wanted to burden my parents or my brothers with my problems, which I now know was the wrong road to follow. We

233

all need to reach out to the people who love us most when we need help most. For some of us, that may mean going to stay with family or friends or even entering a shelter for a short period of time.

I know people inevitably change and evolve over time, sometimes for the better and sometimes for the worse. We don't have control over what other people say and do, but we are responsible for our own words and actions. Our childhood has a profound effect upon not only who we become but also how well we navigate our way through the often-treacherous waters of life. I am very thankful that I had a good start in life and was saved at a young age.

I know for sure that nothing can improve until it is brought out into the light of day. When the light is turned on, darkness disappears. In the Gospel of John 8:12, Jesus said, "I am the light of the world. Whoever follows me will never walk in darkness but will have the light of life." Trying to keep dark secrets hidden is almost always a mistake, as the truth will always come out in the end. Most importantly, true healing involves trying to forgive not only ourselves but also other people who have wronged us. This is a process, and it usually takes time. Sometimes you must also walk away from that person, knowing that you are ultimately better off without them in your life.

The pathway to achieving good mental health and overcoming addiction is a journey with many twists and turns along the way. Although I could not do so initially, I can now feel empathy for Jake's situation. I have no idea when the infidelity began in our marriage, but after talking with our friends, I believe it may have started as early as when we lived in Newfoundland. How do I know this? Our friend Jon, who was a coworker of Jake's, found a drawerful of motel keys in his office after Jake left his job. I can only surmise that they were souvenirs from his double life. As his loving, trusting, and unsuspecting wife, I was an open book but was completely clueless as to what was going on behind my back, until his behavior started to escalate. Ultimately, it was God who orchestrated certain events to happen at certain times, bringing everything out into the light of day.

As Christians, we must try to follow the purpose and path that God has set out for each one of us. Despite my failure to always do this, God has never turned His back on me and has brought me through it all. He revealed things to me at just the right moment, opening certain doors while closing others. He sent me both heavenly and earthly angels in the form of family and friends, who helped me and protected me when I needed it most. For that, I am eternally grateful and happy to be alive. Discouragement and negative thinking are my worst enemies, but I am still learning to trust and obey God each day and to never give up on life. That is the essence of a life filled with faith—the assurance of things hoped for, the conviction of things not seen (Hebrews 11:1).

The Year of the Lord's Favor:

The Spirit of the Sovereign Lord is on me,
because the Lord has anointed me
to preach good news to the poor.
He has sent me to bind up the brokenhearted,
to proclaim freedom for the captives
and release from darkness for the prisoners,
to proclaim the year of the Lord's favor
and the day of vengeance of our God,
to comfort all who mourn,
and provide for those who grieve in Zion—
to bestow on them a crown of beauty
instead of ashes,
the oil of gladness
instead of mourning,
and a garment of praise
instead of a spirit of despair.
They will be called oaks of righteousness,
a planting of the Lord
for the display of his splendor. (Isaiah 61:1–3)

Printed in the USA
CPSIA information can be obtained
at www.ICGtesting.com
JSHW021630101023
49639JS00003B/3